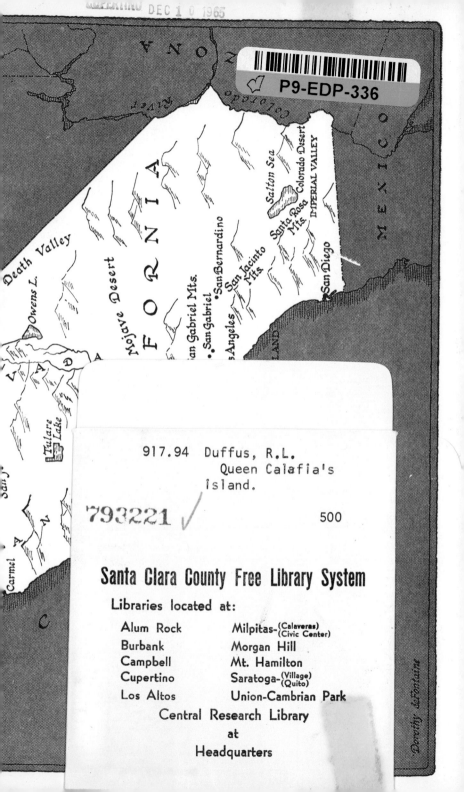

CUPERTINO DEC 1 0 1965

P9-EDP-336

Dorothy laFontaine

QUEEN

CALAFIA'S

ISLAND

QUEEN CALAFIA'S ISLAND

R. L. DUFFUS

W · W · NORTON & COMPANY · INC · *New York*

Contents

☼ ☼ ☼ ☼ ☼

Prelude

This book is not a history of California, although I have found it convenient to arrange the material in a roughly chronological order. There are enough histories of California already. My printed sources are familiar, for, as I have tried to explain in a bibliographical note at the end of the volume, I have used what came nearest to hand.

I have not excavated into what I was taught many years ago to call source material, except as such material is contained in my own memories. My eye-witness acquaintance with California, or parts of it, began in 1906, when I came as a freshman student to Stanford University; continued there for five years, while I took an A.B. and an M.A. in history; was prolonged for nearly eight years as a newspaperman in San Francisco; and has been renewed at various times and seasons since. When I returned to the state in January, 1964, as a permanent resident (in so far as one can be called permanent in this vale of change) I began to wonder about the extraordinary changes I saw about me and read about in the newspapers. There had been, among other alterations, an almost tenfold increase in population since 1906.

I could not help speculating as to the state's future. This book is the result. It is the future that matters most; we look at the past only to get perspective.

Literate citizens of Los Angeles reading this book will perhaps feel I have been unfair to their city. I may have been, for I like San Francisco better. But Los Angeles may be nearer to tomorrow's type of city and San Francisco, greatly beloved though she is, the urban Model T.

R. L. Duffus

Palo Alto, 1965.

QUEEN CALAFIA'S ISLAND

☼ *I* ☼ ☼ ☼

The Name Came First

The name California came out of that fine age of the world in which much of the earth's surface was unknown to geographers and explorers, and in which it was therefore possible to make up enchanting stories about areas the old map makers candidly used to refer to as *terra incognita*. Africa not much over a century ago, the polar regions more recently, were largely indicated in this way. The New World was a matter of speculation before the voyages of Columbus—and afterwards, too. It was approached with preparations and precautions, such as we now take for granted when we consider landing on the moon or Mars.

Where the explorers had not yet penetrated, the writers of fiction and romance could stake out their claims. Thus it happened that a Spanish romancer, Garcí Ordóñez de Montalvo, got out a popular book, whose title may be roughly translated as "The Exploits of Esplandián." In this book allusion was made, as Josiah Royce said, "to a fabulous island, described as near the Indies and 'very near the Terrestrial Paradise.'" A pleasant place, in fact. The island was ruled by a black queen named Calafia and inhabited, or at least controlled, by Amazons. The Spaniards were always looking for Amazons, just why I don't know—women didn't overtly rule Spain, unless they belonged to the royal family.

I shall not attempt to summarize Montalvo's scenario, partly because I haven't read it and partly because I don't intend to. But the Montalvo book was known before Cortez landed in Mexico; and California was christened after its legendary queen, and lied about before (as well as after) it was known to exist.

A more dismal theory is that the Spaniards found the pleasant-sounding word acceptable when they first experienced what then seemed to be the Californian climate—in Lower California, taking it as a modified combination of the Spanish terms for "hot" and "furnace." These innuendos would have fitted the tip of Lower California, where Cortez briefly maintained a colony in 1535–36. They would not be inappropriate for some parts of the future state, farther north, at some seasons.

In the time of Cortez there was no visible gold, no Amazons, and no evidence of an earthly Paradise in the lower peninsula. There was an abundance of sand, cactus, rattlesnakes, lizards, and horned toads, but these, as Coronado showed, could be found in plenty elsewhere.

2

So, for a long time, the Spaniards were not especially interested in Montalvo's "island" (for an island they long believed it to be) much less in the valuable real estate on the mainland farther north. They turned south, on both sides of South America, by-passing the Portuguese-held bulge of Brazil. They held and developed Mexico. They established a university at Mexico City and one in Lima, Peru, in the same year, 1541—more than three-quarters of a century before the Pilgrims hauled their boats up on Plymouth Beach.

Their instincts were similar to those of their far-off successors in California—the forty-niners: they wanted easy money and the power and glory that go with it. Whenever they heard of gold, anywhere, they went hunting for it. There had been gold, already extracted and ready to hand, in Mexico and Peru; it did not seem wrong to take this gold away from the natives, who were idolators and sinners. Why shouldn't there be gold in Quivira, the desert, plains, and prairie country which Coronado explored in 1540–41? There wasn't, to be sure. But nobody, except the professional yarn-spinner Montalvo, had said there was gold in California. They didn't even know that what they called California really was California. For their purposes, in the sixteenth, seventeenth and early eighteenth centuries, there wasn't any gold there, and wouldn't have been, even though they had gone straight to the future site of Sutter's Mill.

As a matter of fact, these Conquistadores, though brave and hearty men, did not really like to dig. They preferred to leave that chore to the natives.

So Coronado returned from his long wanderings around the Great Plains, discouraged and discredited, and the true California, with a climate and soil every bit as good as they are today, slept peacefully on for some generations. Nobody wanted California, not for a long while, except the dark-brown native sons who lived there in happy ignorance of the rest of the world. They were a backward people; they did not even fight very much.

The Spanish did go up the eastern shore of Lower California— Francisco de Ulloa to the head of the Gulf in 1538, Hernando de Alarcón 200 miles up the Colorado in small boats in 1540. This should have proved that the peninsula was not an island, but the Jesuit Father Eusebio Kino had to prove it all over again more than half a century later.

Very slowly, the Spanish priests and soldiers pushed northward along the unpicturesque and unprofitable stretch of land that we now call Lower California. The priests, being missionaries, were looking for converts. The soldiers and their commanders were not looking very hopefully for real estate. There was plenty of real estate lying around elsewhere. What they needed was ports. They also thought that a water connection, the Straits of Anian, might lead from the Pacific into the Atlantic. (The French, on the other side of the continent, were looking for the same thing, with the same lack of success.) So the myth of the Northwest (or Northeast) Passage became tied in with the other myths and misapprehensions of California's early history, or lack of history.

Toward the end of the sixteenth century the Spaniards were trading with some islands they had picked up in the Western Pacific—the Philippines. Every year a great galleon made the run from Manila to the coast of Mexico—a slow, cumbersome vessel that like most other ships of that time had trouble sailing against the wind. The voyage from Manila took weeks and months, and though it is interesting to read about, it could have had little glamour for those who took it. Navigation at that time was not accurate by today's standards. The galleon captain could be sure of hitting the western coast of North America somewhere, but he was rarely quite sure as to where.

Usually the captains aimed to sight the coast above Mazatlan, in Mexico, for the reason that the prevailing winds were (and still are) in the northern quarter. It was therefore helpful for them to know something about the shoreline of what is now called California, and no doubt they hoped some day to come upon the mythical Straits of Anian.

It was to look for possible ports that these galleons were sent for an occasional trip up the West Coast. Occasional is the word for it, for these waters were never crowded. Juan Rodriguez Cabrillo made the try in 1542, on orders from the Viceroy of New Spain, Don Antonio de Mendoza, and seems to have plowed his way as far north as Point Concepcion, with stops at what were later called San Diego, San Pedro, Santa Monica, and Ventura. Cabrillo and his men may have been "the first Europeans to set foot on the shore of Alta California" (that is, today's state of California), as that excellent historian, Robert Glass Cleland, thought, but they left no abiding footprints. These were practical men. They had no immediate use for California. And they were not equipped to conquer it, even if conquering had been desirable.

Next to arrive was that English patriot and freebooter, Sir Francis Drake, who came up from the Straits of Magellan in the *Golden Hind*, took much loot from Spanish vessels encountered on the way, and judged it wise not to return by way of the hornets' nest he had stirred up. He went north in search of the Northwest Passage, then came back down the coast to some point north of what is now San Francisco Bay. He did not find the Bay itself. He probably ran into fog, of which there is plenty at most seasons in that latitude, and was glad enough to find a bit of sand and a little shelter, where he could scrape the barnacles off his hull and give his men a rest. To make matters difficult for the map makers and historians the indentation Drake found and which is probably the one today called Drake's Bay (in Marin County, north of the Golden Gate) was long known as San Francisco Bay.

Drake spent most of the summer of 1579 at this point. Indeed, he and his crew may have been the first men from the Western World to spend a vacation on this spot. After taking possession of the neighborhood, in the custom of the time, making friends—or at least harmless acquaintances—of the Indians and setting up a "plate of brasse," Drake put to sea again. Queen Elizabeth was pleased enough to have some new subjects, or so it seems, and even more pleased to have some Spanish gold to support the currency. But she soon had the Spanish Armada and other difficulties to deal with, and never took up Drake's option on New Albion.

It is strange that Drake's men did not wander up on the hills and catch sight of the real San Francisco Bay. If they did this they forgot to mention it. The "plate of brasse," picked up three and a half centuries later, was judged the genuine article by an expert in the field, Professor Herbert E. Bolton of the University of California at Berkeley. But it was hard for the Spaniards to believe in the Bay of San Francisco, even after they had found it.

At any rate, the English did not undertake a settlement in California, though they did continue to meander around the Northeastern Pacific, looking for Spanish ships which, on account of political and religious differences, they considered it ethical to plunder. One enterprising Britisher, Thomas Cavendish, intercepted the Manila galleon off the southeastern point of Lower California in 1587 and relieved it of its valuable cargo.

This episode reminded the Spaniards that a safe port on the Upper California shore might be useful, and eight years later (it always took time for people to make up their minds in those days) they sent Sebastian Rodriguez Cermanho (or Cermaño) to look into the matter. He too stood far enough out to sea on the westward-slanting coast to miss the great port, but he does seem to have found Drake's Bay, to which he gave the name of—yes, San Francisco. Then he lost his ship and had to bring his crew home in small boats. In a negative way he had succeeded: he had discovered a stretch of shore that galleon captains would wisely avoid.

Seven years rolled by—there were plenty of years at that time. Then, in May, 1602, the quest was taken up by Sebastian Vizcaino, who made way stops at Catalina Island, sailed up the Santa Barbara Channel, and visited the site of Monterey, which he rashly spoke of as "the best port that could be desired." Going or coming, he appears also to have called at San Diego, though, not knowing his geography as a modern school boy might, he called it San Miguel.

Vizcaino was accompanied by a friar, Father Ascension, who wrote a report urging that Upper California be settled. This, he pointed out, would not only be good for the souls and morals of the aborigines, who could be converted to Christianity, but should also be profitable in a business way.

This document was duly filed, but it did not produce immediate results. It was more than a century before missions were established in Lower California, where there were few souls to be saved and little profit to be had. It was more than a century and a half before the string of missions and presidios began to crawl up the mainland of Alta California.

Nobody seemed to want California enough to suffer for it and spend money on it. The power of Spain, after the destruction of the Armada and a few other misfortunes, was declining. The very gold she had taken out of the New World had cursed her by inflating her currency. Her industries at home declined or failed to develop. She had all she could do, for the time being, to retain her distant overseas properties. There was no pressure in the northeastern Pacific. People didn't believe so much in the Terrestrial Paradise. Some of them, by the early seventeenth century, had read an iconoclastic book called *Don Quixote*, by an author named Cervantes. The Paradise superstition, so far as it applied to California, lapsed, and was not revived until a modern species of romancers known as real estate salesmen went into operation in Southern California in the late nineteenth century.

3

Upper California was too hard to get to. That was one reason why the Spaniards, who had settled and to some extent developed such countries as Mexico, the Argentine, Chile, and Peru, did not get up there in large numbers. If they had known about the Mother Lode, history would have been different.

The whole history, or rather lack of history, of early California may suggest to those who believe in fate that the area was being saved for the future, in some calculated fashion. My own theory of history in this case, as in others, is that what is going to happen eventually happens. For many generations there was no reason for anything to happen to or in California. If it had been where Virginia is, or if the people of China had been moved to sail eastward, California would have been settled in a twinkling—that is to say, by sailing-ship standards, in about a century after it was discovered. But it just wasn't accessible, and it just wasn't needed.

By land, as a glance at any geophysical map will show, or as can be proven by the adventurous narratives of persons who got there in the primitive years, it was formidably guarded; it was hemmed in by deserts and rimmed by desolate mountains. There simply was no easy route for people on horseback or on foot. The Spanish-Americans, who were at times the most persistent and most long-suffering pioneers this earth has ever seen, took enormous trouble and risks to get to what is now New Mexico and Arizona. They never tried in any organized way to reach Upper California until settlements had been made there by the sea approach.

And the sea approach itself, until the invention of the steamboat, was at least an ordeal, at worst a disaster. Even in the nineteenth century the American whalers and hide ships made heavy going of it—as we shall see. In 1769, before these improved sailing craft appeared, the Inspector-General of New Spain, Jose de Galvez, sent two ships from the Mexican port of San Blas to support the Portola land expedition. One of these, the *San Antonio*, reached San Diego in fifty-four days, and this was considered good traveling. The other, the *San Carlos*, took a hundred and ten days and arrived with most of the crew and passengers dead or dying of scurvy. The Spanish ships of that day just couldn't make headway against contrary winds.

Those contrary winds were still blowing when Richard Henry Dana, three-quarters of a century later, made the voyage which he was to describe in *Two Years before the Mast*. When the ship *Alert* tried to get up from Santa Barbara to San Francisco she met with heavy gales, which blew her, as Dana says, "half the distance to the Sandwich [or Hawaiian] Islands," and it took twenty days to reach the northern port. Dana adds that the destination had been Monterey but that the ship had been north of that point when "the wind hauled ahead and we made a fair wind for San Francisco."

The *Alert* was of course a far handier craft than such medieval battle wagons as the *San Antonio* and the *San Carlos*, but it is clear that until the steamships made their appearance it was hard to populate and supply California by sea. Or to govern it, either, from such a distant capital as Mexico City.

It was almost as difficult to populate and provision the future commonwealth by land, as was shown by the efforts of Anza and others to open a trail across the southern deserts. An intelligent observer at that time might have thought the land would be saved for a slow, leisurely, beautiful development, over a long space of years. Today we can let our imaginations play, if we like, just as did Montalvo when he wrote about Queen Calafia and her domain. We can picture a New Greece, with temples, a literature, legends, language, and none of the blithering idiocy that led to the civil wars that destroyed the older Greece. And nobody can prove us wrong if we use the conditional form of the verb.

But this would have taken a long time, and there wasn't enough time. The Indians of primitive California, considered in the most favorable light, gave no evidence that they were contemplating a high culture and civilization. They had no agriculture. One may find traces of their activities on the shores, all up and down, where they did some fishing, and also pounded clam, abalone, and mussel shells to get at the meat. They had bows, arrows, and spears and could kill game on the hills and in the woods. They had some sort of religion.

For them there were souls in trees, rocks, mountains, clouds, the sun, the night—all the forms and manifestations of nature. They left few traces, for they built no permanent homes. They may have had their favorite camping places. There is a big rock on a steep hillside below Monterey and the Big Sur (unless it has been blasted out by the highway builders since I last saw it); it thrusts outward, leaving a shallow ash-floored cave at the bottom; and if you like to believe in fantastic things you will not laugh when people tell you that no matter how deeply you find it convenient to dig at the foot of the rock you will never come to the end of the ashes. It would have been a pleasant spot from which to watch the sea in good weather, at night, with the coals glowing; and perhaps hold some sort of religious service. For that region would have been hospitable to the right sort of tribal gods.

Presumably the California Indians would never have risen to the level of the Pueblo tribes, who had well-built and permanent houses, or to that of the Aztec and the Maya; or even to the stage reached by the Sioux and other Plains communities, who used skilfully every part of the buffalo, raised a little corn, and had a language of words and signs. Parkman thought the Sioux might have established a sort of empire in America if they had had time; we saw to it, of course, that they did not have time. The Californians—the real Native Sons—had time enough but no inclination.

They were not especially energetic—they did not need to be in their generally pleasant environment. Nor were they warlike until in later years they turned upon the trespassing white man. They had a good thing of it, even though they did not know this. Doubtless they were wretched when it rained, but along the coast the rain didn't last too long at a time. Meanwhile, the tribes—or *rancherias*, as the Spaniards called them—seem to have respected each other's territories, and they got along, like so many retired Iowa farmers in later times, without doing much work.

They could sit on the beach or the shore rocks, and many of them did, as the simple surviving relics testify. They could sit there and eat shellfish, or pound acorns in a hollow in the stone, watch the water and think of nothing. They may have had as good a time as a tourist has today, but a different kind of good time. Sometimes in the long later years they might see a huge water bird, so they might think of it, floating by, far out at sea; they might wonder what it was, but this would not worry them.

Occasionally the big water birds anchored near shore, and a strange sort of man landed from them. These men observed, as Captain Gali of one of the galleons put it, that California was "a very fair and high land with many trees"—which, as seen from the water, it often was. There would be more trees, however, north of Point Reyes than in the south—and fewer accessible beaches. But the strange visitors sailed by, or briefly landed; this was a neighborhood hard to settle, and land was still abundant in the Western Hemisphere. The real estate business languished. When California passed out of their hands, later on, the Indians did not get as much as twenty-four dollars' worth of beads for it.

Chaplain Fletcher of Drake's *Golden Hind* said that a "multitude" of natives came down to the stockade the Englishmen had built at the time of the 1579 visit, taking it for granted that the Englishmen were gods. How, in spite of the difference in language, this thought was made plain the good preacher does not indicate. The Reverend Fletcher added that the Indian chief "and divers others made several orations" and asked Drake to "take the kingdom into his hand and become their king and patron." This Drake consented to do, setting up the brass plate previously mentioned, with a proclamation to that effect. This was, of course, the usual procedure at that time. It was assumed that any savage or barbaric race would be only too glad to be taken over by an Englishman, a Frenchman, or a Spaniard, especially if the second parties to the bargain did not possess fire arms.

Whether or not the Indians realized that they had just become subjects of Queen Elizabeth I is not clear; or rather it is clear they could not have done so. The facts, such as they were, could not bother them, for neither Elizabeth nor any other foreign potentate interfered with the placid tenor of their lives. For nearly two centuries longer they and their descendants could go fishing with an easy mind.

This incident is worth recalling because it indicates that the Indians around Drake's Bay, under the lee of Point Reyes in what is now Marin County, were not hostile to strange visitors from the sea, and could, unless the chaplain was throwing in a little local color, "sing and dance."

These early Californians would not have understood a community constantly in motion or persons who went out on dangerous and uncomfortable voyages when they could just as well have stayed home. A California Indian of the pre-Conquistadores days was limited to his own tribal hunting and fishing grounds. If he trespassed on another tribe's preserves he might have to fight, and these Indians did not enjoy fighting. Moreover, these early native sons are said to have had more than 135 dialects, varieties of a smaller number of languages. Thus anybody who got too far from home couldn't communicate, except in sign language, with the strangers he met.

Usually the Indians were docile in their attitudes toward the Spaniards. The rising at San Diego toward the end of 1775, which cost some lives, including a priest's, was a rare sort of occurrence. It may have been due to woman trouble, as was often the case when unwillingly celibate soldiers and sailors went ashore in primitive lands. But the Spaniards in California had learned not to be needlessly cruel or oppressive. The friars tried to keep the missions and the presidio garrisons reasonably far apart. What they did—and in the case of the missionaries surely with the best of intentions—was to subject the native to a regime hard for him to endure.

Prior to the arrival of Europeans the California Indian had not experienced tuberculosis, influenza, small pox, measles, syphilis, or the common cold; now these were among the fruits of civilization generously and warmheartedly brought to him. He died by thousands—but not because the newcomers desired it. The friars attended him in his misery and did what they could to ease the parting of his soul.

But all this came after the settlement. The California Indian, according to that excellent authority, Zoeth S. Eldredge, was "of all the Indians of America . . . perhaps the least capable of exercising the rights and privileges of citizenship." Thomas Hobbes, in his grand and superior way, would doubtless have included him in his description of man in a state of nature as leading a life "poor, nasty, brutish and short." A life totally unlike that of proper Englishmen in the seventeenth century, one may presume.

Yet, as has been pointed out, the Spaniards made builders of these people, taught them to speak Castilian, initiated them into the art of music, taught them to cultivate the soil. In other words, they could be waked up out of their happy lethargy—but whether this was a gain or a loss who knows? In spite of the friars' efforts to keep the soldiers at the presidio away from the female neophytes at the mission there may be some mixed Indian, Mexican, and Spanish blood in California today, and possibly this mixing was a good experiment.

I don't wish to grow sentimental over these poor people of the presettlement era in California; they are gone like the Etruscans in pre-Roman Italy. Never in historic time would they have built pyramids, worshipped gods that demanded human sacrifices, mined gold, or created cities. They showed no signs of learning to write or to calculate, though in a few thousand years, if left alone, they might have come to these mysteries. They would not have invented the steam engine, aseptic surgery, or the atom bomb.

But they got along. I don't know how to define happiness; I don't know whether there is any such thing in normal life for any length of time. But I shouldn't wonder if these California Indians, especially those who could get down to the southern beaches and eat clams and get sand in their hair, prior to the white man's arrival, weren't happier than their remote contemporaries, the slum dwellers of London, Paris, and Rome.

This is the sort of myth that has troubled civilized men ever since the days of Rousseau. It might also interest followers of the late Dr. Freud. As for me, I can't help speculating as to what the Big Sur Indians thought about as they sat around the fire in the shelter of that ancient rock.

But the California Indians were not going to be let alone forever.

The Long Walk

There is probably no colonizing effort in history that left so few abiding and tangible results, in comparison with the courage, energy, devotion, and publicity that went into it, as the Spanish movement into Upper California toward the end of the eighteenth century.

The place names (and beautiful names they usually are) survive, as do the lovely ruins of most of the missions; some missions have been carefully restored; some Spanish terms are used in California today, even more than in other parts of the old Spanish-Mexican Southwest; cities occupy most of the sites that the friars and the military *commandantes* wisely picked out; but it is not the Spanish or the Spanish-Americans who gave California its actual and characteristic traits; they had their brief day and were inundated by a human breed that in few ways resembled them.

However, this first little army, these pioneers whose work was mostly lost, are the romance: a moonlit, cobwebby romance that their successors have shrewdly bought and sold in a calculated market. They were in their fashion admirable, in some respects beautiful, but now they are a story that is told and a song that is sung. Yet this is a song and story that keeps one wondering, what would they have done if they had had time? Observe, this is the same question that comes up about the Indian.

One also wonders, to be sure, what would have happened if the power of Spain had been on the rise in the final quarter of the eighteenth century; or if the Mexican Government, after Mexico became independent in 1821, had had the men and energy to resist the American advance. But as usual romance could not tip the scales against the heavy odds of men and materials. Spain in California is a prelude only.

The names and events will linger just the same, in all our memories. The story marches to the slow beat of far-away drums. Even though its heroism was largely wasted, it remains a shining example of what men can dare and do. They tried so hard, they meant so well, they were sometimes cruel and sometimes stupid, and now, except in names and a few walls, the glory has departed.

2

California belonged to the Spanish because the Spanish said so. It also belonged to England because Drake had said so. The natives, as was customary, were not asked: they only lived there. The Spaniards were alarmed because the English might drop in again at any minute. The Russians were pushing along the Aleutians and down the Coast, taking sea otter and anything else that was not nailed down and that could be sold at a profit; and apparently they had thought, as a Russian might well have, of getting into warmer water.

In 1765 Charles III of Spain sent Jose de Galvez to America to stir things up, take steps to guard the frontier of "New Spain," get a little money for the royal treasury, and, as it turned out, to do something about Upper California. It wasn't so much, apparently, that Spain wanted this land but that it did not wish any troublesome neighbors to take it over.

Thus there was set in motion a chain of events which eventually created twenty-one missions in Upper California—today's California—and made that area, briefly, a part of the Spanish Empire. California under at least nominal Spanish control lasted half a century; under Mexican jurisdiction, with even less direct rule from Mexico City, it endured about a quarter of a century more. This was the result of heroic pioneering by a very few astoundingly persistent and long-suffering leaders, some clerical, some military and political. They endured as much, suffered as much, risked as much, as the Anglo-Saxons who were in time to take over most of North America. They failed, indeed, but they failed magnificently, and not for lack of any pioneering virtues such as we like to ascribe to the later comers.

3

Galvez, bearing the title of Inspector-General, probably had more authority than the phrase implied. His mission was to see what was wrong and make it right, what was undone and get it done. He was the man from the home office, sent to stir up the branch managers.

He turned first to the project of reaching San Diego by way of Lower California. On the map, it looks as though all you had to do was to ride or walk up the peninsula until you got there. Or you could go by sea, if you liked sailing. The unluckier members of the four expeditions he sent out went by sea in the *San Carlos* and *San Antonio*. Many among their crews died from scurvy and other diseases, though the ships finally got into port.

Two other parties rode or walked, coming up from La Paz through a hostile but not impossible desert. Since they first had to reach La Paz by sea they did not wholly escape the fantastic discomforts of voyagers in those primitive days.

In the end, out of three hundred men on the two ships and in the two land parties, a third were dead from the hardships of the journey, and only sixty-four were in the party that Gaspar de Portola led northward from San Diego toward (as he hoped) Monterey in July, 1769. At San Diego Father Junipero Serra, middle-aged, in pain from a diseased leg but warm with a missionary zeal that anybody of any faith or no faith must recognize as totally unselfish, founded the first mission—San Diego de Alcala.

For Portola, compared with other expeditions he had made and was to make, this was a picnic. But we get a notion of how far off California had been, how little disturbed, when we learn that Portola expected to recognize the Bay of Monterey—"a fine harbor sheltered from all winds," which it wasn't and isn't—from the description of Vizcaino, written more than a century and a half earlier. No reliable person had checked the Vizcaino narrative.

Portola therefore continued northward or northwestward, hoping to come on some landmark that would fit Vizcaino's report. He passed Monterey Bay and from a hill in what is now San Francisco got sight of Point Reyes, a landmark to Spanish explorers. However, the route to Point Reyes and beyond was barred by a great estuary. In other words, the harbor which we called Drake's Bay and which the Spanish called San Francisco Bay could not be reached by Portola's land expedition because the real Bay of San Francisco blocked the way.

There was nothing more to do at that moment; nobody without infinite time at his disposal could walk around the true Bay of San Francisco and reach Point Reyes. These brave and devoted men therefore turned on their tracks and set out again for San Diego. Food ran out, cold and rainy weather arrived, the Indians no longer came around camp with victuals, and for the last twelve days Portola and his faithful followers were reduced to eating their mules—one mule a day. Their reports suggest that after that they never cared much for mule meat.

Such was the first recorded round trip, by land, between San Diego and San Francisco. It established Vizcaino, whose description of Monterey could not be made to fit the facts, as one of the first of the California boosters. Even then, there seems to have been something about California that made people careless with the truth.

4

The returning pilgrims found San Diego in a discouraged mood because of lack of food, presumbly even of mule meat, and there seemed a chance that the search for Monterey might have to be given up. Fortunately the supply ship *San Antonio*, which had been down to San Blas for provisions, came into port just in time.

Her captain had run past San Diego on his way north and had had to turn around and come back to hunt for it. It may seem curious that after so many years of sailing along this coast the Spanish navigators still could not identify harbor entrances, but they had to go largely by landmarks, their instruments were primitive, they had no reliable charts, and sometimes they ran into fog, or into storms that forced them offshore for safety's sake.

Of course they could have learned the coast if they had had the time, the energy, and the money to give to it. The manifest reason for all their fumbling, guessing, and second thinking is that nobody had been sufficiently interested in the Upper California area as a place to find gold or to settle. When the Spanish stopped fooling around, as they were now about to do, they learned a great deal.

Portola tried again, leading a land force in person and sending the *San Antonio* to hunt for Monterey. It took the ship a week longer than the riders and walkers to get there, but they all did. Everything was clear now. This was Monterey, and the intrepid Serra, who came up on the ship, could found his mission. The spot above the Monterey beach where he celebrated his first mass in Monterey is said to have been the same where Vizcaino's party had held a similar service in 1602. One may see a commemorative bronze plate today on a stone reasonably near the shore as it must have been before the later highway and railroad blocked it off.

Inspector-General Galvez was so pleased when news of this success reached Mexico City that he ordered a "general ringing of the bells" to indicate his state of mind. The mission was founded on June 3, 1770, in honor of San Carlos Borromeo, and later moved over the hill to what is now Carmel. Father Serra wrote to Father Palou: "If you will come I shall be content to live and die in this spot." Those who love the natural shape, color, and beauty of that shore will understand the words; and Father Serra had in addition the hope of saving many Indian souls. In Carmel he lived, except when he was on his arduous tours among the other missions. There he died in 1784, at the age of seventy one, after a long life for a man who had lived and worked so hard and endured so much.

Galvez, a practical man, wanted presidios, just as Father Serra, and his brother Franciscans wanted more Indians to save and civilize. The difficulties of getting anything done in a hurry, even when these energetic and impetuous men put their minds to it, are illustrated by the fact that it took about five months for news of the founding of Monterey to reach Mexico City and another six months for orders to come back for the establishment of a mission and presidio at San Francisco. Wherever it was, the orders might have said, for nobody was really sure of anything but the name. Meanwhile, Portola, who, unlike Vizcaino, was not a California booster, had returned to Mexico and Pedro Fages reigned in his place as commandante.

Fages in 1771 had a garrison of nineteen men at Monterey, and his subordinate at San Diego, Fernando Rivera y Moncado, had twenty-two. "This," as Eldredge says, "was the entire military force in California." Rivera did not dare weaken his tiny garrison, so unfriendly were the Indians in his precinct. Fages had to wait until March, 1772, before he was able to scrape together twelve soldiers to guard his pack train north. Father Juan Crespi went with the party.

Fages was still pursuing the old will o' the wisp—the false Bay of San Francisco under Point Reyes. He did not reach it, for again that immutable fact of nature, the true Bay of San Francisco, got in his way. After sighting what we call today Mount Tamalpais and loading it with the title of *La Sierra de Nuestro Padre de San Francisco* Fages went back to Monterey. Fame had been in his grasp but he cleverly avoided it. He had to report to Mexico City that he could not reach the so-called Bay of San Francisco—there was too much water in the way.

In August, 1773, this melancholy news reached the Viceroy Bucareli in Mexico City. The command in California had now passed to Rivera, who on Bucareli's orders received in November, made another try to establish something at some place that might be called San Francisco. Rivera was at Monterey.

The party set out on November 23, 1774. Five days later they were at the site of the modern city of Palo Alto, thirty miles southeast of San Francisco, near what is now Stanford University. Six days later they set up a cross at Point Lobos (not to be confused with the promontory of the same name near Carmel); it was cold and rainy and they gave up and returned to Monterey. Deserts didn't seem to bother these men, but they did hate to get wet.

The winter of 1774–75 went by, and on June 11, 1775, the frigate *San Carlos* reached Monterey, after a passage of one hundred and one days from San Blas, on the northwest coast of Mexico. On July 7th the *San Carlos* sailed for San Francisco—the real San Francisco, although even yet it was not so labeled—and made it eleven days later, a dizzy speed as things went in those days. This was the first ship, as far as we know, ever to enter that port. Under the command of Don Manuel de Ayala, the explorers investigated the harbor, giving names to Angel Island, Alcatraz, and other islands and points, and making friends with the Indians. The Spaniards were still looking for absolute safety for their ships and were not sure that even the snug cove later called Richardson's Bay, the very door to the future city, was secure against the northwest wind.

The Bay was, in fact, too vast for them, or for anybody in their places, to grasp. However, the Ayala party mapped it carefully —and a good map it was. It does not show modern streets, cities, or freeways, but it picks out shorelines almost well enough for a modern navigator to follow.

On his way out of the port Ayala may have been careless with his soundings, for he hit a rock and had to stay a few days longer to fix up his damaged rudder. He finally got clear on September 13, 1775, after forty-four days in and around the future city, and reached Monterey the next day—a fact which indicates that when even a small clumsy craft got the wind behind it, it could do well.

San Francisco Bay was now identified and mapped and would never again be lost in the fog. The spotlight now turns onto a truly remarkable man, Juan Batista de Anza, who was convinced that Upper California, though a prize possession, could never be held and supplied without a land route from Mexico City. And Anza's adventures, though he did find the needed road, suggest again why California was so long thinly held and vaguely administered—why, to recall Queen Calafia again, it stayed so long an island.

5

Anza's father and grandfather had been pioneers and fighters; his father had tried his luck once too often and had been killed by the Apaches. This tragedy did not make Anza timid about Indians or anything else. He now proposed to find a route from Mexico City across the mountains and deserts to the California coast. He had learned from the Yuma and Pima tribes that there were white men in California—which proved that the Indians along the lower Colorado had some way of getting through.

Moreover, Anza knew an extraordinary friar and missionary, Father Francisco Garces, whose headquarters were at San Xavier del Bac, near present-day Tucson. Garces was a sort of ecclesiastical Davy Crockett, and headquarters, for him, was a place from which to start out and to which to return, not a place to settle down and be comfortable. He was as devout and blithe a spirit —and those two adjectives can seldom be applied to the same man—as can be found in the frontier history of North America.

Governor Sastre of Sonora, Mexico, wrote of Father Garces: "Moved by a higher impulse, with no other provisions than a little pinole, a little chocolate and a fews strips of jerked beef, and with no other escort than his guardian angel" (the citation is from Professor Bolton's *Outpost of Empire*), he thrice walked out into the uncharted wilderness, going down to the Gila River, then crossing the deserts to the eastern side of the San Jacinto Range. Father Garces really reached California in his stroll, as the state line is now drawn.

A man of peace, he had no trouble in making friends with the Indians, though later they turned against him in a furious assault on all Spaniards. But he had an incredible career, of a sort that makes some of the later heroes of the Wild West look silly. He went with Anza to San Gabriel in 1774; later he was the discoverer of the Kern River and Tulare Lake. He was only forty-three years old when he was killed—but they were good years.

Anza had other guides, but Father Garces was the best of them, the most buoyant of them, the most fearless of them, and the longest remembered. He missed being an American folk hero by not being an Anglo-Saxon and by being born about a generation too soon.

The story of the Anza expeditions has been told and retold. Its essence is that Anza and his companions were of extremely tough stock, that except when plundered by the Apaches he lost no lives or goods, and that he succeeded in carrying a colonizing expedition, including women and children, across some of the most appalling wastelands in the world.

His route did not prove practicable in the end. But to say that his valor and skill were wasted would be wrong, for Anza did make the Spanish settlements in Upper California a reality, twice crossing and recrossing the desert between Sonor and Monterey and opening a useful, though impermanent road. He might be regarded as the actual founder of San Francisco, though he was not present when Jose Joaquin Moraga took possession for Spain on September 17, 1776. The battered old frigate *San Carlos* had again pulled into that port, nearly a month earlier; she had taken seventy-three days to come up from Monterey. (As we have seen, she had made it in eleven days the year before—an example of the vagaries of California weather.) In this instance she had been blown so far south and west that her prudent captain had headed her northward, when the winds permitted, to a point so far above San Francisco that he had sailed a distance, as Bolton estimates, of "some two thousand miles."

Overland passages were rough and dangerous but more predictable. Yet Upper California remained still isolated, still an island —still, for the outer world, a land of myth and mystery. Anza, in his first trip from Tubac (in what is now Arizona) to Monterey, took two and a half months and had to cover, going and coming, two thousand miles. By horse, mule, or on foot, a good day's journey was fifteen miles—and so remained until the Americans began to cross the continent by stage coaches and the pony express. Modern travelers who ride into Southern California today by the Salt Lake Line, the Santa Fe, the Southern Pacific, or the big motor roads may be able to imagine what the early Mexican-Spanish adventurers endured; they merely have to conceive themselves on foot or animalback in the sand, with no road and no dependable landmarks.

Unlike the Santa Fe, California, and Oregon Trails of later days, the Sonora-Monterey-San Francisco Trail laid out by Anza and his companions lasted only briefly. Specifically, it lasted only until the Yuma uprising in 1781, led by a chief who had been a warm friend of Anza, made it impassable.

Under these circumstances of difficult access by land and sea California could not grow rapidly in population—indeed, the Indian population dwindled year by year. The land could grow in wealth only as the soil was cultivated, stock brought in, and small industries developed—the pattern of feudal Europe. To compensate for these deficiencies the fur trade and later the hide trade developed, and ships became somewhat more dependable.

At the end of the eighteenth century the easiest way to get to California seemed to be to come in from the west by way of the Sandwich Islands, as the State of Hawaii was then known. But how to get to that turning point was another question.

Queen Calafia held out long past the time when she might have been expected to abdicate her imaginary throne on her imaginary island.

6

The forces of change were of course at work, however sluggishly. There was a slow infusion of western culture. The missions were one by one established, until finally there were twenty-one of them—ranging in order of foundation from San Diego in 1769 to Sonoma in 1823.

Then, with Father Serra long in his grave and with the establishment of the Mexican Republic, the drive to "secularize" the missions were inevitable. The last of them to undergo this process was Santa Clara, after an existence of less than sixty years. The mission Indians, thus "liberated," do not seem always to have enjoyed their new freedom. They nominally got a share of the missions' lands and wealth, which indeed they had helped to maintain or create, but they were not businessmen and rarely managed to hold on to this small inheritance.

If the Indians were not all landless and poor by the time the lordly Anglo-Saxon took over the country, they soon became so; the North Americans were more abrupt in their methods and more contemptuous of what they took to be the lesser breeds than the Spaniards had ever been.

Dana in 1836 found the Santa Barbara mission still in operation as a place of worship, but it was "a large and deserted-looking place, the out-buildings going to ruin and everything giving the impression of decayed grandeur." Yet it is said that Mass has been said daily at this mission, in spite of political conditions, earthquakes, and epidemics, since 1786. The buildings could be wrecked, as they were in the 1925 earthquake, but the mission continued.

Yet the great days and the great power of the missions were over in the middle 1830s. It was not until the North Americans had come in, taken the land, and gradually mellowed into a more sentimental phase that the old establishments were preserved or restored, and became, even for nonbelievers, objects of pilgrimage. But in these latter days the Indians were names on tombstones; and the hills where they had hunted and the rocks where they had gathered abalone and mussels would not have been accessible to them, even if they had ventured to trespass there.

It is not easy to find out what happened to these neophytes, who once worked, prayed, and sang at the missions. Many must have gone back to the wilderness, where they could not be counted by any census taker. John Marsh estimated that in 1845 California had seven thousand persons of Spanish (or Mexican-Spanish) blood, and about ten thousand "domesticated" Indians. Royce's figures, based on Bancroft's are about the same for the population of Spanish blood. Of the so-called "Spanish" blood, some individuals may have represented a mixture of Europeans with the Maya, the Aztec, and the Indians of California itself. The grandees may have kept themselves unadulterated; designated lower orders no doubt did not. It is not possible to believe that the Spanish-Mexican soldiers in California were resolutely celibate. There may be more Indian blood in the area than appears at first glance.

But again, it is all a story that is told, a song that is finished. The California Indian of latter days was a tragic and pathetic figure, sometimes violent but not often, deprived of his old way of life and unschooled in any new one, without rights or hopes in the land that had once been his. Some shining virtues show in the lives of the Missionary Fathers, but they could not save a doomed race from the gathering storm of western civilization.

Ironically, the first breath and ripple of that storm was not much: it was one of the last expressions of the dying power of a once great empire, Spain.

The fabulous California before the American occupation, the trapper influx, and the trickle of American settlers that was beginning around the second quarter of the nineteenth century— these, in terms of people, were a small matter, indeed. Given the risk and trouble, few cared to come to California. Few knew much about the region, and many of those found it lonesome and desolate.

There was a sort of "Golden Age" before the Gold Rush that began in 1848. How golden was this gilded dream? How romantic was this period over which so many millions of Californians of these latter times grow moist-eyed?

The Pre-Gold "Golden Age"

The romantic vision of California prior to the American occupation runs somewhat as follows: it was a land of pastoral simplicity; of instinctive hospitality toward all comers, whether or not strangers; of beautiful women and gallant men; of exquisite manners; of a life simple but contented. The legend is that a traveler could ride the whole length of this imaginary lotus land and count on being entertained at every rancho; that these ranchos, like the missions, were spaced about a comfortable day's journey apart; and—as a fascinating final touch—that a dish containing silver coins would be left where the visitor could help himself if he cared to and was short of funds. These coins, it is added, were never counted; they were merely replenished when they ran low.

California, under the Spanish-Americans and Mexicans, was in fact recognizably feudal, but of the most genial type of feudalism, not seriously bothered by the theoretical central government in Mexico and not menaced until the last by danger of outside attack. Nobody, even the poorest, worked beyond his strength, and even the work that had to be done was often picturesque and adventurous. If digging or cultivating were required the Indians did it.

If a person wishes to find out, in a general way, what society was like he might visit some South American backwoods area today—and then eliminate any modern inventions, especially in the field of medicine and education, that he may find there.

Spanish-Mexican California did produce some remarkable men, as the records show and as the tourist may observe in the faces— many of them photographed—in the Colton Hall exhibit in Monterey, and elsewhere. At their best they were far more civilized than the wild men from the Missouri River frontier who came over the mountains. They were more humane than that famous frontier man Kit Carson. They were not as fatuous as that renowned glory-chaser, John C. Frémont.

Still, there weren't many such men in Spanish-American California. By the law of averages, there couldn't be. Out of a population of a few thousand with some Spanish blood in their veins— the equivalent of a small village—the Californians of colonial days did well to produce a dozen or a score of this high stature.

What these people had sounds alluring, provided one does not also list what they did not have. For food they had beef in abundance, wheat, which was always planted around the missions, poultry and mutton, grapes, wine (which the missions had but which the feudal lords were buying in American ports in Dana's time), an orange once in a while, a few vegetables, and of course fish and wild game. By today's standards their diet—and, let us face it, their whole existence—would seem monotonous. And I don't suppose any population would be more bored by the way their "romantic" predecessors had to live than would the present population of California, whose chief occupation, when practicable, is a frantic effort to get away from boredom of a slightly different and more sophisticated sort.

The richer Californians, in the "Golden Age," were all dressed up, lace and silks for the woman, silver buttons for the men, whether or not they had a place to go. They were elaborately garbed on ceremonial occasions, men as well as women. The materials must of course have been imported from the outer world. The men enjoyed the comparatively noncerebral sport of cockfighting, as well as a bloody pastime in which a bull and a bear were lashed together and left to batter it out. There was a good deal of dancing—fun for the young and good for the digestions of the elderly.

Everybody rode horseback, there being no satisfactory vehicles and few good roads for them to travel on. Dana in the 1830s, Robert Louis Stevenson in the late 1870s, observed that though the saddle and bridle were expensive the horse was cheap; and that no Californian of the old stock would as much as walk down the street if a horse—any horse, anybody's horse—were handy.

This way of life in its thin splendor, reminds one a little of a planter's life in the magnolia-and-cotton days of our own Old South, before the Civil War; though it was never so cruel or so self-conscious. Perhaps to relieve the monotony, some of the Californian hidalgos occasionally rebelled, in a mild and bloodless way, against the demands of Mexico City. Not much could be done to them, or by them. California couldn't really be governed by remote control from Mexico. It wasn't really governed at all, though it had governors. It was controlled, as in earlier forms of feudalism, by those who controlled the land—including eventually thousands of acres sequestered from the missions.

2

The Golden Age illusion is aided and abetted by the violent, though comparatively bloodless, transformation that occurred when the United States took over California and when the world learned that a different kind of gold was to be found there. Thousands of energetic and acquisitive young men thereupon poured into the country. The Gold Rush had its own heroic aspects, and some sordid ones, but it was not Arcadian. So in the later years of the nineteenth century many persons began to look back to the pastoral period, as some of us today look back to the "Golden Nineties." Unconsciously, as a rule, they began telling lies about it, just as some of us tell lies about how pleasant it was when there were no automobiles or television sets.

The question we have to ask is not how the pastoral age looks from a distance but how it seemed to those who lived with it in its prime.

For young Richard Henry Dana, seeing it as a sailor before the mast (and also as an exiled Boston Brahmin), the social system was blatantly aristocratic. There were, he said, but few pure-blooded Spanish families in California, and these formed "the upper class, intermarrying and keeping up an exclusive system in every respect. . . . Generally speaking, each person's caste is decided by the quality of his blood, which shows itself, too plainly to be concealed at first sight. Yet the least drop of Spanish blood . . . is sufficient to raise one from the position of a serf and entitle him to a suit of clothes . . . and to call himself Español, and to hold property if he can get any." Dana saw pure-blooded Indians running around "with nothing on but a small piece of cloth, kept up by a wide leathern strap around the waist." (He might have seen more and found classification more difficult on a California beach today, but that is another story.)

Dana reported that the secularization of the missions had stripped the priests of "all their possessions" but that the Indians remained "virtually serfs, as much as they ever were." The missions themselves, in 1836 (certainly a part of the alleged Golden Age) "were going rapidly to decay."

For the youthful Harvard undergraduate, who went to sea to cure an eye ailment, a great deal of pastoral California was dreary and forlorn. He liked Monterey and disliked Santa Barbara and San Pedro, partly because Monterey, though not a first class harbor, was less exposed to most winds. At the other two ports a quick shift in the weather called sleeping sailors from the watch to "bear a hand" in slipping the anchor cable and making sail to get out to the safety of deep water. He found San Diego comfortable as a mooring ground but in no respect "romantic," and was glad to get away after some time on shore curing hides.

In Dana's time, as he says, "revolutions were matters of frequent occurrence in California. They are gotten up [he continues] by men who are at the foot of the ladder and in desperate circumstances. . . . As for justice they know little law but will and fear. . . . In their domestic relations these people are not better than in their public. The men are shiftless, proud, extravagant and very much given to gaming; and the women have but little education and a good deal of beauty, and their morality, of course, is none of the best; yet the instances of infidelity are much less frequent than one would at first suppose." We should remember, to be sure, that this is a boy speaking, just past twenty when he was in California, twenty-five when he wrote his famous book.

Dana went on to speculate: "In the hands of an enterprising people what a country this might be!" Then he wondered (as well he might, I should say) how long people of North American or English stock would remain "enterprising" if they lived in this environment.

The most idyllic passage Dana wrote about California was his account of the wedding of the ship's agent, Alfred Robinson, in Santa Barbara, in 1936, to Doña Anita de la Guerra. Dana didn't like Robinson, and said so, but he praised the beauty of the bride's sister, Doña Angustia ("a handsome woman and a general favorite") and long remembered the "sound of violins and guitars." And this, no doubt, was the best of the older California—a clear night, a happy occasion, music and dancing, and everybody in a jovial mood. Even the bars of caste were a little lowered; everybody, rich or poor, could come to such celebrations, though only a few were expected to step inside for refreshments.

The other face of the picture might be sailors ashore in San Diego or Monterey; at San Diego a one-eyed Fall River Yankee kept a *pulpería* where each sailor was expected to stand treat, man and man about, at twelve and a half cents a drink. The Californians were still importing wine, although they had the good "mission grapes." They were also exporting leather and importing shoes. Dana continued to think them "an idle, thriftless people." Humanitarian though he was, he could not shake off his strict New England preconceptions.

One way to reconcile the memory of pastoral California as an earthly paradise with these comments of Dana's is to bear in mind that idleness and thriftlessness are sometimes pleasant to remember. The small Spanish-Mexican community in California's colonial days didn't have to work as hard as their contemporaries on the coast of Massachusetts, for they had no real winter. Nor did they worry too much about money, because in spite of the abundance of silver coins the real wealth was in land and cattle. The Spanish-Mexicans rode horses and supervised other men who were usually on foot and who really did work; the land owners and their retinue kept busy enough but in a pleasant and healthful way.

The Indians, not being as a rule literate, wrote no memoirs. If they had done so, they might have described the situation as somewhat less idyllic than the one that had existed before the white men arrived. Probably they were materially better off under the Padres, and maybe under the civil government, than when they were loose in the woods and hills; they could be flogged if they were recalcitrant, but they usually had enough to eat and some handy place to sleep. But we shall never know whether they looked back to some previous period as a golden age; they would not have been human if they had not done so.

Some of them ran away and were forcibly brought back. Some stayed on the mission lands and became good artisans, farmers, and musicians. They could have driven the Spanish-Americans out if they had organized for the purpose, for the alien "army" in the vast area between San Diego and what is now the Oregon line was never more than a few score strong. But though they attempted a revolt now and then they were never a serious threat to the Spanish or Mexican power.

The California of 1776–1846 (the last seventy years of even nominal rule from Mexico City) seems to me as I read about it picturesque, colorful, unambitious—and dull. Yet it was changing rapidly: the connection with Mexico was weakening, especially after the Mexican Revolution of 1821; foreign trading ships were coming regularly on the coast; the Russians were making what turned out to be futile efforts to work their way south; the English had their eyes on this underdeveloped area, as we should now call it, but they were busy elsewhere; and anybody with the prophetic gift could see, even before the Mexican War and the Gold Rush, that this was real estate the United States would find good moral and practical reasons to take over, subdivide, and settle.

3

Population grew by means of a heavy birth rate among the Spanish-Americans. It was also expanded, though not fast enough to scare anybody, by a trickle of runaway sailors and a few traders whom the California administration at Monterey was often glad enough to accept if each would adopt the Roman Catholic religion and marry a local girl. By the time Dana made his visit to the coast, American ships were buying hides—"California bank notes," as Dana and others tell us they were called—and exchanging American manufactured goods for them. Dana gives a graphic account of the way in which some of the captains bypassed the customs officers without fulfilling the legal requirement to put the goods ashore; he tells us also how a trade room and counter were fitted up on the *Pilgrim* as she lay at Monterey —for all the world, one thinks, like an old-fashioned village store.

"For a week or ten days," he writes, "all was life on board. The people came off to look and to buy—men, women and children; and we were continually going in the boats. . . . Our cargo was an assorted one; that is, it consisted of everything under the sun. We had spirits (sold by the cask), teas, coffee, sugars, spices, raisins, molasses, hardware, crockery ware, tin ware, cutlery, clothing of all kinds, boots and shoes from Lynn, calicoes and cottons from Lowell, crepes, silks, scarfs, necklaces, jewelry and combs for the women; furniture, and, in fact, everything that can be imagined, from Chinese fireworks to English cart wheels—of which we had a dozen pairs with their iron tires on."

Thus the Golden Age began to hanker for commodities that California could not or would not produce. And the need for something to vary the monotony of life, something from the outside world, led the local authorities to overlook a certain amount of smuggling, and possibly, on occasion, to accept open or left-handed bribes. Moreover, since the Californians were not bred to business, they almost had to permit some foreigners—usually North Americans—to carry it on for them.

An American sailor, Thomas W. Doak, so Eldredge says, was

the first of his nationality to settle in California; this was in 1816. Two Englishmen, William A. Richardson, who built the first store in San Francisco, and Robert Livermore, who gave his name to the Livermore Valley, arrived not long afterwards. Abel Stearns, Nathan Spear, and Alfred Robinson (the same ship's agent whose wedding Dana saw at Santa Barbara) were other Americans who established themselves in California when their special talents were needed and welcome. Most of them did well, indeed.

These facts may remind the observer that the simple, kindly Arcadia of legends was never fixed and never undiluted: from the beginning it was in turmoil, it was never satisfied with itself, it always wanted more than it had—and eventually got more than it wanted.

Yankee and British merchants, as a rule, were men who wanted to marry, settle down, conform to the customs of the country, and make money. It was only in the last respect that they resembled the trappers—or "mountain men"—who began to come over the big hills from the East in the 1820s.

The trappers were the final generation of professional wilderness men in our history. They had to have steady and unflinching courage, coolness in time of danger, which for them was practically all the time, long training and experience, infinite knowledge of the savage environment in which they moved, a capacity for getting on with at least one tribe of Indians (often they married an Indian squaw), and ability to live and work alone when necessary. When they got to town, or to the annual rendezvous where they could exchange their furs for other sorts of goods, they were likely to engage in gorgeous sprees. But they couldn't afford to carry much liquor on the trail, nor would they, under circumstances requiring constant vigilance, dare do so.

They must also have been men of a peculiar type, with a distrust or dislike of the ordinary ways and customs of civilization. A modern psychiatrist could have had a rich time studying some of them. They seemed like supermen in the exercise of their trade, which lasted a few brief years when the skin of the beaver was used for making hats and declined when the beaver hat went out of style and the beaver himself diminished in number.

Many of these trappers could be, and were, a disorderly element when they got into a settled community, especially a community settled, as California was, by people of a race and culture different from their own. To them (and I am speaking of the Anglo-Saxon breed of trapper rather than the more adaptable French-Canadian) different meant inferior. (We catch reflections of this attitude in California, even today, but I don't blame the trappers for it.) The trappers could act, and sometimes did act, like ruffians and bums. No doubt it was their way of relaxing.

A shining exception to all such generalities was Jedediah Smith, who was the first trapper and hunter of record to reach California by passage over the Sierras. Smith arrived at San Gabriel in December, 1826, leading a party of about fifteen men.

Smith was not only a man of courage and endurance, to a degree extraordinary even among trappers, he was also a man of high character, who did not drink and who carried a Bible with him on his wilderness trips. He got into trouble with the Mexican Governor, Echandia, who threw him into jail in San Diego on a charge of illegal entry. He was such an obviously good man that he was soon released, but on a second trip he was seized again, this time at Monterey. (Remember, this was still the Golden Age in California.) Again no blemish could be found on his record or character, and he was permitted to go free. Pushing forward through Northern California and into Oregon, his entire party, except for himself and two men, were killed in an Indian ambush. He survived to get back to more familiar territory, only to be killed by the Comanches on the Santa Fe Trail, in 1831, at a water hole in the Cimarron Valley.

Smith was described as a "well-bred, intelligent, and Christian gentleman," who once warned a young man who asked his advice about becoming a trapper that the dangers were extreme, and that if the young man survived them he "would be ruined for anything else in life than such things as would be agreeable to the passions of a semisavage." If all the mountain men who drifted into early California had been like Jedediah Smith—well, we can see that history in that area would have been more edifying.

More in the conventional tradition was James Ohio Pattie, who

with his father, Sylvester Pattie, wandered into Southern California in late 1827. They encountered the same irascible Governor
Echandia who had made life difficult for Jedediah Smith, and the
elder Pattie died in jail at San Diego. Up to this point the Pattie
narrative, which was published in 1831, isn't too hard to believe.
But one has to stretch his imagination to accept some other elements in it: for instance, that young Pattie wangled his own re-
lease from jail by offering to give smallpox vaccinations from a
store he happened to have with him; and that he subsequently
vaccinated ten thousand inhabitants. In 1830 Governor Echandia
gratefully let him go, and he returned home through Mexico—
finding in Cincinnati, it is clear, an imaginative ghost writer as
well as a publisher. A man was safe in lying about California in
those days, so few people had been there. Later, one had to be
more careful.

Such were the beginnings of the trapper movement into the region. Once the trails were roughly known it was no great trick for
these tough frontiersmen to follow them, and California, for
mountain men who didn't care to go all the way back to St.
Louis, was a pleasant place in which to spend the winter. As indeed it still is. Moreover, the streams in the Rockies were getting
beavered out, and the beaver market wasn't what it had been.

In 1839 Captain John Augustus Sutter arrived, just in time to
span the gap between the two golden ages. And he was something new and peculiar, neither a mountain man nor a sailor off a
ship.

4

Captain Sutter (he was called by that title, because he had
once served in the Swiss army, and because he said he had once
served in the French army) arrived at what seemed to be a favorable time. In fact, it has always seemed odd that a man who
had failed in business, as he had done in his own country (Germany) should have had the means to set up as a sort of emperor
in California.

But Sutter did have the means, the assurance, or the credit that
was just as good. He got to California by leading a party from St.

Louis to Oregon, then taking ship to Honolulu, then returning to San Francisco as supercargo on a trading vessel. He had an astounding set of recommendations from Russian, British, and Hawaiian sources, and easily persuaded Governor Alvarado (a kindlier man than the Governor Echandia, who had shut up the Patties and imprisoned the saintly Jedediah Smith) to promise him a huge grant on the Sacramento River. In 1841 he was given the documents for eleven square leagues, or nearly 40,000 acres. He also bought the Russian post at Fort Ross. Eldredge says he was "described by visitors of that period as living in a principality sixty miles long by twelve broad in a state of virtual independence."

Who put up the cash or credit? This factor remains vague—to me, at least. Undoubtedly Alvarado counted on Sutter to hold the northern frontier. Undoubtedly, also, the United States Government, (President Monroe had warned Europeans against further colonization in this hemisphere) had colonization plans of its own.

Captain Sutter couldn't have been sent out by our Government. If he had been, he wouldn't have taken so many months and such an indirect course to get to California—and anyhow an American citizen would have been chosen. (Sutter had become a Mexican.) But the moment Sutter got established at Sutter's Fort, at what is now Sacramento, his usefulness to such American plans as existed was clear.

Though Governor Alvarado had given him his grant he was not fantastically loyal to Alvarado—or to any other Mexican governor. He served such government as there was by fortifying his post, equipping it with cannon, and maintaining a species of militia; but every sign indicated that he was chiefly loyal to John A. Sutter. It was not in any sacrificial mood that he bought out the Russians and discouraged the Hudson's Bay Company trappers, who were working south into California.

When he had to have friends he chose American friends. Toward Yankee trappers, hunters, and would-be settlers he displayed the greatest hospitality, and when the time came, as it soon did, he provided a rallying point for American action against the Mexican provincial regime at Monterey. Every traveler who came over the mountains from the East was sure to find a kindly reception at Sutter's Fort. When Frémont blundered through in early 1844, barely escaping the Sierra snows, Sutter gave him the supplies he required—taking Frémont's drafts on the United States Topographical Bureau at a twenty per cent discount. Thus Captain Sutter, though helpful, was also thrifty.

By this time nobody who knew the facts could doubt that the United States and Mexico would soon come to blows, with the Texas boundary as an excuse. Nor could it be doubted that California would go the way Texas had, perhaps to independence first, then to annexation and statehood.

In this development Sutter was to play his part, but not in a way he had foreseen, nor, in spite of the fact that he lived on the edge of an almost unimaginable treasureland, a profitable one for him.

Nobody knew about gold in California—not yet. Nevertheless we can be sure that in due time the same urge that settled Oregon would have populated the fertile valleys of California even though nothing more precious than iron sulphide had ever been discovered in the foothills of the Sierra Nevada. What old Senator Benton called "manifest destiny" was in the air and in men's minds; and it seemed to mean that whatever the Republic of the United States wanted it was justified in taking.

The process of absorption was beginning when the first stationary traders—the ship's agents, the keepers of stores—settled near the coast. It would have continued as the mountain men wandered in, once the beaver supply and the beaverpelt market were exhausted, and took each a bit of land. At the very best even a Rocky Mountain trapper couldn't have spent his old age in the mountains, and he might have preferred to take his chances in California rather than in a shabby back street in St. Louis. And the land-hungry farmers, who actually did settle Oregon, would have tried California, gold or no gold, if they had been able to get land. This was one aspect of manifest destiny of which Senator Benton, who happened to be John Charles Frémont's father-in-law, was fond of talking.

As early as 1840, Antoine Robideaux, a French-Canadian resident in Missouri, was using what later came to be familiar terms in urging his neighbors to migrate to the "perfect paradise, the perpetual spring" beyond the Sierras. In 1841 John Bidwell, barely old enough to vote, arrived at Sutter's Fort as leader of a party from Sapling Grove, Missouri. Rolle estimates that as many as 1,500 immigrants entered California between 1843 and 1846, another 5,500 going to the Oregon Territory. California, of course, was Mexican soil until 1848. The Americans were beginning to settle the country without the formal consent of its legal owners—or even, in all cases, of its semi-independent occupants.

With or without war, with or without gold in the hills, the golden age in California was being brought to an end. The Americans of our own generation would idealize this "golden" period, but the Americans of the 1840s didn't especially care for it. They wanted to make something different and new in their own pattern, and they did.

5

It is considered subversive, in the State of California, to question the integrity of John Charles Frémont or to belittle the land-grabbing raid known as the Bear Flag Revolt. To this day the Bear Flag, below the Stars and Stripes, to be sure, flies over every public building of the State in California. Possibly this does no harm, but it is not an accurate symbol of what happened in California in 1846.

The truth is that Frémont, who was in California on an errand having no reasonable connection with politics or foreign policy, helped raise the flag of rebellion against the Mexican Government in California in an unnecessary and lawless way before he knew that the United States and Mexico were at war.

Frémont was not a regular army officer but a commander of a small force sent to survey parts of California. But he was ambitious; he had the support of his father-in-law, Senator Benton of Missouri; he always showed a disposition to evade orders he did not like; and he had under his control, besides a few surveyors, a force of civilian Americans, not formally enlisted in any legitimate army and in many cases out to take any land or property they could lay hands on. Frémont himself was a vain poseur, like one or two other generals in our national history. His chief virtues on the trail were that he was a good surveyor and a good note-taker. Never by any stretch of the imagination did he merit the epithet of "Pathfinder" popularly given him; the only good paths he found were already well known to the mountain men. His later career included his futile race for the Presidency on the first Republican national ticket in 1856 and his dismissal by Lincoln from the command of the Western Department, in St. Louis, in the first year of the Civil War, for insubordination.

He had been in California in 1844, abandoning in the Sierras a brass howitzer his party had surreptitiously obtained from the Army ordnance division and painfully dragged across the Plains —to survey with, one supposes. In January, 1846, on his third expedition, he was back again, at Sutter's Fort; from here he went south to visit Consul Larkin at Monterey; thence he retired a few miles to an elevation called the Gavilan Peak, above the Salinas Valley, built a fort, and ran up the Stars and Stripes.

Governor Castro objected, as he had a right and duty to do, and word came that a Mexican-Californian force was being organized to attack Frémont's small army of topographers, mountain men, and "patriots." And self-proclaimed "patriotism," then as now, could be exactly what Dr. Samuel Johnson called it, "the last refuge of a scoundrel."

Frémont thereupon reluctantly gave up his minor Bunker Hill without a fight, passed over into the San Joaquin Valley, and started slowly for Oregon. On the way an American officer of marines, bearing letters and dispatches from Washington, overtook him. These dispatches, which included a message from his father-in-law, Senator Benton, made Frémont "know distinctly that at last the time had come when England must not get a foothold. I was to act, discreetly but positively."

Since Army topographical engineers were not under the command of United States Senators or organized for warfare, the reference is a peculiar one. However, Frémont turned about and hotfooted it back to the Sacramento Valley where another patriot, a settler named William B. Ide, headed a band which had been stealing Mexican horses; Ide had also arrested the Mexican commander at Sonora, California, Mariano G. Vallejo, a man well known for his friendly attitude toward the Americans. On June 14, 1846, Ide and some companions proclaimed a California Republic and ran up the famous Bear Flag. Frémont did not go to Sonoma with the raiders, but it is certain that he did not discourage them.

Meanwhile United States Consul Larkin at Monterey had received a slightly ambiguous letter from Secretary of State Buchanan in Washington. The message stated that "this Government has no ambitious aspirations to gratify and no desire to extend our Federal system over more territory than we already possess, unless by the free and spontaneous wish of the independent people of adjoining territories." Mr. Buchanan then obliquely referred to possible attempts to transfer such peoples and territories "without their consent, to Great Britain or France." What he meant, it is now clear, is that the United States intended to take California, with or without anybody's consent. When this letter was written the United States was still nominally at peace with Mexico. Nor was there any real danger that either England or France would interfere with this vast real estate transaction. It was in this very year, in fact, that England relinquished all claim to any part of the Pacific Coast below the present northern boundary of Oregon.

Mr. Larkin, so the Secretary of State intimated, was to do his best to make the transfer friendly and peaceable. And the Bear Flag revolters, coming under the leadership of John Charles Frémont, did *their* best to make the change rough, unfriendly, and bloody.

California could easily have been taken over by the United States without any help at all from Frémont or his unwashed contingent of mountain men and surveyors. The Navy had warships available, first under Commodore Sloat, then under Commodore Stockton. The Army was in due season represented by that doughty warrior, General Stephen Watts Kearny, who brought a small but effective force across the continent from the

Missouri River, by way of Santa Fe. Frémont wasn't needed. The Bear Flag Revolt was superfluous—although Stockton did make use of Frémont and his ragged contingent when he took command in Monterey. On January, 1847, Stockton named Frémont civil Governor. Less than two months later Kearny, who had now arrived on the scene, took over as civil as well as military Governor; and when Frémont refused to obey orders from him, he sent the young explorer home to stand court martial for insubordination.

I have omitted many details in this account of Frémont's exploits. He made a great stir, he acted as though he and his companions had won great encounters and endured sufferings comparable only with those of Washington's troops at Valley Forge; yet he never fought a pitched battle in California or contributed to the maintenance of good feeling between the conquerors and the conquered.

However, he went home as a hero. Convicted by a lenient court martial, with all penalties remitted except a formal rebuke from President Polk, Frémont resigned his commission. Nine years later he still had enough prestige to be the first Republican nominee for President. It now seems fortunate for the country that he was not elected.

Some charges against him will be longer remembered than the charge of insubordination toward that old-fashioned martinet, Stephen Kearny. One that will not be forgotten is that he allowed three innocent and unarmed Californians, Jose Berryesa and two brothers, Francisco and Ramon de Haro, to be shot down in cold blood at his camp near San Rafael, in June, 1846. Kit Carson had a part in this atrocity and was reported long afterwards to have bitterly repented it. Several other men died unnecessarily because of Frémont's thirst for military glory.

Why subsequent generations of Californians should have glorified Frémont it is hard to say. But they did—and some still do. I do not see any reason at this late time for being sentimental about him. I believe he would have served his country well if he had confined himself to surveying and making topographical notes and left strategy and politics to wiser men. He might not then

have had a chance to make a dismal failure as a Presidential candidate and later as a Union General in Missouri, but he would
have come much nearer to being the shining knight he had hoped
to be—and as his beautiful young wife, the former Jessie Benton,
thought him.

The taking of California by the United States was not a struggle for liberty. It came from two forces: first, our westward
march, which could not be averted; second, our material superiority over any possible Mexican resistance. It could have been more
peaceful and less costly in blood and treasure than it was.

Frémont may later have understood how it felt to be a victim
of the Westward Movement, for he had troubles with American
miners on his forty-thousand-acre estate in the Sierra foothills. He
had moved in on the Mexican Californians, and now his brother
Americans moved in on him.

☼ *4* ☼ ☼ ☼

The Age of Gold

It is a great irony that the Spaniards, who found so much gold in the New World and looked so hard for it in places where it wasn't, such as Kansas, should have missed the richest source of all—the California Mother Lode. But they did.

It is likewise an irony that Mexico ceded California and other real estate to the United States in a treaty signed a little over a week after James Marshall discovered gold at Sutter's Mill at Coloma. But such was the case.

As King Midas found, gold cannot be eaten or drunk. Its industrial uses are important but limited. Too much gold will produce inflation, just as will too much paper money. Gold is a drug, curing some ailments and causing others. For California, it did more good than harm, since it stimulated the production of other and more useful forms of wealth; but it was also a calamity, since it destroyed an old society without at first creating a healthy new one; it inflated prices; it perpetuated the gambling spirit; it brought in crime and violence; and it encouraged a dangerous way of dealing with violence.

California would normally have grown far more slowly in population if gold had not been found. Gold transformed San Francisco, in a year or so, from a sleepy pueblo of a few hundred souls, into a howling city of forty thousand. Gold made California a state with brief apprenticeship as a territory. Gold helped support the Union armies during the Civil War. Gold brought better roads, a route across Panama, regular passenger steamships, and, within two decades, a transcontinental railroad.

Gold gave California a new legend, and a new set of lies, to balance—and contrast with—the old legends and lies of the Spanish pastoral lords. Gold brought and preserved democratic government, often corrupt, sometimes arbitrary, but better than the bungling, lazy, caballero type that had preceded it.

Modern Californians, in their love of romance that contrasts so strangely with the eager realism of their economic lives, grow sentimental over the Spanish-Mexican days of roses, stock raising, guitar playing, and fiestas; also over the sterling qualities of Frémont's mountain men and topographical surveyors, who held the Gavilan Peak against a nonexistent enemy—and then ran away; also over the rugged and picturesque virtues of the gold miners.

There is, of course, some basis for the sentiment. Some of the Spanish landowners were admirable men, some were true statesmen. Many of the miners, before mining was organized, centralized and capitalized, and before the dredgers began their systematic ruination of many acres of California land, were heroic individuals. They had to be such to reach California at all, whether they came by land, by sea around the Horn, or through the fever-haunted woods of the Isthmus of Panama.

Mark Twain, coming to California a decade and a half after the Gold Rush, met many of the survivors and out of his own experience understood them. He, too, had prospected—and failed. He wrote of the dead towns of California, those that had been the centers of a vigorous and hilarious life, and then, as the gold was mined out, had faded away. Remnants of such towns can be seen today; one of them, Columbia, in Tuolumne County, is now a state park. But it was the men—for there were few women—who were important, tragic, comic, and infinitely sad. For California's great fortunes did not begin with gold dug by hand out of the earth. In a large way, it was the merchants, hotelkeepers, gambling house operators, saloonkeepers, and speculators who got ahead.

Mark Twain wrote (in *Roughing It*): "It was a driving, vigorous, restless population in those days. . . . It was the *only* population of the kind that the world has ever seen gathered together, and it is not likely that the world will ever see its like again. . . . For, observe, it was an assemblage of two hundred thousand *young* men . . . brimful of push and energy, and royally endowed with every attribute that goes to make up a peerless and magnificent manhood—the very pick and choice of the world's glorious ones . . . the strangest population, the finest population, the most gallant host that ever trooped down the startled solitudes of an unpeopled land. And where are they now [1872, or thereabouts]? . . . All gone, or nearly all—victims devoted upon the altar of the golden calf—the noblest holocaust that ever wafted its sacrificial incense heavenward."

Mark Twain was here pulling out all the stops in a way he seldom did. He must have dropped a tear or two. Not that there is no truth in his picture. Weaklings just didn't get to California, except by accident, during the Gold Rush. But our author overlooked some of the things, not always noble, that the forty-niners did to the Indians, the Chinese, and the Chileans, and to one another. And he makes the Gold Rush a crusade—which it wasn't.

2

There have been gold rushes, silver rushes, diamond rushes, uranium rushes, and, of course, land rushes. Some day some psychologist must explain why this sort of thing happens. Many men left settled and fairly comfortable lives and wandered into the unknown or imperfectly known wilderness of California; doctors left their practices; lawyers abandoned their clients; farmers left their farms and crops; businessmen gave up a moderate security for an immense possiblity. Why?

Some, no doubt, were bored—and it was easy indeed to be bored amid the stodgy social conventions, the poverty-stricken country villages and city alleys, the arrogance of the rich and

wellborn in the older states, even the follies and reform movements of the late 1840s and early 1850s.

It was a disturbed period in the East, for the quarrel between
North and South was growing hotter. Wise men foresaw that the
nation was proceeding to trial by battle, but the young and hopeful, the sons of pioneers who longed for the frontier tradition,
may have longed to break with it all. And in their minds would
be the dream of getting rich in some Sierra foothill gulley rather
than clerking in the village store or working as a hired man and
marrying the farmer's daughter.

But it still wasn't a crusade. (The crusades weren't always crusades, either, when practical men got into them.)

The gold seekers, by definition, wanted gold. They wanted to
shorten the slow, old-fashioned roads to wealth and prestige.
They were tired of playing safe, for small stakes. They had no political urge. As they toiled across the prairies and plains, as they
struggled up and down the mountains, as they sweated up the
Chagres, crossing Panama, as they were tossed in the wild seas off
Cape Horn—in all these circumstances they were buoyed up by
the hope of quick and easy riches. Even in the rough young democracy of the 1840s, the social and economic frontiers were
strictly drawn; and from these, no doubt, many longed to escape.
They laid down their lives, many of them, on their journeys and
voyages and under the hardships of the mining camps, with the
cheerfulness of martyrs in a holy cause.

But it was not a holy cause, nor an unholy one, either. They
had had religious tolerance at home. They had had the town
meeting and other democratic mechanisms at home. What they
felt they lacked was opportunity. What they wanted was money
—the great cure-all, then as now.

We do not in time of peace do this sort of thing today, though,
as the recent records show, young men can still be found who will
risk as much and endure as much in time of war.

The Gold Rush, therefore, takes some imagining. We have to
realize, to begin with, how inaccessible California still was in
1849. We also have to realize how bad things were, or seemed, at
home, to induce people to go through what most of the forty-

niners endured in order to get away. For this was the last great mass movement of its kind. The Comstock Lode did not populate Nevada as swiftly or as much as the American River and other rich diggings populated California. Nor did the Alaska and Klondike gold rushes precipitate much permanent settlement.

The catch in the California Gold Rush was that countless youngsters who came to make their pile and then go home stayed to do something more prosaic; they worked at trades, they farmed, they kept store, just as they might have done at home.

Some of them didn't come for the purpose of digging gold, anyhow; they came to take an honest advantage of the needs, follies, and weaknesses of those who did dig gold.

And some, no doubt, having arrived, liked the climate. In meditating on California, its history and its lore we must never forget the climate.

3

The landing of the Pilgrims in 1620, and the tough and tragic times that followed, gave New England a grim spiritual quality that it took a long while to outgrow. The Gold Rush did not do this to California. There was no struggle for liberty in this new land: there was rather a long and painful effort (not yet complete, even in these glowing, modern electronic times) to organize human and natural resources.

Evelyn Wells (who, with the late Harry C. Peterson, wrote *The '49ers*) tells us that the forty-niner "had spent his last cent, as a rule, for food, equipment and supplies, and his ticket to California, and likely as not he would be robbed of most of his possessions along the way." All accounts agree that gamblers, liquor sellers, and ladies whose affections were briefly available at retail prices were on hand wherever men with gold dust gathered. Prices of supplies, meals, and lodgings were extraordinary by the standards of the time. A miner who took out fifty or a hundred dollars a day in early forms of pocket or placer mining was accommodated if he wished to celebrate on Saturday night.

Some of the prices he paid seem high to us today, others do not. Bayard Taylor's estimate of five dollars for a dinner in a San

Francisco restaurant in 1849 "if we are at all epicurean in our tastes" wouldn't startle us. Sixty years later San Francisco restaurants on Market Street would be offering a "course dinner" with wine for seventy-five cents—but not today. In this new age, this modern gold rush, prices are back close to the levels of more than a century ago.

Mr. Taylor and his fellow traveler were not robbed all the time. They were able to rent a double room with two beds in the City Hotel, on Portsmouth Plaza, for twenty-five dollars a week, plus twenty dollars a week for board; this they could not do today. New York newspapers, weeks old, brought by steamer, cost a dollar apiece—as much as a big New York Sunday newspaper, shot out by air, may do now. But Mr. Taylor and his friends would have been surprised to find a New York newspaper, any date, on sale for twenty-five cents a copy, as was the case in 1964. Another item: a laborer might get as much as twenty dollars a day—a sum not unheard of for fairly unskilled services in our own era.

With the coming of the gold hunters real estate in San Francisco whooshed upward in price—a phenomenon that gave Henry George his first serious thoughts about what he later called the Single Tax. A plot bought for $20,000 at the beginning of the Rush was sold for $300,000 a year later. Interest rates, according to Taylor, ran as high as 10 to 15 per cent *per month*. Gambling was open and general—it went with the spirit that had brought the immigrants to California; the profits must have been adequate, though they were not openly and reliably reported.

One may profitably consider the vast and assorted businesses, legitimate and otherwise, that rose with the flow of gold into this market. This drama of precious metal, of heroism and endurance, might suggest what has been said of the theatrical business in New York City today: something goes to the author, the producer, the director, and the actors, but the speculators get the most. In California the easy money was for those who found out what the miner had to buy or most desired to buy and then sold it to him. The iron laws of competition began to work after a while, but not right away.

For the shrewd and above all the unscrupulous, the Mother

Lode was in the miners' pockets.

To him that hath shall be given. It is easier to arrogate possession of a tract of good real estate, or to add an unlimited profit to
a limited supply of tough range beef, or to corner (if that is the
right word) the only barrel of sauerkraut in San Francisco, which
actually happened—it is easier to do all this than it is to get up
early in the morning and spend the long day working a "cradle"
for the extraction of a little gold from a lot of sand and gravel.

But there is another and larger aspect of the Gold Rush. If
California's swift increase in population had not taken place the
area would not have become almost instantly a state; if California
had not become a state when she did the friends of slavery might
have gained control, and the Union might have lost the equivalent of a battle, a campaign, or a war. The gold of California
helped make viable and immortal the words of the Gettysburg
Address.

The intermountain states had to wait. They didn't have the
visible gold. They didn't have the climate.

4

When the war with Mexico ended, the affairs of California
were administered first by General Kearny, then, after Kearny
had been ordered home, by Colonel Richard B. Mason. Mason
took formal command at the end of May, 1848. When news of the
gold discovery at Sutter's Mill came to him at Monterey he acted
like a good officer and went up to find out. He then wrote to
Washington: "I have no hesitation in saying that there is more
gold in the country drained by the Sacramento and San Joaquin
Rivers than will pay the cost of the present war with Mexico a
hundred times over."

A country with so much gold in it and so many immigrants
rushing in to get their share had to have a permanent civilian
government. When Mason asked to be relieved of the California
post, probably because of illness, Major-General Bennet Riley,
who had distinguished himself in the Mexican fighting, succeeded
him; and Riley ordered an election on August 1, 1849, to a constitutional convention to meet on September 1 at Monterey.

Colton Hall, where the convention held its sessions, has been happily preserved—though like some of the old adobe buildings in Monterey it was long neglected. It is a place of pilgrimage, and should be. The visitor may feel in it some of the emotion he has felt in visiting Philadelphia's Independence Hall. Here, in the first place, an American military commander voluntarily relinquished his duties as a civil governor. Here, in a commonwealth that a few years later had a substantial and dangerous proslavery minority, the forty-eight convention members voted unanimously that "neither slavery nor involuntary servitude, except for punishment of crime, shall ever be tolerated in this state." These forty-eight Californians, Spanish as well as Anglo-Saxon, were foreshadowing the Thirteenth Amendment. Finally, let it be noted that at this convention enlightened representatives of the conquerors and the conquered sat down and reasoned together. There was a magnanimity on both sides that one does not find on every page of California history.

Practice was not then, and for a long time would not be, wholly consistent with the Monterey Convention's high principles. The pioneer Gold Rushers did not look on any dark-skinned person as their equal; they called the Californians of Mexican origin, the Chileans, and the Sandwich Islanders "foreigners" or "natives," and dealt with them accordingly; they killed the Indians who got in their way and were occasionally killed by other Indians in revenge; in later years the children and grandchildren of the pioneers abused the Chinese and the Japanese.

But the institution of slavery did not exist in California. Calhoun and the other Southern fire-eaters of the pre-Civil-War period were backed in California by a number of self-styled aristocrats and other inspired jackasses, but California stood by the Union and supported the cause of freedom by large majorities.

So Colton Hall is an impressive place to visit. If conquest is ever good this stands for conquest at its best. Photographs make it possible for us to realize the personal appearance of the actors in this drama, as we cannot so easily do with those who wrote the Federal Constitution. Quite naturally, they had more variety in their make-up than the Founding Fathers of 1787; they did not belong in most cases to a long-established ruling class; some were rough-hewn adventurers who had come up from the ranks; some had to have interpreters to translate their Spanish into English.

Frémont was not there, though he and William M. Gwin were later in the year to be chosen to be the new State's first Senators, and they did in fact get to Washington before California was admitted to the Union.

I do not doubt that Frémont would have enjoyed riding up the high front steps of Colton Hall on horseback and taking over the joy of running the convention, but he was no longer even a titular Governor but only a resigned officer of the Topographical Engineers. The Monterey Convention was presided over by Dr. Robert Semple of Sonoma, formerly part owner of a San Francisco newspaper (the first in that city, it was said); Dr. Semple was a lanky individual, six feet and a half tall; he presided rather ably after insisting that he didn't know how.

Somehow this gathering seems almost the highest point in early California history. It makes the melodrama of the Bear Flag Revolt seem by contrast pathetic and tawdry. Its excellent work was ratified by such Californians as were able and willing to vote, by a majority of 12,064 to 811.

This did not end the story, for California statehood became entangled in the slavery issue in Washington, D.C., and had the honor of being opposed by Calhoun himself. The Compromise of 1850 ended the long debate, and President Fillmore signed the statehood bill on September 9, 1850. Because of the long time it took to get messages through from the national capital, the Californians did not immediately learn this news, but this is the day their descendants and successors now celebrate: Admission Day is September 9.

Meanwhile, the Convention went ahead to elect a Governor, Peter H. Burnett, a legislature, and various state officials. General Riley recognized these transactions, certified the legislature as qualified to pass laws, resigned his own gubernatorial powers, and went home.

California was now on her own. The United States Government would have had at that moment as much trouble in coercing her as the Mexican Government had had. Fortunately, no such crisis arose. The population was flowing in, by such means of travel as there were, including feet. From less than 100,000 in 1850 the new state would rise to nearly 400,000 in 1860.

A lot of things could happen to California in addition to the continued production of gold—and most of them did. But the wild fervor of the first rush was dying down. It didn't last long.

5

Gold rushes are started in the belief that somewhere one man or a small group, working with pick, shovel, pan, or perhaps a little powder, can take out the equivalent of a great deal of cash. The most alluring gold-digging stories concern prospectors who sit down on a rock to rest, absent-mindedly dig their picks into it and discover it is almost solid gold; or who poke among the roots of a fallen tree and come out with more nuggets than they can easily carry; or who pan out a curious black mud that has previously been thrown away and find it heavy with precious metal—if not gold, then silver; or who slide a pocketknife into the crevices of a quartz vein and enrich themselves in minutes; or who shovel by chance or good guessing into the only "pocket" within ten miles and collect a fortune in gold dust or nuggets as boys might collect raspberries in New England in July.

But this kind of mining is soon used up. The cradle replaces the pan. Capital begins to be needed for machines to replace the cradle and for other machines to crush and refine the ore. Mark Twain knew a pocket miner who would hunt patiently for eight months at a time "and then find a pocket and take out of it two thousand dollars in two dips of his shovel." Looking for "color" in soil where there wasn't enough to pay wages was maddening. But working in a mill that took gold and silver out of crushed quartz, which Mark Twain also described, was no fun at all, except for those who got the profits. And the owners didn't get rich over night. Sometimes they sold stock, which brought in money for them—but not necessarily for the credulous persons who bought the nicely engraved certificates. The gambling risk went out of the actual extraction of gold; it became a business.

This was bound to happen, of course. It was illogical and wasteful to have a multitude of men poking about the landscape trying to find precious metal. The great days had to pass. The Chinese and the Chileans reworked the old diggings and took out some gold by hand. I once saw a stream in the Trinity Mountains that had recently been worked over; this was a long time ago, but not so long ago as 1849. I have been told that some unreformed thirty-three'ers, as we might have to call the victims of the depression of the 1930s, took a few dollars a day—enough for pork and beans, coffee and molasses—out of the gravel of the Sierra foothills.

But gold mining not only became a business but a small one compared with some other California businesses. As early as 1860, as William H. Brewer wrote after a series of exhaustive surveys (*Up and Down California*), "gold mining had passed from one phase to another, and disorganized individual enterprise had given way to corporate organization, capital outlay and engineering skill." Nevertheless, as Brewer went on to say, "the old gambling spirit persisted, stimulated by occasional rich strikes." It has persisted to this day in the California psychology, though in later years it has expressed itself less in gold mining than in real estate speculation, ridiculously costly motion picture productions, oil extravaganzas, and other ways of making or losing, as the saying goes, a fast buck.

California has never ceased to be a combined earthly paradise, plush gambling saloon, house of prostitution, and shrine of democracy. This seems like a large order, but California is a large and varied state.

6

The Age of Gold flowered in one of the greatest achievements of the nineteenth century: the building of a transcontinental railroad. The manner in which the promoters of this essential enterprise were paid and the unholy system by which they long held an autocratic power stand out as one of the most magnificent goldbrick operations in the history of the time.

The whole history of California and the Californians down to 1869 shows how greatly needed this facility was, and the methods by which the facility was financed, built, and administered indicate how recklessly the nineteeth century in America dealt with such needs.

East and West, this was an era of corruption. The corruption may have been worse in the West than in the East, for the West, the California part of it, at least, had been populated by men who had gambled on getting as much as they could for as little as possible.

We have to modernize our concepts of human nature in order fully to understand what went on. Even then, we are not likely to understand all of it, for what we often see is good men doing bad things. The land grabbers, the manipulators of mining stock, the individuals who regarded railroads as mainly an opportunity for private gain, were no more wicked than their fellows, nor than most of us who try in various manners to get ahead in the world today. They were energetic, courageous, and young; they often fought among themselves; their ethical concepts did not require them to call in their neighbors when they came on a rich pocket of gold or a stream glittering with yellow specks. They believed in the private enterprise which they were in fact trying to abolish; they took what values were in sight, just as the gold miner did, and they appear to have had few twinges of conscience. And they were looked up to, respected, and admired by a generation that worshipped wealth even more than we do now. In the secular field, California had nothing else to worship. Discounting a few Spanish grandees, it had as yet no old families.

The Age of Gold brought about the age of communication. A golden spike linked the Union and Central Pacific at Promontory Point, Utah, but in a larger sense every rail between California and the Missouri River was plated with gold.

Gold brought Queen Calafia's Island into the big world. Gold did what all the bold captains, by land and sea, could not. Gold swiftly completed a conquest that without it would have been little more than a romantic adventure. Gold, not Frémont, not even Jedediah Smith, not even Anza, not even Serra, not all the hardships endured by the heroism of named and nameless men from the padres to the gaunt Missourians from the other side of the mountains, laid out the new paths that eventually turned into roads of steel. Gold itself—and the insane, poetic, splendid, dreadful love of it.

✪   *5*   ✪   ✪   ✪

Promontory Point

There had been no really good way of getting
to California: let us continue to bear this in mind. The Spanish
and Mexicans had found ways, but not good ways—hence three
centuries after California's discovery there were only a handful of
inhabitants of European or partially European ancestry living
there in practical independence.

Trappers and hunters and a few farmers of American stock had
found ways to get in, but they were no better than the old Spanish trails and sea routes. If there was a real difference from generation to generation, before the Gold Rush, it was that the ships
got a little better and could sail closer to the wind.

The first real American settlers, coming overland, endured severe hardships at the best; at the worst, in the case of the Donner
Party, nearly half of a group of over eighty died. The Gold Rush
across the plains brought other casualties, and anybody who came
that way was disposed—justifiably, I would say—to brag about it
all his life.

If the gold seekers came by sea they might cross the Isthmus of
Panama, which exposed them to various diseases and was expensive: this was the rich man's route, this was luxury. Or they might

take a sailing ship around the Horn, which was uncomfortable, not altogether safe, and costly in both time and money. Some early settlers or prospective prospectors came from the Sandwich Island, Chile, and Australia. Before the railroad was open a considerable number of Chinese appeared: in fact, they helped build the railroad, on wages and under conditions a white man would not accept.

But until the Gold Rush was over, though gold mining still continued, there was no quick and easy way of traveling or communicating between San Francisco and the Eastern seaboard. Carrier pigeons might have been thought of, but they weren't.

It lay in the American temperament to repair these shortcomings with the least possible delay, and so it was done. The heroism, the cost, and the corruption were taken for granted.

2

What was travel to California like during the 1850s and most of the 1860s? For those who could afford to pay, the Panama route was practicable. Steamships eliminated most of the tediousness of beating north under sail against head winds. Bayard Taylor, in 1849, a reporter with a gaudy expense account, came this way in fifty-one days between New York and San Francisco. Joseph W. Gregory noted in the following year that while the route around the Horn still took five or six months the journey by the Isthmus route "is accomplished in as many weeks."

By 1850 a railroad financed by American capital ran across the Isthmus, so that a traveler could go by steam power, with no risk of hardship and not much danger of infectious disease, from New York to San Francisco. But this was still not fast enough for business communication or for military purposes.

The way to bring California really and not just figuratively into the Union was to carry mails and passengers quickly and directly across the Plains from the Missouri River ports; these could now be reached by rail from the Eastern seaboard.

On the eve of the Civil War politics were unavoidable. Or maybe they would have been, anyhow. There was, therefore, a wrangle between North and South, first as to where the stage ought to run, and second where the rail route, when and if opened, ought to run.

The Southern view was that the proposed stage route should strike southwestward from St. Louis, in a big swing, passing through parts of what are now Oklahoma, Texas, New Mexico, and Arizona, reaching California by way of Yuma. Much of this route would be, as the slave owners hoped, under their control in time of trouble. And since the South had a disproportionate political influence (Southerners had, as they themselves modestly admitted, the "habit of command") the southern route was the first one tried by the transcontinental stages.

John Butterfield, an experienced operator, got the contract to carry the mail by this detour. He did it very well, though his coaches had a long way roundabout to go before they reached the gold fields and the then most important cities of California. It should be noted that the mines were central or north-central, and that, though Los Angeles existed, it was a small city compared even with Sacramento. There was no real sense, except the political one, and the fact that there was less snow and more sand in the southwest, in this so-called Ox-Bow Route.

And this route, for carrying the United States mails, could not of course be continued after the Southern States seceded. Nor was it, in the engineering sense, as good as the line the Union Pacific later followed, over the continental divide at the South Pass. Mr. Butterfield did his best, but nobody's best, under the historic circumstances, was good enough.

The other route was from St. Joseph, Missouri (St. Joe to the pioneers), and this was the one Mark Twain took in the trip he describes in *Roughing It*. It led along the Platte, over to Salt Lake City, across the Sierras by way of Carson City and Placerville, and so down to Sacramento. At Sacramento the river steamboats could take over.

Mark Twain rode in "a great swinging and swaying stage," of the "most sumptuous description . . . . an imposing cradle on wheels . . . drawn by six handsome horses." At least, that was how he started out. He had been a printer and a lordly Mississippi River pilot and was in his middle twenties, but he seems to have entered into this new experience with almost boyish enthusiasm. I doubt if anybody gets more fun out of a jet ride to Nevada or California today.

This stage changed horses every ten miles, "and fairly flew over the hard, level road." In the first part of the journey, that is. On this run the clumsy vehicle made it from St. Joseph to Fort Kearney, Nebraska, a distance of three hundred miles, in fifty-six hours. When Mark Twain wrote about this trip a decade or so later the railroad was making an equivalent three hundred miles in fifteen hours and forty minutes west of Omaha. He "could hardly comprehend the new state of things."

The old state of things had its less luxurious moments. On the nineteenth day out of St. Joseph (counting a two-day layoff at Salt Lake City) Mark Twain traversed the "Great American Desert" (his name for it)—forty miles, walking "most of the way across" in order to save the horses. He did not describe this part of the journey as "sumptuous." On the twentieth day the stage reached Carson City, the territorial capital of Nevada then as it is the state capital today.

The traveler in this case did not go on to San Francisco at that time, but this took only a day or two longer. From the Missouri River to the Coast, with the final leg by steamship from Sacramento, the time required seems to have been three weeks or a little more, depending on weather. This was faster traveling than by steamship via Panama, it was safe enough when the Indians were not feeling hostile, and it was dependable enough when there was no snow in the mountains. But it wasn't sufficient.

Something better was needed, and of course something better was on the way. It was more important then to bring California closer in time to the rest of the Union than it is for us today to prospect the moon—and so the thing was done.

The pony express was already operating. Mark Twain has left a famous account of the first rider his west-bound stage encountered. He had been impressed by accounts of what these men (or boys, for they had to be pint-sized to save weight) did: "a little bit of a man, brimful of spirit and endurance," "always ready to leap into the saddle and be off like the wind," "riding fifty miles without stopping, by daylight, moonlight, starlight or through the blackness of darkness, just as it happened; he rode a splendid horse that was born for a racer . . . kept him at his utmost speed for ten miles," and then "came crashing up to the station."

The traveler saw one of these lads, somewhere east of Scott's Bluff, in Western Nebraska, but what was real about this encounter were "a wave of the rider's hand" and "the flake of white foam left quivering and perishing on a mail-sack." The riders were carrying letters at the rate of five dollars a half ounce (this rate was reduced after a few months to one dollar); and with relays of men and horses they did as much as two hundred and fifty miles in twenty-four hours; they carried Lincoln's first inaugural address from St. Joe to Sacramento in less than eight days.

The pony express, the air mail of the early 1860s, was a famous incident in our frontier history, but it was hardly more than an incident. It lasted only sixteen months, from April, 1860, till October, 1861, it is said to have cost the contractors, Russell, Majors, and Waddell, a loss estimated as high as $200,000, and it was, of course, superseded by the telegraph.

Mark Twain, to whom we have to return for a few more useful footnotes, not only saw the pony express in operation in 1861 but also came on a gang of men stringing wires at Reese River Station. From this point his brother, who was going out to be territorial Secretary of State (at the mganificent salary of eighteen hundred dollars a year), "sent a message to Governor Nye at Carson City (distant one hundred and fifty miles)." Since San Francisco was already connected by telegraph with Carson City, this meant that the pony express riders' beat was being nibbled away.

As was done later with the transcontinental railroad, the telegraph lines were constructed simultaneously from Nevada east and from Omaha west. The line was open from Virginia City to Salt Lake City on October 22, 1861. On October 24 the Omaha party arrived with its poles and wires, and the hook-up at Salt Lake opened communication between the two coasts. The Confederates had won the Battle of Bull Run, but now, a few months later, the North had gained a victory in what may have been the far more important battle of the wires.

In the first eastbound message Chief Justice Stephen J. Field of California assured President Lincoln that the new telegraph would be "the means of strengthening the attachment which binds both the East and the West to the Union."

The Plains Indians broke loose during the Civil War, sometimes attacking telegraph stations and sometimes (as any ex-child who ever saw a Wild West show can testify) going after the stage coaches. But stage coaches, "mule mail," and wires kept operating; the main trouble with them was that they could not carry cheaply enough and safely enough the increasingly heavy load of words, freight, and passengers. There were plenty of brave men to take the risk, but bravery was not sufficient. California was only partially opened up.

It took a railroad to throw it wide open—with consequences visible in today's many-millioned commonwealth. The meeting of the wires at Salt Lake City in 1861 was the prelude to the meeting of the rails at Promontory Point, not far west of Salt Lake, eight years later. And that was the prelude to a story of which all that had happened before was only the first and simplest chapter.

Queen Calafia, remembered as a dark lady on a golden throne, might not have been too much disturbed by what had happened so far, but every year it would have been—assuming that she existed—a more difficult task for her to maintain her aloofness. Something had begun that would reach a climax a long time afterwards—but it had begun.

3

Gold, but more silver, had been discovered in what was called the Pike's Peak region, Colorado, and also in Nevada, about a decade after the California Gold Rush. These attractions helped make up for the many miles of desert, or seeming desert, that long made California comparatively inaccessible.

Henry Villard wrote in 1860 that "nothing is more likely to render the realization of the great national project—a Pacific railroad—more certain than the opening of extensive gold fields half way between the Atlantic and the Pacific Oceans."

The Comstock Lode was discovered in 1859, so that by 1860

the western country had come to stand in many minds for something more adventurous and rewarding than raising corn and wheat. There was land in seemingly limitless quantities and also the means to reap where one had not sowed and to dig more precious crops out of the once infertile ground. Of the two gold fields (soon to be silver fields) the more important was the Comstock—especially to California.

The drive toward a transcontinental trail on which no one would grow weary, no one would be caught in the snow, no one would die of hunger or thirst, no one would be killed by Indians, became irresistible. It had also become practicable, for the engineers of 1860 could conquer even the forbidding Sierras; the South Pass was an easy road over the Rockies, the locomotive had proved itself; and a generation of experience had shown how railways could be and should be put together. If the capital had been on hand the transcontinental railway could have been built by 1859—ten years sooner than it actually was.

But the builders had to wait for the moment in time when all things came together: the technology, the economic desirability, the political necessity. The transcontinental railroad appeared because it had to. It was as inevitable as the discovery (or rediscovery) of America in 1492. The task had to be accomplished by fallible and extremely human men, because these were the only ones available. And the gold the "Big Four" dug out of this tremendous enterprise, this inescapable necessity, was the richest "pocket" California ever yielded.

The Central (later Union) Pacific was advocated for years by various persons. It was actually organized by Theodore D. Judah, who got small profit and little game out of it. Judah had been engineer in charge of a project of the future General William T. Sherman to build a railroad from Sacramento to Marysville, on the Feather River. A few miles of this line did get built between 1855 and 1856. Then the enterprise bogged down for lack of money—this was a costly undertaking, since the heavy material had to be hauled round the Horn. Judah, full of energy and enthusiasm, turned toward a bolder dream.

For this purpose, he got together a group of businessmen in

Sacramento, and out of this grouping came those who were later to be known as the Big Four. These were actually not much "bigger" than their neighbors, but the time was to come when almost limitless power would be in their hands. Originally they seem to have expected many more California businessmen to join the group; this plan failed, and they were left, so to speak, holding the bag. It turned out to be a big bag and full of nuggets and dust.

One of them was Leland Stanford, an antislavery man who was elected Governor on the Republican ticket in 1861 and was later a United States Senator. He had been a small storekeeper, but eventually he had money enough to raise blooded horses and later to establish the University that carries his name. The other three were Charles Crocker, a miner turned merchant; Collis P. Huntington, who gave up mining to go into the hardware business in Sacramento, and Mark Hopkins, who started out as Huntington's partner in the hardware store. They had all been successful enough to have a little money to invest and a great deal of credit.

Judah went east, and by July 1, 1862, President Lincoln had signed a bill authorizing Judah's company, then called the Central Pacific, to build east from Sacramento, and another company, the Union Pacific, to build west from Omaha.

This bill carried subsidies that were rich indeed: aside from a guaranteed right of way, there were Federal funds available as loans from $16,000 to $48,000 a mile, according to the nature of the terrain; and outright grants of land that in 1864 rose to twenty square miles for each mile of line. Having driven this magnificent bargain, Judah returned to California, where he found that his partners proposed to increase their available cash by exaggerating the ruggedness of the route between Sacramento and the foothills. They also suggested what Judah regarded as unjustifiable economies in construction. A dispute ended in his selling out for small change—$100,000. He then departed for the East by way of Panama, caught yellow fever, and died soon after reaching New York. Crocker took over as chief engineer. What he didn't know about engineering he learned as he went along.

It was to the partners' interest to build as much track as they could as fast as they could, since the Federal loans and grants were going, on a mileage basis, to the Union Pacific building west, as well as to the Central Pacific building east. Crocker worked with characteristic energy and directness. He used the latest engineering methods to carve his ledges and drive his tunnels in the Sierras, and when white labor proved too scarce or too demanding he imported Chinese coolies. These cost him forty dollars a month apiece, which was cheap indeed compared with the wages white Californians were accustomed to. The Chinese did not organize Western-style labor unions. They had been maltreated by white miners in the old diggings, and if they now worked twelve hours a day for Crocker nobody protested. Nor did any protective laws, including the kindly statutes of workmen's compensation, operate in their behalf.

Mr. Crocker and his friends had their troubles, then and later, but when General Dodge's Union Pacific roughnecks met them, at Promontory Point (or Promontory Summit) they were within fifty-three miles of Ogden.

When the final day came, May 10, 1869, everybody made speeches, Bret Harte wrote a poem, spikes of iron, silver, and gold, and one of pure gold and a plate of pure silver were put in place, and cars from the East and from the West were solemnly hauled back and forth across what had been the gap.

The completion of the transcontinental line of course made it easier and cheaper to build others, inside California. Locomotives, rolling stock, and rails no longer had to be brought around the Horn or loaded and unloaded at Panama. Some intrastate railroad building had already been done. The line from Sacramento to Marysville was one of these. As early as 1863 there was a line between San Francisco and San Jose—a distance of about fifty miles.

California was thus hooked into the expanding railways systems of the nation. The railways took roots and threw out branches, dominated trade and travel, kept a firm hand on skittish State and Federal legislatures. It would be another forty years before public highways, thronged with private vehicles, would begin to bind the nation more tightly together; longer still before the airlines began to compete.

California may have been discovered, in a fashion, by 1542. "Discovery" is a loose word, for Cabrillo learned very little about the region. Nor did Anza, Father Serra, the mountain men, even the gold hunters, even the men and women who rode or drove covered wagons, really comprehend what they had stumbled into. They couldn't, for they hadn't today's knowledge or perspective. What they had really come into was a new world—one of the last of earth's new worlds.

For practical purposes, for use as an outlet for population, California was discovered when the two lines of rails were joined at Promontory Point in 1869. After 1869, an even more important date than 1849, the word California meant something different from what it had meant before. We may even postpone the date of the actual discovery—the moment of total realization and exploitation—into the generation of living men.

But poor old Queen Calafia and her Amazonian maidens had no more substance and authority after 1869.

☼ ☼ ☼ ☼

The Age of Silver

The discovery of rich gold and silver deposits in Nevada—as in Colorado, the silver turned out to be overwhelmingly the more important—sent California miners, in the historic year 1859, rushing eastward.

The profits, on the other hand, tended to flow westward, to the nearest big city. If the Gold Rush had been California's first big spree, this was its second and bigger. Certainly it prolonged for some years the adolescent fervor of the first mining excitement. It also made it possible for middle-aged juveniles, with paunches, beards, and bald heads, to speculate in mining stocks and thus, in some cases, avoid the hard work of speculating with a shovel along the fringes of the Mother Lode.

The actual money taken out does not impress us today. The "Big Bonanza" vein, for example, is said to have produced two hundred million dollars' worth of silver in twenty years. Today this sum would pay the expenses of California's State Government for about three weeks. The value of the dollar has greatly declined, the population has fabulously increased; still, the silver mines of Nevada, like the old gold mines of California, were a shot in the arm rather than a square meal. California prospered (when it did) by goods of value produced or manufactured in the state, not by symbols of value represented by precious metals.

One might go as far as to say that mining is a state of mind when all that is taken out is gold or silver. Mining kept people excited. Cattle and wheat, root vegetables, the orange, the apricot, the humble prune, the apple, the pear, these, plus the scenery and the climate, were what made California burgeon after the Civil War was over and the transcontinental railways were spiked together. Scenery and climate were for a long time the most important things California, and especially Southern California, had to sell. They were more important than wheat, cattle, or the orange—except as orange trees are decorative and, to an Easterner, surprising.

2

One gets the impression that the Conquest, the discovery of gold, the influence of the Comstock Lode, and the increase of population (up to 560,000 by 1870) left everybody a little stunned. One effect was that for some years Southern California lagged and drowsed, while Central and Northern California, where the gold was and into which the silver flowed, flourished. Half a century after the discovery of gold a Californian, when he spoke of "going to the city," always meant San Francisco—he never meant Los Angeles.

William H. Brewer, later for nearly forty years professor of agriculture at Yale, brings out interesting sidelights in his letters and journals, written during his work as a member of the California State Geographical Survey between 1860 and 1864. He came out, as did all who could afford it at that time, by steamer, crossing the Isthmus by rail from Aspinwall to Panama City, and reaching San Francisco after a journey of twenty-three days. He was astounded, as other observers of that time were, by San Francisco's growth from a town of huddled shacks to a metropolis of "large streets, magnificent buildings of brick and even many of granite, built in the most substantial manner [with] a look of much greater age than the city has." He landed just after the arrival of the pony express rider (by steamer from Sacramento) with news of Lincoln's election; he went out to "see fireworks, processions, etc.," in a celebration long remembered.

The south-bound coastal steamer which took the surveying party where their work was to begin, stopped at the Port for San Luis Obispo, where freight had to be lightered out, and at Santa Barbara. At San Pedro the party took stages for Los Angeles, where they bought supplies, and Mr. Brewer went to church. "We had," he wrote, "a congregation of about thirty or forty, I should think."

While waiting to take the trail the party camped "on a hill near the town, perhaps a mile distant, a pretty place." Los Angeles' first motel, no doubt.

The town's population at the beginning of 1861 was under four thousand. Brewer was among the first to note what the Southern California boosters later proclaimed to the four winds: "The effect of the pepper, fig, olive and plum trees in the foreground, with the snow in the distance, is very unusual." He also lists oranges, lemons, and grapes.

He goes on to say that "this Southern California is still unsettled." He did not mean so much that it had a tiny population, though it had, but that there had been many murders, and that the best-behaved of men, even clergymen, thought it prudent to go armed.

In 1861 Santa Barbara was in the dumps. "Here were whole streets of buildings, built of adobe, their roofs gone, their walls tumbling, squirrels burrowing in them—all now desolate, ruined, deserted." The Spanish culture (as it seemed to a bustling Yankee) was out of date, and the American culture had not made itself felt in that goldless region. No American had yet got to a point of sentimentalism over the old days when the padres and the leather-jacketed soldiers from Mexico ran the show. But this is the Santa Barbara that modern romanticists have been trying to restore—with roofs, of course, and no squirrels.

People were prospecting all over the state—near Santa Barbara they hoped to find coal. In the foothills of the Santa Clara Valley they did find quicksilver, which shortened the lives of the men who mined it but enriched those who owned it. But the South remained "sparsely populated," and would be so, Brewer thought, "so long as it is mostly divided into ranches so large that they are never spoken of by the *acre* but always by the *square league*."

Brewer comes back again and again to the land situation, to the confusion caused by the vague terms of the old Spanish grants, and to the violence and corruption that appeared as the conquering Americans took over. A new feudalism was being built on the ruins of the old—though when Brewer wrote the political road agents of the Southern Pacific (the "Espee machine" of later years) had not yet gotten to work.

Brewer speaks of a Spanish grant that had covered 8,800 acres, with "certain privileges on the *sobrante* or 'outside lands.'" Then, he continues, "the lawyers (those curses of California agriculture), after getting the grant of 8,800 acres, went to work and got all the rest . . . amounting to over 48,000 acres additional, and now hold it." Squatters had settled in the meantime. They were driven off, "and the houses are now unoccupied."

Brewer was not a politician and, indeed, touched the fringes of politics only when the State held back money needed for the salaries and expenses of the survey it had contracted for. He wrote, as his twentieth-century editor, Russell H. Chittenden said, "primarily for the benefit of friends at home." His book is facts as he saw them—not propaganda.

The squatters in Mr. Brewer's anecdote were tossed off the land. Sometimes they won. Poor Frémont, a little past the first brightness of his fame, held a gold-bearing estate of 40,000 acres on the Mariposa, but he was pestered and suffered severe losses from prospectors who moved in on him and panned his gravel. He was a friend of freedom and ran on the freedom ticket in 1856, but this was anarchy which he could not be expected to like.

The Chinese had no rights at all, anywhere at any time, except as they might be hired to build a railroad or do the laundry. The Indians were even worse off. Brewer speaks of the "innumerable wrongs they have endured from the mining population of whites." He adds that they were a "low, very low, brutal-looking race." It was the old story: no savage, even the lordly Sioux, is at his best after the white man has taken his land and made a reservation—a sort of outdoor poor house—out of the least valuable portion of it, for him to live on. The Indians of California learned the white man's vices, including a fondness for hard liquor, lost their own old, simple, and perhaps brutish way of living, and were driven off their hunting grounds, beaches, and fishing places whenever the white man wanted such. After all, what claim did they have? They were only the original settlers.

We will never know how the white race looked to the Indians. At any rate, the California Indian, whether under the control of the padres (who really did have a fatherly affection for him, even when they chastened him), under the Spanish-Mexican civilian authorities, or under the conquering and self-righteous Americans, could never have been as easy in his mind and emotions as he was when he was a pitiful savage living in part on acorns, shellfish and grasshoppers; dirty, indolent, short-lived—savage, yes, but a free savage.

The Negro was not a local issue in California in the 1860s; he was merely a part of the national issue that had led the South to secede. Slavery had been made illegal within the State by the Constitution of 1849. California did indeed have its secessionists. Some of these were honorable men who accepted the results of elections. One of the most honorable of all was an Army officer, Albert Sidney Johnson, United States Commander on the Pacific Coast. Johnson refused to break his oath of service; instead, he resigned, handed over his post to a duly appointed and loyal successor, and went home, to die under the Confederate flag at the Battle of Shiloh.

On the Union side were such solid politicians as Leland Stanford, governor at the beginning of the Civil War; a few preachers, notable among them the flaming Thomas Starr King, whose eloquence and magnetism were long remembered; many editors, and a majority of red-shirted, booted, sweating citizens who were not kindly to the pigmented individuals who got in their way, whether Indians, Chinese, or Mexicans, but who did not care for slave owners, either.

These miners and sons of miners were not impressed nor attracted by the swagger of what was called, for short, "The chivalry." California was not a natural region for chattel slavery, though from time to time in the years and decades that followed there were to be self-selected lords of creation who tried to put and keep the common man in his place, and workingmen who took pickhandles and other weapons to make life difficult for their brothers under the skin. In short, the millennium was not introduced by the Constitututional Convention of 1849, by the admission of California to the Union in 1850, or by the Northern victory in the Civil War. (It hasn't arrived yet.)

Brewer gives a good summing up of the Civil War situation in the state: "There are many more Secessionists than you in the East believe, and many of them are desperadoes ready for anything in the shape of a row." The desperadoes did not win any help for the South, but they must have continued in existence after the surrender at Appomattox—and they did not raise the community's moral tone.

California did not become an earthly paradise after Lee's surrender, nor with the arrival of the first transcontinental locomotive four years later, nor with the discovery of silver in Nevada. The Silver Age, like the Golden Age, was marred by human frailty and greed. History seems to work that way, in California and elsewhere.

3

But the myth spinners did begin to form the image of an idyllic California. Brewer didn't have this. When in 1861 he spoke of the "large desperado population" he also referred to the Mexican minority, "but semi-civilized at best, who as a class hate the Americans with an inveterate hatred."

The end of the Civil War and the formation of a sounder State Government—perhaps also the activities of several overrated, overdramatized "vigilante committees"—put an end to the violence Brewer described. Latter-day Californians, during the Silver Age and afterwards, found nonviolent ways of separating the careless or indolent citizen from his money.

In July, 1862, Brewer visited Benicia, which had been promoted by land agents men and which for one legislative session had been the state capital. It had, he said, "dwindled to a little, dull, miserable town of not over five hundred inhabitants," kept alive because there was a United States arsenal there, and because the Panama steamers had repairs done there. He commented: "All speculated and none built—the same old California story." (If Mr. Brewer had been able to wait a century he would have found Benicia not even yet a great city, but not dull or miserable, and with a population a dozen times as big as when he saw it.)

Speculation could not succeed until there was an obviously prosperous future, and this California did not have in the 1860s. When Brewer writes about the Chinese he says: "They come not as other immigrants, to settle; they come as other Californians come, to make money and return." The cult of California had not begun as the 1860s waned: the 1860 population of a little under 380,000 had reached only 560,000 ten years later. By 1880 it had risen to nearly 865,000, but this growth is not remarkable when the opening of the transcontinental railways is considered.

The reason for this relatively slow increase is doubtless that settlers looking for land rather than gold did not have to come all the way to California to find it. For instance, Iowa, which was later to furnish so many retired farmers to Southern California, nearly doubled its population—and with *young* farmers—between 1860 and 1870; Kansas more than tripled its population during the same period. Except when the railroads got into rate wars, it was for a long time fairly expensive, in proportion to average incomes, to cross the continent.

But the railroads helped. The Placerville Road between the Nevada mines and California carried at its peak a regular traffic employing five thousand teams, with twenty-five thousand horses or mules to haul them. A "team" did not mean two horses, but, as Brewer explains, often as many as eight or ten horses or mules, "carrying loads of three to eight tons, on huge, cumbersome wagons." Passengers along this route rode the Overland stage in what must have been, during the dry season, almost continuous dust. The California part of the highway had been built by the

state, but not well built; contractors were then authorized to im-
prove it and charge tolls—thirty-odd dollars a trip. There was
profit in keeping it open in winter.

The railroads could bring in more people and more goods, but
for some years there was some question as to what they were
bringing them to. A state as large as California, still shut off by
deserts from most of the rest of the Union, with its get-rich-quick
attractions largely used up or appropriated, and with a population that could be dropped into today's Los Angeles with hardly a
splash, had to grow up before it could attract newcomers in any
great numbers. And it couldn't grow up without attracting newcomers.

The Santa Clara Valley in the mid-sixties could flood the San
Francisco market with fruits and vegetables, the great Central
Valley could produce almost limitless quantities of food; but ship-
ping rates by sea or land were kept too high for a profitable export trade. Nevada silver flowed into the state, but Eastern capital was cautious. Drought, which could be a calamity before water storage and irrigation systems had been widely developed,
could come every year—as it still does. The famous California
climate, with the rains carefully allocated during the winter
months, followed by a long, dry summer, was whimsical—some
years there would be floods all over the southern and central
areas, and some years the dust would begin to blow in those areas
in the early spring. The Sierra snows fed the valleys, but in the
1860s and 1870s, as today, the amount of snow that fell varied
from year to year enormously.

Thus it took hard work, and ultimately a great deal of high-
flown advertising, to make California seem to multitudes of
people an "earthly paradise." It took half a century (1860 to
1910) to get the population well past the two-million mark, and
the state's population explosion did not begin until after the Second World War.

A little more integrity and foresight might have helped build a
more solid economic and social structure. A little common hon-
esty among the multiplying breed of boosters and manipulators

might have been useful. California was by nature a noble, a majestic region; it was not really necessary to sell it like a patent medicine. But this was what began to happen.

4

Let us take another look at Nevada's Comstock Lode as it entered into the California situation and stimulated the tendency I have just mentioned. As I have said, the first result of the discoveries in the Nevada area (Washoe, as it was then generally called) was to produce the customary "rush." This one came largely from California, over the Sierras, by way of Placerville chiefly. Men who had been boys in forty-nine were not yet too old to handle a pick, a shovel, and a pan.

But gold miners did not know how to mine silver, even when they found that the heavy blue stuff that got in a man's way when he was looking for gold actually was silver. The veins of the Big Bonanza were fifty to sixty feet wide and (so Mark Twain says) as high as a church steeple. The excavation, the timbering, taking out the ore, extracting the silver (plus a little gold), all required capital.

The capital could be raised by selling "feet"—that is, shares in the mine. Prospectors scratched holes in the ground, and took up "feet"; and after that they needed money. "It was the friendly custom," to quote Mark Twain again, "to run straight up to the newspaper offices, give the reporters forty or fifty 'feet' and get them to go and examine the mine and publish a notice of it." The reporter could pay his bills with "feet." Anybody could. Nobody was poor in Virginia City in those days.

All this made for a happy, carefree life in Nevada, for a few years, but its effect in San Francisco was spectacular. C. B. Glasscock, in *The Big Bonanza*, compares the speculation in Comstock securities with that which preceded this century's great depression of the 1930s.

The mine owners had their worries. At times during the 1860s they seemed to be running out of ore. In 1873 the vein that came to be known as the Big Bonanza sent all mine stocks skyrocketing. Fire wrecked Virginia City—western style, the town was soon rebuilt. Fire wrecked mines and chambers, which were heavily timbered, and there was loss of miners' lives.

Meanwhile, for years on end, Adolf Sutro, possibly the most famous, hated, and admired man the Comstock ever knew, had labored, at home, in San Francisco, in Washington, and abroad, to put through his famous tunnel—a practicable device to draw water out of the mines by means of a tunnel and to bring ore out at a smaller cost. He won his long fight, but not until July, 1878. His was a sensible proposal, and it worked as he predicted; but somehow it got into politics and people argued about it as they might over a high moral issue.

The men who ruled Virginia City and its metallic underworld made money out of silver, but rather more money, it now appears, out of manipulating the market. They could sell stock when they were about to pass a dividend. They could buy stock when, as insiders, they knew they were on the edge of a new pocket of rich ore. They could form subsidiary companies and roll up money on the contracts they thereafter made with themselves as mine owners. They made money when other businessmen and industrialists were scurrying for cover. Business ethics were not as high as they are today—at least, they were different. At that time, if a man could get away with the kind of tricks and subterfuges the Nevada magnates practiced he might not be loved, but people admired his sagacity. The same was true of men who played poker really well.

But the effect of all this was to make a tragic joke out of what had been the romance of mining. Its effect, also, was to concentrate economic power on the Pacific Coast, and especially in California, to a point where there was relatively little left for the old-style variety of pioneer. The Big Four of the Comstock and the Big Four of the Southern Pacific had much to answer for in determining an unhealthy trend in the state.

It is hardly necessary to bring back the details of the Comstock's internecine war. We need not try to sort out the personalities of Fair, Mackay, Flood, O'Brien, Sharon, and Sutro and so determine which did California (and incidentally Nevada) the least harm or the most good. Sutro certainly had an altruistic streak in him, such as was hard to detect in some of the others. Sharon, one-time master of the Comstock, lost his power, though not all his money; his estate furnished the basis for a famous lawsuit in which a beautiful blonde lady claimed it as his long-standing consort under a secret compact.

Sutro is remembered in San Francisco for his development of the sand dunes on the ocean front; for the library he spent many years accumulating; for his fight with the Southern Pacific outfit; and possibly for the term he served as Mayor. Except for Stanford, who gave a university to the public, Sutro was possibly the outstanding individual among the magnates produced by the mines and the railroads—by gold, silver, and the golden spike.

5

What all this comes down to is that California in the 1870s and 1880s had points of swift and ruthless growth and areas of frustration, tragedy, and decay. In this respect it had resemblances to the rest of the United States, particularly the Middle West. The late William Allen White, in one of his saddest moments, wrote of Kansas farmers who actually made their livings, over a long period of time, not by raising corn but by waiting for the price of land to go up. A difference was that in California much of the land was in large holdings, controlled either by the railroads or by those who had grabbed the Spanish land grants.

There was a squeeze on the man of limited means who wanted to work his land for a modest living. Frank Norris's *Octopus* told some of the story fictionally. What has been called the "Battle of Mussel Slough" was tragic realism. Farmers had settled an undeveloped railroad land grant in the Southern San Joaquin with the understanding that it would be sold to them later at a low price per acre. Meanwhile, the railroad postponed registering title to the areas involved, in order, it was said, to avoid paying taxes. The settlers prospered after a hard struggle with nature, and in the late 1870s the railroad company took over, with a call upon the farmers for $25 to $40 an acre instead of the $5 an acre originally stipulated.

The settlers, being in this way asked to buy the improvements they themselves had made, brought suit in the Federal courts. Pending the result of this case (later withdrawn after it had reached the Supreme Court) the railroad company secured eviction orders. There were clashes between old and new settlers and finally the "battle," in which five farmers and one member of a United States Marshall's posse were killed.

In the older settlements, in New England, upper New York, Pennsylvania, Kentucky, Michigan, and Illinois the settlers had had to contend with Indians; the same thing had happened along the trails across the Great Basin, and in Arizona, Oregon, and the State of Washington. The California settlers toward the end of the nineteenth century had very little trouble with Indians—these were sometimes used as labor, more often pushed aside to make room for the conquering white man, and savagely repressed when they resorted to violence. There were squabbles and outrages, murders and reprisals, but nothing like the fight in which Custer allowed himself and a good part of the Seventh Cavalry to be decoyed and destroyed. California had no Indians comparable in fighting quality with the Sioux, the Cheyenne, the Apache, or the Navajo. And the California Indians had already been exposed to nearly a century of white domination before the Americans arrived.

In California the real Indians that made the lives of the American pioneers hard if not dangerous were the Anglo-Saxon heirs to the Spanish grants.

The railway tyranny—the "Octopus"—was not a simple thing. Spokesmen for the railroads explained, unofficially, that they had to corrupt the legislature in order to prevent that businesslike body from passing unfair laws. Unfair to the railroads, that is. It was unquestionably true that competition between the Southern Pacific system and the Santa Fe forced rates down and helped populate the region. But the original Big Four, for a long time, frankly charged what the traffic would bear, and this twisted the state's development.

The result, even at this late date, is that though democratically intended mass movements have flourished in California, and though the state, especially in the South, has generated countless fads and fancies, right or left, only a few of which made sense, the old individualistic democracy of the prospector who did not give a damn for any other man's pride and power did not survive. Or it has survived only as a legend.

As the years went by California did not attract people hungry for a homestead—there were no forest lands of importance for homesteading; on the other hand, great lumbering companies came into existence. There were few fertile acres that could conveniently be turned into small farms—the emphasis was on great cattle ranches, great wheat farms, and in time very expensive citrus orchards and vineyards. Farming in California never was and is not today a poor man's opportunity. The old-fashioned general farm—the subsistence farm, as it has been called— doesn't fit into the modern world. In California it never did fit in.

What did develop in California was a demand for wage earners to work the great estates for a small part of each year— and, much later and more wholesomely, in the state's growing industries. California, to which so many ambitious young men had come in search of wealth, became an area in which the propertyless citizen could earn a living most of the time, but not a place where he could generally hope to grow rich.

California was also a place for the tourist, for persons with a moderate amount of skill or capital; later, and especially around Los Angeles, a place for a retired person with enough savings to keep him from becoming a public charge.

Southern California was the Land of Sunshine—and so remained until in quite recent years the sun was dimmed by smog. Sixty years or more ago the California propaganda in New England (this I saw as a small boy) was dramatized by a sort of exhibition car that was left on the sidings for a day or two at many a small town on a short branch; here were California fruits (in jars), pictures of California scenery that made one think unfavorably of Heaven, and descriptive material that might tempt a rheumatic farmer to sell his land at once and move to Pasadena or San Bernardino.

7

The Land of Sunshine

The list of sentimental books about San Francisco is as long as your arm—and often they are written by persons who are not in other respects sentimental. The list of such books about Los Angeles can usually be carried in a pocket notebook. The books may praise its climate (though this is slightly out of date); they may glorify its energy (it has been called a second Pittsburgh); but they don't make one's eyes moisten as easily as the books about San Francisco do. And if one really wishes to be in style the way to write about Los Angeles is to jeer at it, make fun of it, or accuse it. This can be overdone, too.

In modern times serious Angelenos are adopting a new tone. They are beginning to glorify its formidable qualities: its great size, its more than normal traffic, its fabulously inept transportation system, its industrial giants, its fantastic cults, its extremes of the right and (with a shudder) of the left. Does anybody love Los Angeles as many love San Francisco? Probably a person can manage to love parts of it, just as others love parts, but not all, of New York City.

All this is a matter not so much of people as it is of history. And there are fewer histories and memoirs of Los Angeles than there are of San Francisco. In a way, the history of Los Angeles is just beginning. Most of us will not be around, I believe, to read the best and the worst of it.

The wealth that came to Los Angeles with the Gold Rush was the result of a rise in the price of beef. When the hide ships were operating on the coast the meat of the slaughtered cattle was often left to the buzzards. Now there were thousands of new customers for it, and these, unlike the buzzards, could pay in gold. Hence the herds were driven by the thousands to the mining regions, where the miner, at the peak of the demand, paid the retail equivalent of seventy-five dollars per steer.

This could not last, but for a year or so it gave Los Angeles, as a market town for ranchers, a taste of what the Americans called prosperity. But even a brief prosperity made the land more valuable; thus, when the best of the golden days were over, the conquering Gringo became interested in Southern California real estate—as he has been ever since. And it is safe to affirm that more money for more people has been taken out of Southern California real estate (and possibly more lost in it) than was ever dug from the Mother Lode.

People who owned real estate in Southern California didn't really have to lie very much about it, though occasionally, like their twentieth-century brethren in Florida, they did: they could get along nicely if they just sat and rested their tonsils and waited. There were slumps as well as booms in the southern area, but in the end, sooner or later, the booms won.

2

In Dana's time, in the 1830s, the port of San Pedro "furnished more hides than any port on the coast." He added that "in the interior was a fine plain country, filled with herds of cattle, in the center of which was the Pueblo de los Angeles." And this, he said, was "the largest town in California." The cattle vanished, but it was Los Angeles' destiny to become again "the largest town in California." Why?

One reads the record with a sense of disbelief in the undeniable evidence. Los Angeles was not a natural port. Why not San

Diego, which had always been one? Too shallow, perhaps, too small. The climate of Los Angeles was no better and no worse than that of San Diego, but it was not perfect, even before the smog arrived. For one thing, it was and is monotonous. For persons with a bit of zip and clatter in their make-up, San Francisco, foggy, windy, summer in the sunlight, winter in the shade, would seemingly have greater appeal.

And it is true that Los Angeles did, in the early days of the railway era, attract the aged, the weary, the ill, and the indolent. It was indeed sold to them in such a package, like a bag of Christmas ribbon-candy. Every medium was used—newspapers, magazines, traveling speakers, paid advertisements.

It was sold to them, not as a great metropolis of the dazzling future but as a part of The Land of Sunshine. The magic of this phrase is understandable to those who have lived through a Kansas or New England winter—or, worse yet, the damp part of a rainy Kansas or New England fall. But the Sahara Desert is also a land of sunshine, as is the Mojave.

Some persons don't like sunshine. Too much sunshine is bad for some people's eyes. Dry, hot air may injure the skin. It may impair a lady's complexion—for evidence in favor of dampness let any traveler take notice of the complexions of the people of Britain. Sunshine isn't everything, nor is it for all men—and women.

But the phrase, when it came to be used to entice settlers to Southern California, was irresistible to many persons. It is possible that the lure of California, like that of Florida (except during the hurricane season) reflected a growing distaste for the Puritanic way of life. Increasing numbers could no longer see the use or necessity of being physically uncomfortable. What many sought was a sort of feather-bed pioneering. Such persons highly approved of the men and women who landed on Plymouth Rock, forced their way across the Alleghenies in the face of hostile Indians, cut the trees of Kentucky in order to make farms, shivered with fever and shakes on the banks of the inland rivers, crossed the Plains and the Rockies and the Sierras, took possession of the Pacific Northwest—they approved of them, indeed, but they did not wish to emulate them, or be them. They were Stevenson's

sailors home from the sea, hunters home from the hill: they
needed rest, they thought, they wanted warmth.

They wanted easy living, which Southern California seemed to
offer. Sometimes they wanted romance, which Southern California could dredge up for them out of a misunderstood and partially nonexistent past. They wanted more than an earthly paradise could offer; this made no great difference, for the salesmen of
illusions had this one in stock, too, and were gifted with the hyp-
notic eye. Indeed, some of them, in the words of the late Lincoln
Steffens, believed "their own bunk."

Alas, the state of mind I have tried to describe is now in a way
of becoming historical. Los Angeles and the other communities
south of Santa Barbara had some rugged times before they became
the astounding megalopolis they are today. They are built on
faith—not so much the spiritual kind but rather resembling that
of the patent medicine manufacturer (I knew of such a case)
who took his own nostrum and got well.

The Gold Rush and the competition of the great port of San
Francisco left the South lagging and enfeebled. But the Southern
cities—villages in comparison with what they have now become
—invented a patent medicine of their own, took it faithfully (as
though it were, to borrow a phrase from H. G. Wells, some fabulous "food of the gods"), and grew like weeds.

All this took time, but we are seeing the results today.

3

Los Angeles (which occupies a good bit of Southern California
and is a handy symbol for much of the rest of it) took strength at
first, in the final quarter of the nineteenth century, as a health resort. As a boy I heard fascinating first-hand accounts of the region
from my maternal aunt, who had lived there for a time with her
husband, a tubercular Civil War veteran. Camping in the San
Bernardino Mountains did not cure him, but perhaps it prolonged
his life. I do not recall that she said much about the city of Los
Angeles.

Other invalids, more fortunate, did get well in Southern California. The climate was indeed dry and mellow—most of the

time.

But so were other climates available to invalids who had cash and could travel. What first stimulated the flow of people, sick and well, into Southern California was the competition between the Southern Pacific and the Santa Fe railroads; this was bad for the companies but pleasant indeed for the traveling public; for a brief period in the 1880s it drove passenger fares from the Middle West and East down to almost nothing.

Southern California had already had good years and bad years, wet years and dry years, boom years and depression years. It had busted, with the rest of the nation, during the hungry 1870s. It had gained far less than did San Francisco from the silver treasures of the Comstock Lode. On the other hand, it did attract some settlers from the ever-restless citizens of Northern California.

The result was a population of 50,000 in Los Angeles in 1890, but this did not greatly alarm the lordly burghers of San Francisco. However, Southern California ploughed ahead—selling climate to those willing, able, or foolish enough to buy. The climate of Northern California, and especially of San Francisco, could not be sold in the same way. It needed explaining. What, for example, is so fascinating about fog? It is, indeed, an acquired taste. In the South all a climate salesman had to do, as a rule and in the right season, was to get a prospective buyer into the open and point.

This was, in fact, a kind of miracle of salesmanship, for comparatively little of what may still make Los Angeles the largest city in North America was yet in sight. Los Angeles had few historical side-shows—a dusty plaza, a mission not far away, a memory of squabbles rather than of battles, no secular shrines where men had died for liberty. It had mountains in view, and sun—which the early natives avoided when they could. But somehow the impression got around that this was the last of the outskirts of Paradise, the final available tracts of Queen Calafia's island, in case anybody remembered her, and a bargain at the price.

And pioneering here was different from pioneering elsewhere.

The Southern California pioneer didn't have to chop down a tree, though he might choose to plant a few for shade or profit. The myth of Southern California was poetic. It was magnificent. It was unspeakably silly; but somehow it populated—and in time overpopulated—a significant portion of the United States. People thought, maybe, of the Song of Solomon; "For, lo, the winter is past, the rain is over and gone; the flowers appear on the earth; the time of the singing of birds is come, and the voice of the turtle is heard in our land." This was the impression that the sellers of real estate and other goods tried to create.

Living in Southern California was indeed different from living elsewhere, just as pioneeeing there was different from other pioneering in the more rugged past and in less friendly areas.

Was this growth sound? Not always. Some new arrivals got homesick for lack of variety; they just didn't care for Paradise, once they had reached it. But most of them liked it, most of them stayed, and the result was just as solid as though they had been collected at the point of a gun. The gold of the Mother Lode, the silver of the Comstock were not needed. The Southwest, meeting the sea at San Pedro, was golden enough, sufficiently silver-plated, without the miner's pick or the clamoring dredge.

4

There were several phases in the growth of Los Angeles, one of them the phase represented by Frank Wiggins, the Chamber of Commerce lyricist. I remember the shock I felt when, in the middle 1940s, I was told by a spokesmen of the Los Angeles Chamber of Commerce that the business community was no longer plugging for an increase in population for its own sake. Frank Wiggins had then been dead for over twenty years, but many of us had not realized that his notions and doctrine had died with him. What had been heresy in 1925 was sound policy in 1945— sounder still twenty years later.

Los Angeles had got what it asked for—too much of what it had asked for. The Wiggins immigration had skyrocketed the price of real estate, but it had also inflated the demand for services and facilities—especially for water.

Admittedly it had been fun while it lasted. It had its charm, as did Mr. Wiggins himself. As secretary of the Los Angeles Chamber of Commerce he was full of good will, not only toward owners and prospective purchasers of real estate in the Los Angeles area, but toward the whole human race.

This could not continue. Nobody can make a strong, secure community out of a new population that is running away from something, whether it is the police, a pestilence, or bad weather. What Southern California needed was people who were running *toward* something—and this, in turn, it finally got. The region needed more money more than it needed more people. An Iowa farmer who had sold his acres during a period of increasing farm-land prices in his home bailiwick was more than welcome; he could buy a little land and a little home in Southern California. As later events showed, however, a farmer who had not sold but had abandoned his land in Oklahoma or Arkansas or who had been merely a share cropper and therefore had no money was not welcomed by practical minded Southern Californians. Even Frank Wiggins never gave anything away, so far as the record shows. Southern California always wanted people with purchasing power, and in recent times it has seen the desirability of those with producing power.

But Mr. Wiggins, in his prime, created a sort of New Jerusalem, a Never-Never Land, a revival meeting in which the whole audience came up to the front pews and was saved; and what he and his assistants wrote about it was as good, perhaps, as the ancient romance in which the legendary Queen Calafia was the heroine.

I recall reading, as a boy, something that Mr. Wiggins must have inspired. It drew the picture of the cold-country farmer, getting up before dawn (and this interested me, for I, too, though not working on a farm but in a printing office, did have to get up before dawn on depressing winter mornings), going out to the barn, and warming his hands by milking a dozen cows. The inference was that in California there were no cows that had to be milked (though there were, for I later milked some), no hard work (though there was, for I later did some and saw others doing it, in California, for twenty-five cents an hour), and indeed nothing but a land flowing with orange juice, honey, and strawberry shortcake.

I realize now, as I did not then, that Mr. Wiggins, though a businessman, was also a poet. I do not believe that Mr. Wiggins, in addition to being a poet, was also a liar. He was enthusiastic about Southern California because he had been sick, and it had cured him. He was an ardent supporter of the theory that if the population and bank clearings of a community increase everybody benefits. This is not necessarily so. Los Angeles with a population of about 319,000, which it had when I first saw it, in 1910, may have been a better place in which to live than it is now, with a population ten times as great. The Lord giveth and the Lord taketh away, and perhaps the books balance in the end.

It seems reasonable to suppose, however, that Southern California was an easier area in which to travel to and from work half a century ago than it is now. It was also a better place in which to look at ostriches, roses, mountains, beaches, or sunken gardens. In 1910 Los Angeles had one of the best urban rapid transit systems in the world—the Pacific Electric. If a passenger desired to go from Pasadena to the big depot in Los Angeles he could do so; if he were in a hurry he could take the Short Line; if he were not in a hurry he could take the Orange Grove Line, which really did run through orange groves. He could go to Long Beach and the other beaches. He could go to Venice, which did not much resemble Venice, Italy, but was pleasant enough.

The cars were red. They were comfortable. They sufficed. As Remi Nadeau puts it in his book, *Los Angeles from Mission to Modern City*, "one could ride from Los Angeles to Santa Monica in half an hour, from Los Angeles to Redondo in forty-five minutes—schedules that are more than doubled by traffic congestion and transfer delays of today's buses. It is difficult to imagine Los Angeles of the early 1900s without these sweet-humming electric cars."

I can testify to the truth of these statements, for I rode many times on the Pacific Electric. I did this under happy circumstances, since I was then courting a young lady who lived in

Pasadena, and I believe these trips on the Pacific Electric contributed to the happy outcome. The Pacific Electric had a sort of magic, though no bonds were issued to cover this special commodity. Once we went for dinner to a restaurant then well known called the Casa Verdugo—a famous old name in California history—and felt that the old Spanish days were not wholly forgotten. We went back to the end of the line, walking along a quiet road, and rode the Pacific Electric home to Pasadena. Are there any roads around Los Angeles today as quiet as that one was in 1910? No, there aren't.

Today, if we were young again, we would not take the Pacific Electric, because it isn't there any more and because we would have a car. We would not walk more than from the parking lot to the restaurant, for walking is out of style around cities, though it survives in the hill country. And we would eat at a restaurant called the Green Butterfly, which would resemble a butterfly as much as a building could, and be waited upon by waitresses with green wings. But at the time I mention, of course, we were ourselves butterflies in Mr. Wiggins' heaven.

Mr. Wiggins and his fellow enthusiasts were trying at that time to build up population by representing the Los Angeles area as a restful, beautiful and easy environment—which it was. They could not anticipate just what problems a swift growth of population would bring; nor could they look far enough into the future to foresee the importance of petroleum, the desperate need for water, the symbolism of the motion picture, and its effect on their culture; they could not count the motor cars that would make the metropolitan area a purgatory of travel in the 1960s; and they would have denounced as insane—or, worse yet, subversive—anybody who had a correct second sight in this matter; they seem honestly to have believed that as they spread abroad to a listening and reading world their fantastic doctrines of an earthly heaven they were merely creating more of the same.

Of course they weren't doing this—as I suspect some of the survivors now understand. They were making something new, magnificent and awful; and it did not include much that had been previously described as heaven.

No such thought or intention occurred to the people living around San Francisco Bay. They wanted to be rich, or at least able to eat out every now and then. Otherwise they let Nature take her course. Nature did. This is the basic difference between Los Angeles and San Francisco. It is a handy guide for tourists and intending immigrants.

I leave Los Angeles, for the time being, with the memory of a sad spectacle that once, in the later years, caught my eye there: a huge junk yard filled with the remains of the Pacific Electric's red cars. They had been piled there, evidently, by cranes, and were waiting to be turned into something useful—automobiles, maybe. But they looked like an immense catastrophe—and in a way that was what they were.

8

"Serene, Indifferent of Fate"

Bret Harte wrote a beautiful poem about San Francisco, and then, abandoning his wife and children, went to London. The poem is haunting to this day. What depths of love and hate lay in his reference to "thy hard high lust and wilful deed," to "her faults, her sin and blame" I don't know, and perhaps Bret Harte didn't know, either.

When he said that the city he had inhabited and left was "serene, indifferent of fate," he was wrong if he meant that San Francisco had no struggle, no aspiration and in fact didn't really give a damn. But he was right if he meant that San Francisco had at times a furious energy that did not require the backing of favorable omens. In fact, there was so much stirring in San Francisco, even then, that Harte might be remembered today for something more significant than "The Luck of Roaring Camp" and a few other short stories and poems if he had stayed there.

San Francisco was born with a personality. She did not have to be huckstered to a previously indifferent public, as Los Angeles was. She didn't need and never had a Frank Wiggins. People came to her in triumph, after having wrestled with men and mammon elsewhere. The tumult they made could be heard for miles. People also came to her because she was a lordly port and mother of trade, where goods could be sold for more than they had cost, and what Harte called "the sensual joys and meaner thirft" were equally available.

For many years San Francisco drew a different sort of man from those who were attracted by Los Angeles. Not better. Not worse. Just different. Younger, perhaps. Not so tired.

This would change, but that was the beginning.

2

When San Francisco became a city instead of an outpost against the Russians and then fell swiftly into American hands, she became a center for American trade with the East Coast, and soon, also, for trade with Hawaii and the Orient.

She also became a place to spend money, which Los Angeles at first was not. The forty-niners who arrived in the city returned there if they were successful in the mines. The Comstockers came west out of the big hills when they wished to make a splash. Some of them might go to New York or London later as the big money continued to roll in; but at first a mansion on Nob Hill was adequate; they wanted to show off their affluence, and they did. New York City's brownstone houses on Fifth Avenue were intended for the same purpose, but they weren't so spectacular; when a successful San Franciscan wished to exhibit his affluence and his consequent superiority over other mortals, he could build a hilltop house that would advertise him from the Golden Gate to the Berkeley Hills, from Tamalpais to Diablo and the heights above Burlingame.

San Francisco from the fifties of the past century was not merely a metropolis, she was a three-ring circus. If one looked at her in detail she was often ugly: the still unclothed sand dunes of the earlier days, the dust blowing in the afternoon winds of summer, the creeping fog, the grey houses, the honky-tonk atmosphere of many streets and neighborhoods, ingenious devices for separating the honest miner or other visitor from his gold dust, the noise and dirt. But in her topography, in her impressive meeting of land and water, in her fringe of mountains in three directions, San Francisco has always been, and must always be, superb. Nobody could spoil her, not even a highway engineer or a glass-drunk architect.

Not everybody liked her when she was young, nor does everybody like her to this day. Many, like Bret Harte, both loved and hated her—and this may still be the case. But she has always been an entity, she has been coherent, she has always had some of the attributes of the great city-states, she has always kept her grasp on the contemporary world.

The harbor, the slope of the hills, the contours of the Bay, helped give her this distinction, She did not, like Los Angeles, have to struggle to be a city; she was one. And the reasons that made her naturally a city kept her from being the huge complex that Los Angeles has become. The two cities together, so different one from the other, make California; or they would do so if we did not have to bear in mind the marvelous rivers and plains of the Central Valley, the deserts, the northwestern coastal forests, and the heights and recesses of the Sierras.

It took a long time for Los Angeles to pass San Francisco in population (if not in grace), and the reasons were numerous. Meanwhile, San Francisco grew like a redwood tree, a *sempivirens*, without much ballyhoo. Gold stimulated her, silver ran like a brief madness in her veins; she had her vexatious internecine quarrels, her racial clashes, her corruptions, her crimes and glories; but on the whole she was going through the normal processes of development in an American city. She was not, like Los Angeles, a new and abnormal phenomenon. She was shaped, finished, adapted to her boundaries, before the twentieth century came whooping down the road.

Much sentiment, some of it moist-eyed, all very human, goes into the conventional histories of San Francisco: the Emperor Norton, a harmless neurotic with delusions of grandeur, cherished and provided for by his contemporaries about a century ago; the old Barbary Coast, with its picturesque mantraps; the elegant and learned madames who ran some of the fancy houses; the free lunch that was really free; the lustiness of life in the restaurants, saloons, and other public places. And some of this sentiment is justified and true. Cities, like people, tend to become what they think they are.

San Francisco, at any rate, has always had a dramatic and glamorous surface—as has Chicago, a city which in some respects she resembles and in some other respects fortunately does not resemble. She has been, and is, an outdoor, or at least away-from-home city. In spite of fogs, winds, and winter rains, people in San Francisco have not tended to huddle at home around their stoves and radiators.

The streets and public places were early a part of the parade of life in San Francisco. The nabobs who lived on Nob Hill might be loved or hated, but they put on a good show, and their mansions endured until the earthquake and fire of 1906. The public may have envied this show—especially on the part of the railroad magnates who were taxing the inhabitants of the whole state and to some extent were governing it—but the public also found these antics diverting. This is one of the keys to San Francisco: the miner with his poke full of gold dust may have been robbing sluices or jumping claims, but if he was not caught, and if he got down to San Francisco, alive and with his dust, he could buy admiration and respect.

But the city was not wholly made up of nabobs. Obviously, she couldn't be. Solid virtues and solid types grew up behind the glittering façade. The most horrifyingly fascinating things might be going on: the wildly wicked Barbary Coast, spectacular swindles such as the "Great Diamond Hoax" of the 1870s, race riots, such as the assaults on the Chinese, also in the 1870's, theft in the City Hall, fantastic proceedings on the Stock Exchange. All this could and did happen, but some San Franciscans, exactly like their contemporaries in Boston or Baltimore, were trying hard to be respectable.

Los Angeles was still a small city being forced by the most drastic methods to become a bigger one. San Francisco, like Topsy, was just growing. As Joseph Henry Jackson put it: "The railroad men . . . had built themselves impressive piles of marble or granite or Neo-Gothic scrollwork in wood; the silver kings a little later had done their best in brownstone brought around the Horn. But now in the eighties the modest fortunes were beginning to show. In street after street comfortable houses blossomed with bay windows . . . the dwellings of the respectably successful."

In brief, it was becoming respectable to be respectably successful. The men who were mining the pockets of their fellow citizens in California as the century waned did not, like the original gold miners, spend the contents of a rich placer in a few wild nights and days; they lived prudently, put reserves in the bank, and had a respectably good time, in accordance with the manners and customs of the day and place. And a good time in San Francisco, even for respectable persons, was not quite as stuffy as a contemporaneous good time by similarly respectable parties in Boston or Philadelphia.

A few of these respectable persons' respectable houses, on the far side of Van Ness Avenue, which were not burned out by the fire that followed the 1906 earthquake, tell the story. These residences often seemed exceedingly drab and dull in front, but if you were admitted to them you would be shown gardens in the rear. And some had and still have lovely views across roofs, water, and mountains.

3

If San Francisco had been able to annex the trans-Bay cities of Alameda, Oakland, Piedmont, Berkeley, Richmond, and later the Peninsula cities to the southeast as far as San Jose and the Marin County cities to the north she would have kept longer ahead of Los Angeles in the meaningless race for population. She could not do this, since in California cities cannot cross county lines. The truth is that under no circumstances was the San Francisco area destined to become an urban sprawl; she is more crowded, more traffic-ridden every year, but not so jammed and populous as she would have been if her surface had been smoother and less interrupted by inequalities in the terrain.

A congested area cannot, of course, be self-supporting. It can handle goods, which is a service. It can manufacture goods, from raw or partly processed materials, which is often also a service. It can't grow its own food. So, as a trading center from almost its first urban days, San Francisco could still sell services, just as Los Angeles could sell land. When the railroad arrived San Francisco, as the best available natural port, could tranship from sea to rail and contrariwise. First the gold of the Mother Lode then the silver of the Comstock provided the city with at least a moderate amount of capital. Beneath the surface glamour a great deal of hard, even prosaic work got done.

Gertrude Atherton, famous chiefly as a novelist, spoke of "the social era of the seventies, eighties and nineties" as "one of incredible snobbishness," in San Francisco. What this reflects is probably a yearning for stability that was lacking in Los Angeles. San Francisco was trying to set up a cult of family, or, when this failed, a cult of money. In 1945, so Mrs. Atherton wrote, "snobbery hardly exists." It still existed, but not on the old three-ring circus basis.

On the other side of the shield, in the old days and possibly even quite recently, there was a certain amount of sinfulness, both vulgar and high-toned. The vulgar kind of sinfulness has always seemed to many San Franciscans and commentators on San Francisco as rather dashing: it was nothing of the sort; most of the time it was dirty and unscrupulous. People didn't merely get robbed or shanghaied on the Barbary Coast—they sometimes got maimed or killed.

The high-toned sort of sin was, however, more dangerous to the city's welfare. The ethical concepts of the last quarter of the nineteenth century and the first years of the twentieth, in San Francisco as in most American cities, were not lofty. Essentially the thought was that they who had the power should take and those who could should keep; and I never observed, in my reading or in a brief experience as a leg man for an afternoon newspaper, that San Francisco's great social figures lost standing because they had picked up cash in what I might call an inconsiderate fashion. If they had the money, they got along all right and were invited to parties. Of course some of them such as Adolf Sutro got their money by doing things useful to the community. But in the 1880s and early 1900s, say, this was not the rule.

Mrs. Atherton did not gloss over this aspect of San Francisco's high society in the chapter she wrote on the graft prosecutions just after the turn of the century. Rudolph Spreckles was a member of an able and eminent family. He had also made a fortune in his own right, just to show that he could. But when the trail of corruption led to some impressive and well-padded pocketbooks that had figured in the city's social world he patiently followed it, along with Fremont Older, the fighting editor of *The Bulletin,* Francis J. Heney, and Hiram Johnson. This was considered bad manners. Spreckles was denounced for his impiety, and "Mrs. Spreckles, who had been one of the bright lights of Burlingame society [a rich suburban community, south of San Francisco], found herself ostracized . . . by the wives of men who were in mortal terror of being exposed, tried and sentenced as malefactors."

That was San Francisco, the long and the short of it, the good and the bad of it. Those who today read memoirs of the Gold Rush days, the early railroad days, the Comstock days, and some later days should be on their guard against glamour. Down to very recent times (let us say) there were slums south of Market Street and elsewhere. There was once Dennis Kearney whooping it up against the Chinese, who were harmless except when they worked for low wages and, when inspired to violence, customarily killed each other, not the Anglo-Saxons.

It was a rough, tough world, the San Francisco of the century's end, in the dear, dead days before the earthquake and fire of 1906. And it did not live on spider webs, moonlight, fog, and the memory of things past. It—the city collectively—worked for a living. People quarreled as to how much each should be paid for luck, skill, and sweat. San Francisco was, among other things, a city where the so-called working man (I use the qualifying phrase because it is old, mangy, and meaningless, what with automation coming on and working hours diminishing), this creature of brawn and pride, never willingly bowed his head to any arrogant patrician.

San Francisco had its social traditions. It also had its memory of the rugged miner who would not take off his hat, much less bend his knee, to any man in the world. This miner could be stupid, cruel, even vicious, but there was nothing feudal about him. If he were alive today some of the social columns might amuse him. I hope so.

4

Nor must we allow the glitter of San Francisco life during the 1880s and 1890s to distract our attention from the city's relationship to the surrounding country. The railroad magnates would not permit this relationship to be entirely normal, but if they were to keep their big houses on Nob Hill serviced and supplied they did have to haul some freight and carry some passengers. And until the southern lines of the Southern Pacific and the Santa Fe were completed this freight had to come into or through the San Francisco area. Even when the Big Four were able to charge all the traffic would bear San Francisco got some of the gravy and did some of the work.

Mining continued, not only in Nevada but in the deep veins and medium ores in California, but the state remained for a long time pastoral and agricultural. Henry Miller, who founded the huge livestock business of Miller and Lux, is said to have pastured a million cattle on a million acres, mostly in the San Joaquin Valley. The outlet for this beef was in or through San Francisco. The padres had brought the grapevine and the olive to California, and before long the state started making its own wines —which were and are good, and of which San Francisco drank all it could hold, as well as baking its own bread from its own wheat.

The farm lands near San Francisco were richly endowed. The Santa Clara Valley produced apricots and prunes, as well as grapes. The Napa Valley was celebrated for its wines. The wheat of the Sacramento and San Joaquin Valleys flowed into San Francisco for use and export. San Francisco could feed herself well, and did so increasingly as the years went by. Her restaurants became famous and her people, if they had a dollar or two in the pocket, ate and drank in them.

The city and the region developed industries that were not invariably romantic but did help pay the bills. Lumber was a prime necessity, especially in the period when the city kept burning down every few years and growing when it was not burning. Cutting down a thousand-year-old redwood was not considered wrong in those days—the lumbermen loved Nature, but they loved money more.

California had no good coal deposits and not much iron ore, but San Francisco did exchange grain for a scrap iron, and many raw or semifabricated goods which had once been brought around the Horn were processed in the metropolitan area. As Brewer indicated, there was a great scurrying around for base metals as a means of getting rich when the gold began to give out. Except in the case of quicksilver, this did not amount to much.

It was in a way distressing—it was even a calamity—to find out that fortunes could no longer be made over night by a lucky bit of digging or a speculation in mining stocks. But this was what happened to San Francisco in the 1880s and 1890s. Most people had to work for a living, just as they would have done back East. But they clung to a past glamour (or so it seemed)—and after a fashion still do.

This was the city of make-believe. This was, to paraphase Will Irwin, the City that Never Was. And yet . . .

5

San Francisco, in the end-of-the-century days, was the city of Frank Norris's McTeague. Could anybody anywhere ever live a more dismal life than did McTeague in his phony dental parlors on Polk Street. "These were his only pleasures," Norris wrote, "to eat, to smoke, to sleep and to play upon his concertina." For him this was no gay, dangerous city of the Renaissance. It was not Florence. It might as well have been Omaha.

McTeague was true, of course. There were no doubt thousands of McTeagues in San Francisco. The glory of that city was for those who knew how to take it, as is the case with all cities—even Paris and Golden Samarkand. But the glory was there. It was within the drab houses; it was part of the desolation and abomination of the Barbary Coast; it was perhaps in the hearts of those "laborers trudging past in a straggling file" that McTeague saw from his Polk Street corner; it was in the fog that chilled you and shook you and made you dream dreams.

The written material about San Francisco includes comments not wholly complimentary, but you do not find this kind of material (except possibly in the works of such eccentrics as the late Ambrose Bierce) in the outpourings of born or acquired San Franciscans. A San Franciscan, past or present, may admit that one or two things are wrong with his city, but he will never admit that the city itself is wrong.

The critics are travelers from other parts of California or from the benighted areas beyond the California frontiers. Helen Hunt Jackson wrote: "The city is hopelessly crowded and mixed, and can never look from the water like anything but a toppling town." Anthony Trollope stated flatly: "I do not know that in all my travels I ever visited a city less interesting to the normal tourist." But the Trollope family, mother and son, were hardly ever enthusiastic about anything in the United States. Rudyard Kipling called San Francisco "a mad city—inhabited for the most part by perfectly insane people whose women are of a remarkable beauty." To his proud eye the English, in India or in England, were far more civilized than any San Franciscan. He complained of the city's drinking habits and was mainly allured by its "captivating rush and whirl." But later, when he briefly tried life in the United States, he chose Vermont, not California. (He didn't especially like Vermont, either.)

Ina Coolbrith, with Bret Harte and others, was one of the group that ran the old *Overland Monthly*. In 1928, when she was past seventy, the California legislature honored her by naming her the State's Poet Laureate. Some years earlier I had interviewed her, probably on her birthday; she spoke of the bright early days of the *Monthly*, and went on: "Bret Harte, Sam Clemens, and the others—all went back East. Perhaps I would have been wiser if I had gone, too." What she really meant, I imagine, was that it had been good to be young in San Francisco. The truth was, California in the golden years (whenever they were) was not a good literary market. The writers (and some others) who made successes in San Francisco usually did go East, where there were more people and business was that much better. Some of these persons did not really like California; Mark Twain could have lived anywhere in the world at the height of his career, but he didn't build on Nob Hill; he withdrew to Connecticut or to Europe.

One of the classic tributes to San Francisco was Will Irwin's, who fondly recalled his younger days there as an apprentice reporter. However, he wrote his famous essay "The City That Was" in New York City, two days after the 1906 earthquake. Will Irwin loved the town, every brick, stone, and cinder of it, but the pay was better elsewhere.

Not many cities, not many lands, are loved that way; Los Angeles isn't, to mention one. One theory is that this difference is partly one of magnitude—it is not a good theory, perhaps, for Los Angeles was scarcely a city of romance even when it was smaller than San Francisco. Or its romance, as in the case of the movies, was manufactured and sold by the yard. The Los Angeles romance was peripheral— the beaches, which once were on some days and at some hours almost lonesome; the San Gabriel Mission; some aspects of Pasadena; Mt. Lowe. But the central city of Los Angeles never took on shape and significance.

Has any one ever been happier in a dramatic and magic city than in a plain and practicable one? I don't know. The individual or family life possible in Los Angeles may be more satisfactory than life among the foggy, windy, scraggly hills of the Northern city. But down to the turn of the century, perhaps a little longer, there was more vitality in the North. Even McTeague may have warmed his dreary life with the thought, I am at least a San Franciscan. The period from 1880 to 1906 in Northern California is often taken as one of adventure and romance and, therefore, mourned; but it was certainly not wholly idyllic.

Consider some of its aspects. The railroad giants were still able to see to it that there was no complete democracy anywhere their lines ran. They corrupted legislatures; they ejected settlers who might have been the backbone of a strong and self-supporting yeomanry; they appointed judges; they evaded regulation; they vulgarized life beside the Golden Gate and elsewhere by their arrogance and ostentation; they came near turning the whole state back into a feudal principality. They fought organized labor; and labor in turn became corrupt and vicious and tyrannized as far as it could over the pigmented races. California was developing between 1880 and 1906 but not in an entirely wholesome way.

And yet the rugged spirit of the pioneers stayed alive. San Francisco made its own myths as Florence did under the worst of the Medici and as Naples did when it was a sink of corruption under arbitrary foreign rule. In all these instances, there were always a few rebellious spirits, even among the ruling gentry. When San Francisco's artists and writers organized a club that later became extremely well known, the men who had nothing but cash to recommend them asked, with what I believe was true humility, to be let in; and since artists and writers often needed financial backing the petition was accepted. Genius alone was not quite enough, money alone was not quite enough, but the combination worked well. Among the general public there was widespread tolerance, and even affection, for such eccentrics as the "Emperor" Norton. San Franciscans of all sorts and conditions had a fondness for this kind of drama; the population sometimes seemed to move as to the squeaking of invisible fiddles. The city was crude and sinful, but stuffiness was laughed at, even among the socially elite—more than it is today.

So the years went by. Gentlemen who could afford it built big and hideous houses on Nob Hill; they also drove down the Peninsula, behind what for some reason are referred to as spanking teams of greys, and lodged in huge and sometimes awful country houses. It was not real, any more than was Walter Scott's belated baronial castle at Abbotsford. These persons felt themselves, I am sure, actors in a pageant and tried to live up to the role. And they helped give the city its color and vivacity, as did the lowliest bum drinking himself into a high state of hilarity and manly combativeness in a saloon on Third Street.

Visitors could never be indifferent to such a city. If, like Trollope, their reaction was hostile it was always vigorous. If they loved it, they exaggerated its charms and attributes. Dana, returning in 1859, paid a tribute echoed by many a later observer: he found friends liberated from the old conventions if not the old moralities: the New England deacon once characterized by "the downcast eye, the bated breath, the solemn non-natural voice, the watchful gait, stepping as though he felt responsible for the balance of the moral universe" had put all this away and "become a human being." Robert Louis Stevenson, twenty years later, came down exultantly into "the new day and the new country" and at dawn gloried in the sun rising over Tamalpais. Even Kipling, though he stuck his dagger into the city's vitals, was fascinated by it.

Nobody ever passed through the city, I should say, without an impulse, if he could string sentences together, to pass judgment on it. The danger has always been that San Franciscans would grow complacent, as though living in their metropolis were in itself a virtue. But there was never any doubt that here had been created an entity—made up of natural and human forces and elements combined—that was unique.

But the real boom in the San Francisco legend came after Will Irwin and many others thought the city had been destroyed—that is, after the earthquake and resulting fire of April 18, 1906. Those who lived through that episode in San Francisco, or suffered over it in the far places to which they had removed, could not believe that a community so shaken and burned could be restored.

And of course it could not be, not the physical city. The buildings had to be replaced, and could not be duplicated. Yet the spirit of the community was not changed at all. There was a brief period of chaos, a somewhat longer period when everybody loved everybody else, a fury of rebuilding (with skyscrapers that could move with an earthquake as with a high wind, safely rolling to the punch, as the pugilists say), and then the essential city reemerged; brushing the dust and ashes from her clothing, she went on creating, enjoying, and sinning, as before.

In fact, I would regard it as one of the myths of the history of San Francisco and of California that the catastrophe of 1906 was a determining event. It brought out much heroism; it stimulated the community's energies; it caused some loss of life; it encouraged some new architectural forms; it brought the city painfully down to date; but it did not alter the essential character of the place.

San Francisco, it is customary to say, was never quite the same again. Neither, for very long, was any other American city, even without an earthquake and fire. None of our cities are permanent abiding places. We tear down and rebuild, over and over again, and today's New York, Chicago, St. Louis, Omaha, Salt Lake City, bear little resemblance, except in the street plans, to the same communities in 1906.

A considerable portion of the old San Francisco burned. But time would have done what the fire did. The essence, the soul of the town, lasted; the old informality, the old yearning for fun in the streets and eating away from home, the old memories, the old casual, uncritical love of the forty-niner for the arts, the old whoop-la persisted—and still persists.

☼ *9* ☼ ☼ ☼

The San Andreas Fault

The earthquake that shook San Francisco and neighboring cities and towns in 1906 was caused by a slip in what is called the San Andreas Fault. It rocked quite a few miles of territory, in fact, David Starr Jordan, then President of Stanford University, believed that this weak spot in the earth's crust was "part of a very lengthy ancient break, probably extending through the Bering Sea on the north to Patagonia on the south." The section of this break that shook San Francisco ran from Mendocino County to Mission San Juan Batista. California has other potential cracks in her surface: Santa Barbara was badly shaken in recent years, Los Angeles not so seriously.

This is new country in more senses that that of human history. It faces on a rising coast. The sea once filled the great interior valleys, likewise a shallow arm of San Francisco Bay that runs southeastward from San Francisco toward San Jose and used to be much deeper. There is probably some relationship between this newness of the land and the presence of gold which helped so much to populate it. In ancient days, so the geologists say, the Columbia River reached the ocean by way of San Francisco Bay —though at that time neither bay nor river would have answered to the name. Such changes, it appears, are likely to continue, though so slowly that they may not figure in the measurable time of man.

The San Francisco people may anticipate Nature and gain some land by filling in the southeastern part of the Bay. The region may be—indeed, it is certain to be—shaken by other earthquakes. After the 1906 upheaval many people took it for granted that there would be another of serious importance in another thirty or forty years. This was easy to deduce: there had been a big shake in 1868; Mark Twain, who had witnessed it on an otherwise tranquil Sunday morning, spoke of "a violent jogging up and down" and "a heavy grinding noise as of brick houses rubbing together." There was no great fire in 1868 (although the incident was long spoken of as "the great earthquake"), and there probably will be no great fire if another comes along—as some persons assume will be the case, on the ground that earthquakes are habit-forming. The old-timers in San Francisco shook their heads ominously when they read the tragic news of the Alaskan quake of 1964.

The lesson of all this, no doubt, is that California is not as gentle an environment as the normal climatic arrangements and assumptions would lead us to believe. It has its rugged side. There can be earthquakes—and destructive ones—just as there can be hurricanes on the coast of Florida and tornadoes and blizzards in the Northeast and Middle West. There can be droughts—parts of California are true deserts. There can be snow blocks in the high mountains. There can be smog, if man and Nature cooperate to produce it. And there can also be a revival of what is called the pioneer spirit to deal with these matters.

California is deceptive, as the San Andreas Fault and other items should remind us. If its magnificent gifts are abused, if it becomes overcrowded and overexploited, it can turn into a very grim environment indeed. A few thousand Indians lived here before the white man came and made no provision for the future; but for the twenty million or so people who will soon be there some planning is needed.

This is a "boobyland" only in dreams. In reality California includes some stern facts, not only about earthquakes but about some phases of climate, economics, and resources. My own theory, when I was a green westerner a long time ago, was that California was an admirable and beneficent machine, with which humanity had only to cooperate to be free and prosperous. It had rain at the proper season and usually of an adequate quantity and suitable distribution, a neat arrangement of mountains and parallel valleys that fed the existing and probable population. This was a pretty formula. It was also incorrect, because it was geared to a population of about two million. Nature, like many human engineers, had failed to provide for the long future when she erected the Sierras and arranged for them to serve as automatic reservoirs.

The "boobyland" phase of life in California was indeed passing in 1906, though few suspected this. The state was an excellent boardinghouse but it did not have enough seats at the table nor a big enough chicken on the platter to accommodate more than a fraction of those who were about to arrive.

So the San Andreas Fault, which may still smash some dishes, chimneys, and windows in San Francisco and give the inhabitants a good rattling all the way from Bolinas to Gilroy, seems to me a kind of symbol. It reminded San Franciscans in 1906 and may remind all California again that they are really not living in an earthly Paradise.

Nature stands waiting, here as elsewhere—a kindly mother who sometimes feels it necessary to chastise her children. Neither yesterday's gold nor today's promises to pay on demand can be had for nothing. Human life in California is a bargain, and sometimes a hard bargain, just as it is in other parts of the world.

2

The earthquake was a human tragedy, though it took less than one-third of the lives annually sacrificed by California today to the gods of speed on the state's highways. I am thinking in terms of perhaps twelve hundred persons, many of them nameless, unidentified and never missed, dying in April, 1906, in the wreck and ashes of the cheap lodging houses south of Market Street. San

Francisco then was, and long remained, a place where migrant labor—for instance those who went north every year by ship to work in the salmon packing houses in Alaska—holed up for the winter. This particular part of the California Paradise had in 1906 no stake in the city or the land. They were drifting and, except at short intervals, womanless. The city they remembered, if they lived, was not precisely the one of which Will Irwin so beautifully and poignantly wrote.

The human casualties, though the number I have mentioned was often cited, do not concern us as much after all these years as does the fact that this city of San Francisco, glowing, beautiful, ugly, drab, and infinitely poetic, had its basements and subcellars of misery.

It also had its wild pioneer humor. In the days after the 1906 catastrophe Mary Austin made note of a placard in the burnt district: "Don't Talk Earthquake; Talk Business." Months after that there was a sign on a barracklike building of rough, unpainted lumber, visible from the Southern Pacific trains rolling into the Third and Townsend street station: "Palace Hotel."

The hills of San Francisco, as one saw them from the Oakland Mole (and this I did in August, 1906) were black as coal. One couldn't believe there would ever be a live city there again. But there was. The spirit of the men who spent their gold dust or gambled away their Comstock "feet" in a night was still alive.

I do not intend to be emotional about this phenomenon. I suppose people wanted, as usual, to make money. But they faced with an indomitable eye the act of Nature (assisted, to be sure, by the bright-eyed engineers who had laid water mains near the lines of the San Andreas Fault, and had neglected to provide an auxiliary salt-water pumping system) in wrecking their city. They resolved, collectively, to build another and better one. What they actually built was the same one, more solid and more nearly shakeproof and fireproof—but it was quite a job.

The total loss in the 1906 episode may have been as much as half a billion dollars, on some of which insurance was never paid. The fire swept over 4.7 square miles and destroyed more than twenty-eight thousand buildings. Mrs. Fremont Older, in her *San Francisco: Magic City*, records that "within three months 6,600 new buildings were undergoing construction in the city." Five years later, when I first took a leisurely look around San Francisco, there were still many vacant lots on which had once been houses. Near the site of what is now the Mark Hopkins Hotel there was an arch leading nowhere—later to be set up in Golden Gate Park and labeled "Portals of the Past."

Actually San Franciscans did not need to weep over the past, for their city as rebuilt was probably more attractive than the one that had burned. Robert Louis Stevenson writes somewhere that men always came back to the devastated slopes of a volcano because the soil is good there. The forces that had made San Francisco were still at work in the latter months of 1906, just like those that had created the city in the first place, more than half a century earlier. The earthquake had wiped out buildings, none of them venerable by Old World standards, many of them as ugly as sin, but it had not injured the harbor; the fire had burned up cash money but had not diminished the commercial and financial importance of the location; the city remained because there had to be a city at that meeting of land and sea. Mrs. Older recalled that "banks built sheds over their vaults and did business in their old locations" and that "bank clearings soon surpassed those of the previous year."

3

The trouble with San Francisco was at no time a matter of its bank clearings. It was a sort of economic and social ineptness, a civic fever and shakes, a tendency to move in on somebody else's diggings, a heritage of big and petty larceny, that every now and then came over the town and took control of it, just as the Sydney Coves and the Hounds had briefly done in the golden past.

Not that San Francisco was any more dishonest in her worst phases than were other American cities. Ida M. Tarbell, the crusading journalist, once told me that San Francisco differed from most of the other cities she had studied in being more open and unabashed in its corruption. It was not always, of course, corrupt, and it always had its majority of honest and well-behaved citizens.

But through its life there ran what might be called a San Andreas Fault, economic and social, and out of this fissure there sometimes came an upheaval. This had been happening just before April 18, 1906, and it went on happening after the first few days of brotherly love and good deeds had passed by. San Franciscans could be courageous and big-hearted during an emergency, but not when the struggle for pay dirt or the best water hole was resumed.

San Franciscans had another pioneer quality: they were not easily outraged by normal sexual relations between freely consenting adults of opposite sexes. If a man and a woman rented a private room in what was called a "French restaurant" and there did what Mother Grundy expects men and women in private rooms to do, the articulate voice of San Francisco might regard this as careless but not necessarily wicked.

On the other hand, the acts of one or more city officials in selling for their own benefit rights or franchises that were the property of the public were frowned upon.

Both kinds of corruption were flourishing in the city before and after the earthquake and fire of 1906. Mayor Eugene E. Schmitz, an orchestra leader elected nominally as a union labor representative, was controlled by "Boss" Abe Ruef, and it became evident that everything of value the city had was for sale to furtive and corrupt bidders.

It is easy to believe that the police were taking money from prostitutes and their "protectors" and from the "houses" in which they operated. The public was hardly aware of what this meant in terms of human exploitation. It was the old system, a little more luridly evident in "open towns" of the West than in the possibly more hypocritical contrivances of the older cities of the East.

San Francisco had had a reform wave in the 1870s and another in the 1890s, in a pattern similar to those of other American cities. In the first decade of the twentieth century the "muckraker" drive was nationwide, in spite of Theodore Roosevelt's belittling characterization of it. Now, in San Francisco, it apparently had to be done all over again. And more than the wages of sin on the Barbary Coast was at stake.

The "graft prosecution," which was what the episode came to be called, involved Fremont Older, managing editor (and real editor during a long crusading period) of the San Francisco *Bulletin;* District Attorney William A. Langdon; Rudolph Spreckles, who with no hope of political or other return, put up money to keep the investigation going; Francis J. Heney, an able attorney of whom more would have been heard if a wound received at the hands of a defense witness in a San Francisco courtroom had not temporarily disabled him; Detective William J. Burns; and Hiram Johnson, who stepped in after Heney was shot, became a reform Governor, and ended his days as a United States Senator, not always on the side of liberal causes.

The graft prosecution also helped to give birth to the Progressive Party, although the actual accouchement, so far as California was concerned, may have been in Los Angeles.

As the investigation and prosecution broadened out, they led to indictments and accusations in high places, against the president of the city's privately owned street railway system and against officials of other public utilities. And these were people who moved in what was thought to be the best society, had their names in the society pages, gave pleasant parties, and were greatly looked up to.

None of these persons went to jail. The only accused individual who did that was Abe Ruef, the little boss who was left holding the bag. Editor Older, angered and shamed by the injustice he thought had been done when Ruef was punished while the prominent parties who had bribed him went free, spent some years getting Ruef out of jail again.

The moral and economic San Andreas Fault that ran through the life of San Francisco was not abolished by the graft prosecution or by the statewide reform movement that followed it. I presume it is still there, after a long series of fairly good—or really good—mayors. But I do not suppose the doorknobs and plumb-

ing fixtures at the City hall have ever again been quite so fla-
grantly for sale as they were under Mayor Schmitz and poor
"Boss" Ruef.

And who wants a streetcar franchise any more?

4

The ashes were hardly cool, the streets hardly cleared for such
traffic as there was in those days, the dust of building still in the
air when San Francisco, with characteristic bravado, announced
plans to build a World's Fair to celebrate the opening of the Panama Canal.

A little more than five years after the earthquake, to wit, on
October 14, 1911, President Taft came from Washington (a long
journey in those days) to break ground for the Panama-Pacific
Exposition and make the expected flattering speech. The occasion
took people's minds off memories of the five-year-old catastrophe
as well as thoughts they might still have about Schmitz, Ruef, and
the nameless sinners of half a decade back. It also underlined
San Francisco's position as the Pacific Coast's greatest port—although it was soon to lose this distinction to the artificial bowl of
salt water then under construction at San Pedro.

San Francisco was in some ways an unlucky city, in some ways a
more than ordinarily wicked city; it was full of strife but it was
also rich with aspirations; the Fair was more than a shrewd
business-getter, it was a challenge and an affirmation.

The Fair was not an unqualified success. It did not open until
a year after the first ship went through the Panama Canal. Meanwhile, a World War had begun, although practically everybody
on the Pacific Coast was pretending there was no such war—except as a series of adventure stories in the afternoon newspapers.
On one occasion, however, a German demonstration snake-
danced through the French Pavilion after a French defeat on the
Western Front—and this was not generally considered *gemutlich*.

The opening day was rainy. Old-fashioned San Franciscans did
not take kindly to the silk hats and frock coats the city officials
bought or rented to wear when a distinguished visitor came
through.

But it did seem that everybody who went to the Fair, even in a silk hat, long and lovingly remembered it. It was just right: not too big, not too small. It made people feel happier and more comfortable. It came just at the ticking of history's big clock, before ordinary daily life in big cities had become so remarkable that nobody could easily be surprised any more.

In many ways the Panama-Pacific Exposition was more of a landmark than the earthquake and fire of 1906 had been. It was San Francisco's last gesture of supremacy before it stopped being California's Number One city. In population, that is to say.

The San Andreas Fault was still deep, still building up tensions. It was not in people's minds in 1915.

Los Angeles Grows Up

Meanwhile the Los Angeles area had developed a drive and influence out of all proportion to its population. The city itself in 1900 had only about two hundred thousand people, in spite of all that had been done to sell land and opportunity to Middle Westerners and Easterners looking for an easy life. It was a snug little urban community, as such things go.

But Los Angeles felt neglected. Because it had no adequate port facilities much of its sea-borne commerce had to be carried to San Francisco and then brought back by rail. It called upon Congress to pass one of the juiciest river-and-harbor acts in Federal history. The project had been authorized before the Spanish-American War of 1898, but our accidental and temporary acquisition of the Philippines probably accelerated construction. At that time we were beginning to fancy ourselves a Pacific Power—which indeed we have in these later years reluctantly become.

At any rate, work on a deep-water harbor at San Pedro was actually begun in April, 1899, and to this day pushed and expanded. Early in the present century, therefore, Los Angeles had a harbor, though in the early years not much traffic went through it. The traffic came later, a good share of it for reasons not foreseen in 1899.

The Angelenos went through several stages as they matured in wisdom and experience: first, the climatic stage, when sunshine was sold by the fraction of an acre; second (and overlapping this), the citrus stage, when people from the East were encouraged to buy a few orange trees along with their land while they looked at the snow (at the right season) on Mount Lowe; third, the harbor stage, still continuing, of course, and increasingly important; fourth (with more overlapping), the motion picture epoch; fifth, a great many other developments that left the pathetic wraith of Frank Wiggins far behind and forgotten; finally, in our own day, the turning of Los Angeles and its environs into something never previously dreamed of—something of a gigantic monstrosity and also possibly a foreglimpse of The City of Tomorrow.

All this took time. The great scramble of people, buildings, freeways, highways, and cars that we call Los Angeles in the 1960s came more like a glacier than an avalanche. Let us approach it cautiously.

I was speaking of San Francisco as a city of make-believe, which, with a population of less than 800,000, it still manages to be. San Francisco's make-believe, however, has always been a luxury, indulged in after working hours or as a sort of coffee break; it has kept on trying to act like a mining camp long after it evidently wasn't; like a college undergraduate, it has hoped to seem tougher, wickeder, lighter of heart, than was truly the case. Today it puts on a white tie, a tailcoat, and a selfconscious air of having come over with William the Conqueror, as it attends the opening night of the Opera, but it would also like you to think that it still wears a miner's red shirt underneath.

Los Angeles hasn't any such paradoxes as this, no emotional conflicts over the past. People came to Los Angeles to make money or to be comfortable, not in search of the high romance. What Los Angeles did was calm and businesslike; it imported its glamour and made money out of it; it went east and played the Pied Piper to the infant offspring of the motion picture.

2

Motion pictures of a sort had been drifting around since the late 1890s. I saw a few reels (as I suppose they were called even then) in the small village of Williamstown, Vermont, prior to 1900.

At about this time also one could buy little picture books which, when thumbed rapidly, gave the illusion of motion—a boxer hitting a punching bag, or even another boxer, a horse running, possibly some slightly improper dancing—but of this last I recall little, having been properly brought up.

But when we saw pictures like these, on the screen or in a little book, we did not then associate them with California.

The early days of the motion picture in what was called Hollywood (the time came when land values went so high that the principal studios had to move farther out) have been treated as subjects of mirth and derision. Later, with our customary nostalgia, some among us began to look back upon them somewhat as others do on early Victorian furniture: taken out of the attic and dusted off, they seemed to have an art and reason about them. Some were pantomime at its best. Others were, to be sure, fumbling and grotesque, though they had some of the virtues of the primitive. The marriage of the manners and customs of New York's lower East Side (and I am not sneering at these—they were just different) with those of the real estate dealers and boosters of Los Angeles produced some quaint results. But the real estate operators and the primitive motion picture promoters were alike in two ways: each was working in a mist of make-believe and neither had any accurate perception of the future.

The motion picture entrepreneurs came to Southern California because they could work more handily and cheaply there than they could in the uncertain light of Eastern cities. They did not know what their new industry would turn into—nobody did. They made films in a few days for a few dollars and seem to have been honestly surprised when some of these were taken seriously. They did not know, until they were told so, that they were dealing with an art. And with few exceptions they did not concern themselves primarily with the movies as an art until sound arrived in 1927. Like Shakespeare, they wanted to make money, and the art crept in almost unsuspected. Yet out of this environment, careless and nonchalant, came Chaplin, Sennett, Pickford, Garbo, Fairbanks, John Bunny, and enough others, mostly comedians, to fill out another page or two.

Of course the emergence of sound and the later arrival of television transformed this idyllic system and destroyed a good part of it; for pantomime, whatever you think of it, is not the same art as spoken drama, and the television stage presents different problems from a movie set, outdoors or in.

But what sound and television did to Los Angeles may be noted later. What mattered down to 1927 is what pantomime did. In the first place it showed that persons (including investors) who could go where they wanted to go might choose Southern California. It attracted some capital at first and many millions in the long run. It drew settlers, many of whom worked at something else after they had found that the silent film had no place for them. It gave Los Angeles glamour, which in spite of sunlight, beaches, orange groves, and ragged-looking dusty palms, it had needed.

The movies didn't go to San Francisco, which had and still has too many hours of fog and rain for outdoor shooting. It may be observed that Los Angeles passed San Francisco in population (1910–1920) during the decade when the motion picture industry was getting its real start in Southern California. There were of course many other factors, but this was one of the most important. It wasn't so much the money as it was the prestige.

It was made clear far and wide that Southern California was the home of beautiful women and gallant (or sometimes, even better, comical) men. This made young persons, and not merely wornout farmers from Iowa, wish to go there. It also raised the pulchritude level of clerks in stores and waitresses in restaurants.

3

Growth in the Los Angeles neighborhood meant growing pains. These included a bitter and tragic labor war and a search for water almost all over the Southwest, nearly as ruthless and brutal as the labor war. It led to Mary Austin's savage remark that it would be humanly wiser to use the water of the Colorado River to grow more Arizonans than to produce more of the kind of people then inhabiting Southern California. Whether she would have repeated this dictum had she been still living in 1965 nobody knows.

The labor war and the search for water modified the genial, easy-going picture of Los Angeles and the Sunny Southland that had been planted in many persons' minds during the reign of Frank Wiggins. Labor unionism was weak and under constant attack in Los Angeles, just as it was naturally strong and aggressive in San Francisco. The results could be unhappy in either city, although San Francisco has always had more freedom and often more tolerance.

There are understandable reasons why Los Angeles developed a nonunion tradition. The small farmer, whether from Iowa or somewhere else, had had little experience with labor organizations, even though he might have belonged to a farmers' organization with the same objectives—that is, to get more pay and privileges. The same may be said of the small businessman. And the Los Angeles community was heavily salted with representatives of both these groups.

Harrison Gray Otis, publisher of the *Los Angeles Times*, certainly helped to bring antiunion sentiment in his area to a boil; however, he did not invent it, and in the San Francisco field he might have been helpless; he operated in the right community, for this purpose, and at the right time.

The first decade of the present century was marked by a good deal of unrest and discontent, all over the country, and this unrest affected more than the so-called working man. It affected farmers —including farmers in Iowa. Of course this fact did not make farmers or ex-farmers more tolerant of rising wages or other influences which they feared would increase the cost of living. And in the Los Angeles neighborhood much of the population half a century ago was living wholly or partly on fixed incomes during an era of inflation. The "high cost of living" was just becoming a pat phrase.

Therefore Mr. Otis was applauded by a large section of the population in his neck of the woods when, though he had once carried a union card, he broke with the typographical unions and began a campaign against unions in general. The applause increased when he pointed out, correctly or otherwise, that if industry in Los Angeles permitted itself to be unionized it would be less able to compete with the heavily unionized industry of San Francisco. The moral and the profit arguments ran together—thus making life easier for persons with tender consciences.

Mr. Otis carried on his antiunion campaign when some elements in the labor movement were conducting an equally bitter antiemployer campaign; each group wished the other group to be unorganized and docile. Many wage earners thought Samuel Gompers, the benevolent and careful president of the American Federation of Labor, an old fuddy-duddy. They wanted action. A few of them wanted violent action. This mood did not fit in with the orange blossom and rose scents of Southern California, but it got there just the same.

Los Angeles had already had some tough experiences with labor upheavals. It was these, indeed, that had made Mr. Otis even more belligerent than Nature had created him.

It thus happened that labor's self-styled friends committed one of the most shocking crimes of violence in our industrial history: on October 1, 1910, they blew up the offices of Mr. Otis's *Times*, killing twenty and injuring sixteen employees. Detective William J. Burns, who had operated on what seemed to be the side of the angels in the San Francisco graft investigations, was asked to expand the inquiry he was already making into dynamite cases charged against the unions by the National Erectors' Association.

In April, 1911, Mr. Burns' agents brought about the arrest of Joseph McNamara, secretary-treasurer of the International Iron Workers, and his brother, James B. McNamara. They also laid hands on a character labeled Ortie McManigal, a hanger-on at union headquarters in Indianapolis; and McManigal immediately confessed to a countrywide dynamiting plot against the National Erectors' Association, which did not care for labor unions.

When these arrests were announced, it seemed clear to all union sympathizers that a gigantic frame-up had been manufactured. The pattern was familiar. Labor's friends rallied around the McNamaras. Thousands of dollars were raised to help them. Clarence Darrow went to Los Angeles to throw his powerful weight on their side. Lincoln Steffens rushed to the scene.

The trouble was that the charges were true, as Darrow realized as soon as he had talked with his clients. Thousands of good people had wasted their sympathy on a pair of scoundrels. The only possible argument in extenuation was that the dynamiters had not planned to kill so many people and that a gas leak had turned their childish prank into a horrible disaster. This line of reasoning did not fool many detached observers.

The end came when, on Darrow's advice, James McNamara pleaded guilty to the *Times* bombing and his brother to another dynamiting experiment, which luckily had cost no lives. A political deal on the eve of a Los Angeles municipal election saved James McNamara from the gallows and let Joseph off with a relatively short prison term.

Technically, of course, the bargain made between the McNamara defense and the District Attorney (actually between the Los Angeles labor group and the business group of which Otis was the loudest spokesman) had nothing to do with the imminent mayoralty election.

Actually, the situation was such that as long as the McNamara "boys" could pose as innocent martyrs every left-wing force in Los Angeles (and this phrase didn't mean Communists in those days; they had yet to assume their role of black sheep) would be strengthened. Job Harriman, a former Socialist candidate for Governor of California and for Vice-President of the United States, was running for Mayor against the incumbent, George Alexander, whom he had out-distanced in the primary. The run-off election was held following the confessions, when the streets were still strewn with Harriman buttons which disgusted sympathizers had thrown away. Thus Los Angeles was saved from going Socialist, whatever that might have meant, but it was returned to the control of Harrison Gray Otis and his numerous friends.

All this did not prove, of course, that labor had no grievances or that collective bargaining was a bad thing. It did not prove that all labor leaders approved of terrorism or that some employers and some employers' agencies had not used violent tactics. It did, however, kill for the time being any hope that labor unions, however honest and law-abiding could flourish in Los Angeles. Victory went, at great human cost, to Harrison Gray Otis and company: on the record they were the victims, they were the exploited.

Los Angeles was still only the second city in California, but it could offer a lure not only to climate seekers; it could give a welcoming hand to businessmen "who wanted to run their own businesses in their own way without outside interference"—that is, without real collective bargaining. These businesses gladly came.

But the face that Los Angeles presented to the world had changed. It was not quite so folksy as it had been. It was not quite so genial. It was tougher. It was harder to be sentimental about.

4

The other episode that showed that Los Angeles was no longer solely inhabited (if it ever had been) by jolly Middle Westerners was its aggressive struggle for water. There were a few under 320,000 inhabitants at the time of the McNamara tragedy. If there were to be many more, with the necessary industries to employ them, there would have to be more water. And the struggle for water holes in the Southwest has never been won by the generous and magnanimous.

Most of Southern California was by nature semiarid; some of it was, frankly, desert. It was cattle country—and the Spanish-Mexicans in Dana's time so used it. To turn it into a garden, much more, to turn it into the setting for a modern American city, meant reaching a long way for water. Otherwise it would have remained a mere oasis.

Under the direction of an able water engineer, a self-trained and peppery Irishman named William Mulholland, the city therefore reached more than two hundred and fifty miles and took the Owens River. It did this after a long struggle, by turns legislative, legal, and violent, extending from 1903 to the middle 1930s.

The details are confusing and perhaps are no longer important. The settlers in the Owens River Valley had a thriving community, they were at times as full of democratic fury as the men who stood on Lexington Green and held the bridge at Concord, but they were not numerous enough to fight Los Angeles, either by court action or by dynamiting Mulholland's pipelines—both of which strategies they tried. For how could they hold off the Los Angeles land speculators when the water from the north boosted real estate values in the San Fernando Valley, now a part of the greater city, tenfold, and all the land in Los Angeles County at least twofold?

For the Owens River people this was a famous defeat—and a pathetic one. In the end they were paid what was said to be a fair price for the land they bitterly hated to sell. And Los Angeles by that time was bigger than San Francisco; and population was flowing into Southern California faster than the melted snow down the great acqueduct. Los Angeles speculators—if that is not too flattering a word for men who manipulated land values on inside knowledge of just what the city was planning to do—made a killing on this fantastic deal.

Of course Los Angeles did need the water to grow on, and there were more people in Los Angeles than in the Owens Valley. The majority were served, after a fashion and for value received. The act was possibly a kind of rough democracy, questioned largely by those who did not make any private profit out of it and by those who believed that it was unhealthy to build sprawling cities in dry lands by seizing water and then selling it to tributary communities. Yet this is how Los Angeles grew in area and to a large extent in population. There was no economic or cultural need for an urban sprawl of that size in that area. And a city based on thirst is not necessarily a city at all in the old and familiar sense.

The quest continued. Soon Los Angeles had to have, or so those in control thought, a good share of the Colorado River; it cast lustful eyes on the Feather River, which is northeast of Sacramento, and in the 1960s there began to be hints that Los Angeles would like to have power hauled down from the Columbia River to feed its industrial plants.

These matters will have to be dealt with in years to come, but beginnings have been made. Experiments to take the salt out of sea water have been under study for a long time; the problem is not to prove that it can be done—it can be—but to do it cheaply. Such a miracle will be necessary if we are to have a new sort of urban complex rather than old-fashioned cities—and Los Angeles really is moving in that direction. Perhaps we shall some day have a solid city reaching along the coast from Santa Barbara through Los Angeles to San Diego. Such a city will need water and other basic essentials as no other aggregation of people in the world has ever needed them.

And it is apparent that Los Angeles began at least half a century ago to change not only in size but in substance. When I first saw it in 1910 it was not only a bigger city than it had been in 1900 but it was a different *kind* of city. I thought I detected another change in quality when I saw it six years later, in 1916. I remember an old house, uninhabited in 1916, with a tired palm tree in its brown front yard; somebody had lived there once, I knew, but nobody would ever live there again; it would shelter some cheap kind of business, then it would be torn down and replaced by a shop or store. I don't doubt there is a skyscraper on the site now, unless it has been absorbed into some monstrous coil of the freeway system.

Looking back on what I myself have seen and what others have said and written, I wonder if the basic alteration in Los Angeles did not begin when the Pacific Electric's red cars started to disappear. These cars served very well a city of the size Los Angeles was in 1910—about three hundred thousand—but not one of about twice that size ten years later. And the human values of 1910 were more cherished than those of the 1920 city. This is a debatable subject, perhaps, because one person's human values may not be the same as another's. But I shall continue to believe that the human currency in and around Los Angeles has been, so to speak, inflated: an individual's serenity and comfort are not worth what they used to be.

5

The comparatively modest program to make Southern California a home for the elderly, a Mecca for tourists, and a fruit exporter—all these helped create the booster spirit, but they could not satisfy the spirit of boosterism.

Nor could they fully realize the available bounties of Nature. The Los Angeles area, and Southern California in general, were designed—if that is the proper word—for industrial use. The climate was not only pleasant (most of the time and in most localities); it also made it possible to carry on manufacturing operations of various kinds, indoors and out; snow did not stay the employees from reporting for work; fuel was needed, and Nature, niggardly with coal, thoughtfully provided an abundance of petroleum. Iron usually had to be hauled in from Utah, though there was a small supply, relatively speaking (fifty million tons or more) at Eagle Mountain, and possibly more elsewhere. But industries could spring up, and did so.

Industry brought in a younger population, ambitious and energetic, and therefore not inclined to drowse in the parks or spend the time playing horseshoes. People began to come to California to start a career, not to end one. Meanwhile, there were more and better roads, both inside and outside California, and more trucks and cars to travel them. There were fewer fleas and less dust.

What was happening to Southern California was also happening, though not in such intensity, to Northern California, and to almost the whole United States. Among other things, the automobile age was beginning. But Los Angeles and its near neighbors in the South had the enterprise and good luck to get there (in the old Civil War phrase) fustest with the mostest. They rode the wave.

The community or communities that developed under these circumstances had some peculiar features. Union labor had suffered a serious setback in the McNamara case. Economic and social discontent was therefore under suspicion, even when they did not remotely imply violence. Individuals who wanted to express themselves in unusual ways nevertheless flourished. Religious and various pseudo-healing cults, evangelism, and all sorts and conditions of utopianism broke out all over the place.

Los Angeles, like other American cities, had a normal complement of Protestants, Catholics, and Jews. It also had such personalities as Aimee Semple McPherson, pretty enough and dramatic enough to be in the movies, but more important at the height of her evangelistic career than any motion picture actress or producer. Faith-healers of many kinds were a dime a dozen. It was a common experience to be asked on a street car whether or not you were "saved." But the questioner was usually an elderly party with a red neck, not a machinist or factory worker; and this was an echo of a more leisurely day.

Los Angeles also produced some real and sane liberals—maybe more fifty years ago than today.

Divided They Stand

When the California constitutional conven-
tion met in Monterey in September, 1849, there were three opinions as to how large the proposed new state should be. These
varied greatly. Land was being handed around rather carelessly
in those days; there seemed to be so much of it and so few claim-
ants, and it took so much to keep a cow or a family going in many
parts of the area.

Some people, it may be recalled, wanted to split the commonwealth at a point somewhere in the latitude of Santa Barbara.
The open argument was that the area as proposed and as adopted
was too big for one state government. The real argument may
have been that the land in the south that would thus be excluded
was not worth much, anyhow. It could produce cattle, of course,
but what else? Its inhabitants were lazy, too—many persons said
so.

Wiser opinions prevailed; this was a wise convention. It remained true, however, that there was a Northern California and a
Southern California, and to this day the twain have never quite
met or fully united.

When I was a newspaperman in San Francisco in the second

decade of the present century it was assumed by many politicians that if Northern California had a Governor for a term or two the next Governor ought to come from Southern California. This reminds me of a similar and just as silly tradition that used to influence Vermont politics: if Vermont had a Governor from the eastern side of the mountains he should serve one term and then be followed by a Governor from the western slopes. I do not know that this is still the case in Vermont, for the modern automobile roads have made it possible to cross the Green Mountain range in an hour or so at numerous points, and the separation is not so acutely felt.

In California, however, the situation is and has always been a little different. Southern California does not resemble Northern or Central California in many respects; it does not resemble anything but itself. The two populations come from different breeds of kittens. They are suspicious of each other.

Once in a blue moon, to be sure, they have stood together and, as the saying went, battled for the Lord. One of these occasions was when Hiram Johnson linked California with the Progressive Party and inadvertently caused the two elections of Woodrow Wilson to the Presidency. Another result was, of course, Mr. Johnson's election as Governor and subsequently as United States Senator; there, during the League of Nations fight, he displayed a parochialism one would not have expected of a man from so big a state.

2

I am not writing the history of the Progressive Party in California. It is worth remembering, just the same, that in some ways, for some persons, and for a little while, this movement did bring California's North and South, its sea coast and its valleys, together.

It is difficult, however, to generalize about the California of 1900, the California of 1910, and the California of 1920 (or any subsequent decade), because with each new decennial we are talking about something different and new. The state was changing in the *kind* of population it had as well as in the *size* of its population.

In 1900, for example, the population was 1,485,053; in 1910, it was 2,377,549; in 1920, just after the First World War, 3,426,861. We cannot track these newcomers down by places of origin; since they didn't have to have passports this might be impossible even for the most intelligent computing machines. But Southern California did become less and less a land of lotus eaters; and the North, growing more slowly, did not forget its red-shirted, pick-and-shovel origins.

Both Northern and Southern California did, in a way, get together. Both sections, for a time, wanted reform—which had not become a dirty word. This movement began, not as a program *for* something but as part of the protest against the Southern Pacific Railroad machine. Los Angeles was no more willing to be contolled by this apparatus than San Francisco was. Even Harrison Gray Otis fought the "octopus" when the "Espee," in the person of Collis P. Huntington, proposed to build the Los Angeles port facilities at Santa Monica, where Huntington controlled the approaches, instead of at San Pedro, where he couldn't. And this was one fight that the railroad, in its waning political power, didn't win. The port facilities went where they would be handiest for Los Angeles. And Santa Monica remained a tiny enclave, inside the county but outside the city of Los Angeles.

The San Franciscans were not enthusiastic about using Federal money to make Los Angeles a great port, but it was righteous in their eyes to slap the "Espee" down and give the Santa Fe a chance to compete.

There was, as I have noted, a reform drive in San Francisco during the first decade of the century. It was abortive in that it led chiefly to the conviction of an unimportant figure, Abe Ruef. There was also a movement in Los Angeles, to which the conviction of the McNamaras dealt a deadly blow. If anybody at about that time argued that organized labor ought to have a fair hearing once in a while the answer was, "So you believe in murder, do you?"

Yet somehow the sounder elements in both reform movements survived, were merged for a while, and produced some humani-

tarian legislation. San Francisco remained a city in which the labor unions were strong, Los Angeles a city in which they long
were weak. This was hardly fair, for there were few union men in
Los Angeles or anywhere else who believed in negotiating with
dynamite; but unfair things occasionally happened then, as they
do now.

It would have been easy to carry Central and Northern California on the proposition that members of labor unions are entitled to organize and to bargain collectively through representatives of their own choosing, but after the McNamara trial it
would have been hard to win with this famous phrase in Southern California. The Lincoln-Roosevelt League in those days
stood for some commendable programs, but it did not come to
grips with the real problems of relationships between labor and
management; that required another Roosevelt at a later day.

What the liberals north and south could agree on, in California
around 1910, and what they actually did during the Hiram Johnson governorship, would have seemed like socialism a few years
earlier.

Johnson was an aggressive, ambitious, and dramatic figure,
with a capacity for indignation. His father, Grove Johnson, had
been a politician of the old-fashioned, adaptable type, guaranteed
to stay hitched, and this made the effervescent and irreverent
Hiram all the more picturesque.

Some of the Johnson reforms, in which he had support in the
south as well as upstate, were not especially wise. Others were
admirable. Seemingly most valuable of all was his victory over
the railway machine. In this, however, he was aided by the fact
that he could meet the voters without using the trains; he went
around the state over bad roads in what would seem today a perfectly foolish automobile. The Southern Pacific was dethroned as
much by technology as by politics. Johnson, like Theodore Roosevelt, came at an opportune time, when invention was taking a
hand in undermining some of the old monopolies.

The bills put through under his first administration were magnificently described by Colonel Roosevelt "as the beginning of a
new era in popular government and the most comprehensive pro-

gram of reconstructive legislation ever enacted at a single session of any American legislature." Since Roosevelt had been Governor of New York and had forced through some bills of his own in Albany, this was high and even unselfish praise.

The legislation included: the initiative, referendum, and recall, forms of direct government which, despite their democratic labels, did not always work too well later on; equal suffrage; a civil service law; and various reforms in the field of social services, such as workmen's compensation, an eight hour law for women, a child labor law, and the establishment of commissions to regulate farm marketing, immigration, housing, and public utilities.

The State Railroad Commission was ostensibly an agency by which the State regulated the railroads; it had been an agency by which the railroads regulated the State. Hiram Johnson reversed this situation. The sight of John Eshelman, as chairman of the new commission, doing a little regulating was as inspiring to some who watched and listened to it as a burst of sunshine after a long rainy spell. There was a new spirit and gleam in the air. It is with nostalgia that one recalls all this, now that all public utilities are regulated by State or Federal agencies, or both.

Hiram Johnson carried the State in 1914 as well as in 1910. In 1916 he won a Senatorial seat. In 1920—to his credit but apparently to his lasting regret—he refused to run with the inept Harding as candidate for the Vice-Presidency; if he had done so he would, of course, have become President when Harding died in 1923. What this would have meant to the Republican Party, then in one of its periods of recession and confusion, one can hardly guess. Hiram Johnson was not in his old age a great teacher or an outstanding liberal. The Presidency might have revived his old urges and stimulated his sense of leadership. But he did not lead in the Senate; he sulked.

Meanwhile, the veteran Progressives in California had repented or recanted, and the South had outrun the North in power and arrogance, as well as in population. There would never again be as exact a balance between the two sections of the State as there had been during the brief flowering of the Progressives.

The men who argued at Monterey in 1849 that two states would have been better than one may have been right.

3

But no one, no matter how skilled in crystal gazing, could have foreseen what was about to happen in California; no one could accurately dream of the way in which the old cattle ranges of the South, the land of sunshine and boredom, of slow ageing, of cults and curious digressions, the earthly paradise of wistful seekers after health, was to be transformed. Queen Calafia wanted—and got—a change in her kingdom. For though San Francisco and the North did not change in their basic characteristics, it may be said that the South was completely renovated and made over. Hollywood couldn't have done it better—and of course Hollywood was a part of it.

The key to what happened was, as I have tried to suggest, water. When Nature designed California she had provided for a rainy season and a dry season; and she had so arranged it that the melting winter snows of the Sierras would replenish the dry summer acres of the Central Valley and of all Southern California.

But Nature, as usual, had done what any good engineer would regard as a rough job. The rainfall varies in years and in localities. In Del Norte County, on the coast at the extreme northwest corner of the state, it averages nearly 76 inches a year; in Humboldt County, at Eureka, about 38 inches; in Napa County, a large grape-growing region, 23 inches; in San Francisco about 22 inches; in the Santa Clara Valley about 15 inches; in Tehama County, in the upper Sacramento Valley, more than 23 inches; in San Joaquin County, on the river of that name, from a little over 13 inches at Stockton to nearly 18 inches at Lodi. In Fresno County, if you go far enough into the mountain, you may find a ridge where more than 20 feet of snow falls in an average winter —which helps with the irrigation in summer. (But there are no average winters, even in California.)

So much for Northern and Central California. There are notable differences as you pass from east to west or from sea level to the loftier elevations. The climate on the top of Mount Whitney (elevation 14,495 feet) is not the same as that in nearby Death Valley (at one point 282 feet *below* sea level). But it is in going south or southeast, north or northwest, that one encounters the factors that do most to divide the state into two radically different sections and make references to California's "climate" ridiculous. What climate? Or which?

Here are some average rainfalls for Southern California: Orange County, 12 inches; San Bernardino, in the valley areas, 16 inches; San Diego County, 10 to 13 inches along the coast, 17 inches further inland; Imperial County, a maximum of 3 inches; Kern County, under 9 inches; in Los Angeles County rain falls, on the average, twenty days a year—but you can't count on averages in a wildly diversified human and geological blob, with an area about forty per cent that of Rhode Island, and elevations ranging from sea level to more than 10,000 feet.

Every great city, of course, needs a reliable supply of water; the inhabitants cannot be depended on to catch it in pails or open their mouths and let it run in, no matter how great the precipitation. So both Los Angeles and San Francisco had a legitimate need for outside supply. And both got it.

San Francisco's needs were not as great (or its people were not as ambitious) as those of Los Angeles. It did, however, reach into the Sierras, in a project proposed by James Phelan in 1901 and completed in 1934, to bring in water from the Hetch Hetchy Dam, in the Sierras, over a 186-mile acqueduct. John Muir and other nature lovers did not approve of this project, which from their point of view ruined the Tuolumne River Valley; but a growing city can always outvote the nature lovers. The Bay cities, opposite San Francisco, also went into the hills for their water. Since they were in other counties, San Francisco could not make them submit to annexation as part of the price of selling them water—as I have noted, cities in California cannot cross a county line.

San Franciscans insist that they took only what they needed, for the size of city they were; Los Angeles, on the other hand, took water from the Owens River, later from the Mono Basin, later from the Colorado River, and reached out for the Trinity River and other distant sources; it did this, as I think is evident, not for the size of city it then was but for the size and the population its inhabitants (or its real estate dealers) wanted it to become. There is a difference.

But I believe it is true that any human organism (such as a city) tends to grow to the limit of its possibilities, with little regard for rights and verities. What stops it in the end is a competing organism (another city, perhaps) or an act of Nature. Los Angeles had every facility to become a megalopolis, except water. With water, it was able to aspire to become the biggest city in the United States, possibly in time the biggest city in the world.

In the 1960 census, San Diego was shown to be a larger city, with a little under 600,000 inhabitants, than either San Francisco or Los Angeles had been at the end of the First World War. And San Diego, in a functional sense if not in a political or sentimental reference, was a part of the great Los Angeles community. So was Santa Barbara (population 1960, a little under 59,000), although its people don't like to think so, and Richard Henry Dana, who saw it in 1836, after a long beat to windward from San Diego, would be astounded to hear it.

San Francisco has its great metropolitan area, too—or megapolitan area, if the expression may be used: by census definition in 1960, about 2,783,000, as contrasted with 6,742,000 for a corresponding spread around whatever is the center of Los Angeles. It is dangerous to cite statistics about California, of course—last week's figures, like last week's news dispatches, are of purely historical interest. And some questions are hard to answer; for instance, why do San Francisco's bank clearings run about two-thirds as high as those of Los Angeles, despite the great difference in populations? Is there a banker in the house?

4

But no mathematical calculations or comparisons, no similarity in freeways, no common problems and desperate solutions can make these two cities in the least alike.

San Francisco may not long remain a city in the old, lovable, cultural sense; at times today it seems to be bent on ruining what it has retained; but at the moment of writing (and in California one had better watch all moments, because they slip away so drastically) it is, with all its sins and imperfections, a *city*, whereas Los Angeles, in the older and significant meaning of the word, is not. At best, Los Angeles is Byzantine in all its barbaric glory, whereas at worst San Francisco is Italian—or even Greek.

This is not a matter of virtue or morality any more than is the architecture one chooses for his house. It may not even be a matter of taste, for nobody really planned Los Angeles—nobody could have done so. And nobody really planned San Francisco, beyond laying out the original streets and later filling in the empty spaces. The city was planned by its topography, and that was planned, in turn, by Whosoever laid out this small section of the earth.

But the result is that one community is a true city, with a center and periphery, whereas the other is not. Some persons like the San Francisco plan, or lack of plan, and others do not. Some prefer Los Angeles; I have talked with them. But the point is, there is a difference, not just in quantity but in kind.

I have run ahead of my story. I have also oversimplified. California is not divided precisely into two city-states, one dependent on and governed by Los Angeles, the other the hereditary appanage of San Francisco. Some of the outlying communities are not only fiercely independent but they are inexorably distinct because of the climate (as exemplified by the rainfall differences I have mentioned), their ways of earning a living and the kinds of people they have attracted. To take a single instance, lumbering along the foggy and rainy north coast would have few attractions for an electronic worker in the Santa Clara Valley or a date rancher in the Imperial Valley.

When a Eurekan goes to San Francisco he may feel friendly but not at home; in Los Angeles or San Bernardino he would feel himself in a foreign country. He understands lumbering better than fruit raising.

Go up to Del Norte, with its 76 inches of rain a year; this is not Sunny California. Two-thirds of its area is publicly owned. Try

Trinity County, which is mountainous and has about three persons to the square mile—no population explosion there, except in summer. Napa is pleasant, interesting, and prosperous; its wines are good; it is almost a commuting center for San Francisco, but it isn't rigorously dominated by that kind of business; it is more like what Central California used to be half a century ago—it may not remain so, the population keeps increasing so fast.

Sacramento County grew by more than 81 per cent between 1950 and 1960; the City of Sacramento had about 200,000 people yesterday and will have more tomorrow. It is not only the State Capital but John Sutter's old ranch, and it bears no resemblence to either San Francisco or Los Angeles. The Central Valley cities, Bakersfield, Fresno, Stockton, put your finger where you will, sit and sizzle during certain months of the year, but they are not stereotypes or tributaries of the two big cities, or of one another. They aren't earthly paradises, either—not even a medieval Spanish romancer would mistake them for that.

Even in Southern California, which tends to be lumped in many generalizations (including some in this book), especially in election years, there are wide individualities. Imperial County, for instance, once included in the Colorado River desert, has temperatures running up to 116 degrees in whatever shade there is. Too much sun, even for the sun worshippers from the East. It does not thrive on tourism but on fruits and vegetables; in a good year its agricultural products may be worth $166,000,000. The Imperial is a thing in itself: it does not fit into the picture puzzle of Southern California. Nor, for that matter, does Palm Springs in Riverside County, although the clientele of this popular desert resting place may represent every prosperous element in Southern California life in the course of a "winter" season. Nor does Henry Kaiser's steel plant at Fontana in Riverside County.

However, Los Angeles spreads its influence far, into Orange and Riverside Counties, San Bernardino and San Diego. Industry tends to invade the old grazing and farming spaces, pushing back the frontiers of orchard and garden cultivation. But the new communities differ in many ways from the older and larger aggregations. They draw the young, energetic, and ambitious. They are rarely idealistic or romantic. They are radical in applying new methods and new scientific tools to their buinesses, conservative to the point of stupidity in the political area.

To sum up, California is not one community, it is many. It is as diverse as the Eastern seaboard. There are, on the other hand, two great and disparate cities, and these give a distinctive character to the regions over which they loom. You will not be in the least danger of being misunderstood if you say you do like, or you don't like, one or the other. I don't think anybody could love both.

California is two empires, each with satellites and allies in various degrees of intimacy. It is two civilizations. It is two cultures. I wonder which one Queen Calafia would choose to rule over if she could come back; she couldn't handle both.

12

The Plenteous Years

Howevever, we can't understand what California is—and Queen Calafia couldn't, either—without a few more glances at what it has been. I would like to give some added attention to the decade 1910–20. During these memorable years a few things began to happen that foreshadowed what we see today when we travel a California road or look out of a California window. These included the state's share in—and profit from—the First World War. As in Joseph's time in Egypt there were some extremely good years; there were also strikes, political turmoil, and internecine warfare between North and South, as well as a war with Germany.

I have already alluded to the rise of the Progressive Party and to the career of Hiram Johnson, but these developments were not the whole story, perhaps not even the most important part of it. During this decade, California's population grew at the rate of a little over 44 per cent, that of the nation at 15 per cent. California was pulling ahead but not yet explosively. Southern California was outrunning the North, but not yet enough to keep a San Franciscan awake at night.

Labor unions had a hard row to hoe, especially after the Mc-

Namara outrage, and especially in and around Los Angeles, but the kind of unionism represented by that vast and highly successful producer's organization, the California Fruit Growers Exchange helped straighten out a chaotic agricultural industry. The same worthy citizens who set up this agency took pains to discourage any protective organizations among the migratory workers who harvested their fruit or vegetables—and that was human and natural, if not humane and democratic.

Since California was geographically a long way from the battlefields of the First World War, the natural impact of that conflict on the state was relatively mild. People took sides during the first two years, when it was still practicable to do so. When this was no longer feasible California jumped into the fray with its customary enthusiasm: those who couldn't fight could still hate —often the wrong people; some San Franciscans are ashamed today that they helped ruin a concert tour by the late Fritz Kreisler, violinist, because he had fought, as was his duty, in the Austrian Army on the Italian front.

In a military way California was a great training ground after the United States entered the war in 1917. Troops from the Philippines were brought back, and regiments were expanded into divisions. Some of these soldiers got into the fighting, and others did not; at least there was no heavy gloom of death and wounds hanging over the state. Subsequent developments suggested that some soldiers liked California and stayed there or came back after their service days were over.

Possibly the most important thing that happened to California during the war was the increase in demand for food products. California was able to ship these by land and sea, since the Panama Canal had opened a new water route in 1914. The Port of San Francisco and the new Port of Los Angeles were therefore busier than ever. Except for the soldier, who is never overpaid for what he has to do, California gained more than it lost by that distant adventure. At no time during the war was there a lack of markets for California cereals, fruits, meats, and anything else that could be shipped abroad. The great industrial days of the Second World War were foreshadowed.

2

A newspaperman who was in California during the years from 1911 to 1919 remembers the state as a strange combination of ferocity and pastoral charm. The population increase was going on, but it was still a trickle, not a tidal wave. There were rustic areas within easy reach of the two leading cities. North and South were still fairly well balanced.

The ferocity came out of the labor wars, which affected the migratory workers who were (and are) essential to the production of crops under the California system. Carey McWilliams later wrote of the cruel exportation that occurred under the system in his *Factories in the Field.* I suspect he overdramatized his facts (though the facts themselves were sustained by newspaper writers and by Federal investigators); and possibly he left out some redeeming features.

But the truth was that California was not and could not become a land of small farmers. The great staple crops were harvested by men (and women and children) who were needed, and paid, only a few weeks out of the year. "Following the fruit" from ranch to ranch, from the south northward, was an arduous occupation, even with a succession of crops, not only fruits but small vegetables. One of the worst farm labor conflicts in all California history occurred on a hop ranch—at Wheatland in August, 1913. Wages were pitifully low, living conditions abominable. The beer of California was bitter that year for those who longed for peace and good will among men.

These were the days when the Industrial Workers of the World, the I.W.W. or "Wobblies"—a half-sinister, half-comical group of semirevolutionaries, were scaring the daylights out of conservative people in California. (And elsewhere, of course.) They were not bloodthirsty, though men sometimes got killed in the activities they sponsored; they were not, however, averse to sabotage if they judged it would be good for their cause. The cause was the organization of the unskilled and migratory workers, and it was a thankless one.

I never saw the Wobblies at work, though I talked with newspapermen and others who had seen them. No doubt I did see them, on the road or in the cheap rooming district south of Market Street in San Francisco, without knowing who they were. They had a strange sense of humor, as I gathered from those who had interviewed them and from some of their publications. Sometimes they put on a "free speech" fight, as in San Diego, and enjoyed the joke when the police arrested an innocent bystander, a store clerk or something of the sort, because he was wearing a red necktie; after which, to cap the story, he became a member of the I.W.W. They did some harm and possibly a little good during the "plenteous years" in California.

But they were outside the mainstream of the American labor movement; they had a certain eccentricity, from their very way of life, which would always have prevented them from getting a place among the solid labor unions. In brief, they were doomed to extinction as an active organization, although they did succeed in calling attention to the ills and wrongs endured by unskilled and drifting laborers in California and elsewhere. And this labor, without hope, health, or normal satisfactions, was the very antithesis of the "hired man," so fondly cherished in New England tradition. They had no savings, they had no permanent abiding place, and they never married the boss's daughter.

An even darker shadow than any the I.W.W. wilfully conceived was cast across the land by the frightful "Preparedness Day" explosion in San Francisco, on July 22, 1916. (Labor in San Francisco at that time considered these demonstrations purely an employers' trick to "discipline" them.) Nine persons were killed and about forty injured in this diabolical bombing of innocent marchers in a parade such as had been taking place, with President Wilson's approval, all over the country. I studied testimony in this case long enough to convince me that Tom Mooney, convicted of the crime by perjured witnesses produced by a corrupt district attorney, didn't do it—though at first all of us thought he had.

Who did do it I don't know. The police foiled any logical attempt to find out by arresting the wrong people and dropping the investigation. The reason Mooney could be accused, convicted, and sentenced to death (he was later pardoned) was that he did seem to speak for a certain wild-eyed section of California labor. He wasn't even a likeable man, or a natural leader, but he had gotten it into his bewildered, sulky brain that "capital" was out to destroy organized labor, he had tried in vain to pull a strike on the privately owned streetcar system in San Francisco, and he may have used explosives to wreck power lines. But he was no murderer, and the plot to get him hanged was more than anything else an evidence of the savagely bitter feeling between labor and management in California. Who was the guilty man? Perhaps an old-fashioned anarchist. More likely somebody driven mad by hate—for the people killed were not "capitalists" but employees of various corporations, some of whom were in the parade not because they were excited by "preparedness" but because their employers had suggested it. And it was to have been a paid holiday.

This sort of thing happened on the eve of our entry into the First World War, and similar, though milder, symptoms of unrest were visible during that war and for some years afterwards. The plenteous years were also years of struggle.

Yet California was growing and prospering between 1910 and 1920—and after. Not all of the state's inhabitants shared these good times, but most of them did. The poorest, as usual, wanted more, which is not too surprising.

3

California is a state of about one hundred million acres. In 1915, as a report by Mr. McWilliams indicated, about 28 per cent of this acreage was capable of farm use and about 11 per cent was actually being so used. Ownership was highly concentrated, tenancy and rural day labor were widespread, and, as Mr. McWilliams said, the system "worked infinite harm to many honest, industrious, but oversanguine and credulous homeseekers." The supercrops—perhaps most of the California staples—didn't lend themselves to the homestead type of farming. Such farming, to be sure, was waning in the states east of the Sierras and east of the Rockies. All over the country, except in the plantation states of the old South, the subsistence type of farm, which was tradition-ally the source of so many sturdy democratic virtues, was losing its importance. Nobody expected any longer to make a living out of a potato patch, a corn patch, and a cow—or, in California, a dozen prune or orange trees, or an acre of wheat.

Everywhere the shift from small cultivation to big cultivation was painful. But whatever the human cost the agricultural output of California, which had never been on the small handicraft pat-tern, was becoming under modern methods more diversified and more profitable—profitable to those who invested in it, that is, if not to those who did the hard work. California agriculture was a going concern, even though it certainly wasn't the democratic paradise some had dreamed of.

The *California Information Almanac* lists today "more than two hundred different agricultural products—vegetables, fruits, nuts, field crops, and livestock." Many of these are relatively new in the state's farm economy. Most farms or ranches are special-ized—only a tiny percentage raise general crops. Specialization, with all that this signifies in dependence on weather and markets, makes farming in California a gambling enterprise. Irrigation re-moves some of the weather hazard, though not all. Irrigation (a million acres in 1890, four million in 1920, much more today) had worked its magic by the end of the First World War, but there were—and always must be, until the salt is cheaply taken out of the sea—years when water is scarce and costly, as well as years when there is enough of it, and maybe too much.

One of the newer crops that came to be important after 1910 was cotton; and this was, of course, a profitable item during the First and Second World Wars. Cotton's westward march, since the end of the Civil War, had at last, in the Imperial Valley and in the San Joaquin, almost reached the Pacific. It added greatly to the total wealth of California. Almost everything, from motion pictures to the popularization of the avocado, did that.

As for gold, it continued—and still continues—to be extracted in California, at the rate of about one tenth of one per cent of the annual value of all mineral extraction. Any one who was offered a gold mine in 1920, or might be offered one today, might consider a few acres of land instead—let us say grapes in Napa, Sonoma, or San Joaquin counties. He might be wiser still to put his cash into airplanes or some species of electronic equipment. For California, long the land of sunshine and flapdoodle, was evolving into a solid industrial community. The sunshine remained, and a good deal of the flapdoodle, but the hardware was becoming each year more important. The Federal Government gave this development a lift, but it did not invent it.

4

In 1910 the people of the little city of Los Angeles (as it seems now) had gone to nearby Dominguez Field to see a new kind of circus—the first international "air meet," in which Glenn Curtiss and other early aviation enthusiasts demonstrated that their flimsy contraptions of wire, sticks, and canvas would actually leave the ground. These exhibitions produced a frenzied interest in aviation, and this interest led to the formation of an aviation industry in what was clearly a favorable environment. Glenn Martin began making planes at Santa Ana in what had been a church. Donald Douglas turned an old movie studio into an airplane factory.

This was the beginning. These were the balmy days which men afterwards fondly remembered, after the aviation industry had become a colossus, with huge government contracts, assembly lines, labor disputes, and shares listed on the New York Stock Exchange. It was another one of those intrusions that were to modify the picture of Southern California into something no longer even faintly resembling a lotus land where it was always afternoon.

That petroleum and natural gas existed in California had been known since the first settlements. What to do about them in the primitive days was no problem—one left them alone. Later they were found to have their uses; many of us read by kerosene lamps in our childhood; in a Vermont country printing office shortly after the turn of the century I found myself cleaning type and printing-press rollers with benzine; petroleum could be substituted for coal as a fuel; it had chemical uses in industry; you could rub a petroleum derivative on your chest when you had a cold, and it did you no harm. But the oil business did not become colossal, of course, until the invention of the internal combustion engine. And between 1910 and 1920 the number of automotive vehicles produced in the United States, each with a drunkard's lust for gasoline, rose from 187,000 to 2,227,349.

California was there early, with oil wells not too hard to "bring in." More was happening on the West Coast during the decade from 1910 to 1920 than a brief war. There were more ways to get rich than had been previously dreamed up. Petroleum was one of them—another resource more valuable than all the gold of the Mother Lode.

The smell of oil ran all the way from Richmond, on the Bay of San Francisco, to Los Angeles. As an impressionable traveler, I saw the derricks in the ocean below Santa Barbara as early as 1910 and some remaining pumps at Long Beach, slowly coughing up oil, more than thirty years later. Oil does not smell as good as gold, except to a petroleum engineer, but it is worth more.

The motion picture, half art, half industry, was still silent between 1910 and 1920, but it added a note, a color to Southern California out of all proportion to its industrial value. It also brought there some performers of distinction. As late as 1920 one might catch sight of a motion picture celebrity (or one might think one had done so, which was just as good) on Wiltshire Boulevard, or way downtown (an indefinite locality, but it was said to exist at Fifth and Main or somewhere else), or in a restaurant. Some motion picture kings and queens liked to go about incognito, or relatively so.

In 1916 my wife and I, with some sort of journalistic credentials, could wander in on the making of *The King of Kings* and chat with the twelve Disciples while the cameras were being rigged; a wind machine was being tested, and a melancholy stand-in (I wondered and still wonder how much they paid him), bound to the cross, saved the leading actor from discomfort and fatigue. When sound came, about a decade later, this sort of nonsense had to stop. There might still be stand-ins, because actors and actresses were more valuable than ever, but there couldn't be visitors talking with the actors on the set. The noble art of the "silent drama" died.

And a part of Los Angeles died, too. Hollywood was never the same again. Within the space of a few years motion pictures had stopped being toys or vaudeville interludes, had explored the possibilities of using gestures, had become respectable—and then were transformed by the tumult of color and sound. But all along the years they shed glamour, and this glamour added to the attractions Los Angeles presented—especially for the young. Never was a city so essentially dull and unimaginative so transformed.

Somehow this glamour became of more importance to the city and its environs than its absolute financial basis would have justified. Glamour sent up the price of real estate. Glamour made people understand (or think they did), far more than all of Frank Wiggins' words, how beautiful Southern California was and how wonderful its scenery and climate. Glamour helped sell lots in Pasadena, Riverside and San Bernardino. Glamour built Palm Springs, in the desert east of San Jacinto. The whole region came to be associated with high adventure, in which the bad guys always lost and the good guys always won. (Real tragedy, in which the good and upright man sometimes got his teeth kicked out, came much later—and was regarded as far more artistic.) Comedy and sex were present from the first. Whether or not the movies gave the people what they wanted, they did give them what the producers, who were often men who had gained more education in the streets and market places than in school, thought they wanted. It was all, in a way, very democratic.

California—especially Southern California—was not real, like Michigan or Vermont. It was a haze, a kind of dream, a modern myth. It was, as always, easy on the old; but it was beginning to be stimulating for the young: a presentable youngster, a waitress, a girl clerking in a store, a young man who managed to get a day's work as an extra in a mob scene, any one of these who happened to catch the eye of a director—well, there was no limit to the possibilities. Somebody had to win, for there had to be actors and actresses, and these could not all be plucked off the New York stage, where the infant picture industry was at first regarded as a kind of last resort for failures and the habitually unlucky. Somebody did win, and in time the rewards were fabulous. Those who didn't win could still enjoy the climate. Or, eventually, get jobs making airplanes.

So the war years (the first ones) and the other years went by. I once saw Mary Pickford, in some sort of uniform, coming into a newspaper office in San Francisco; she was doing her bit for the war "effort" of 1917 by acting as a recruiting agent. Madame Schumann-Heink, soon to end her career as a singer, reviewed a divisional parade in (I believe) San Diego and sang the national anthem. There was a coming and going of young soldiers in San Francisco. Forty thousand men trained for military service at Camp Fremont, just across the San Francisquito Creek from Stanford University. A considerable number of youngsters came to Stanford and other colleges and universities to be educated for the fighting services; most of these would have gone into action as officers if the war had not ended when it did. The flu came and killed men at Camp Fremont, as it did in camps and communities all over the United States.

Good and bad things were happening, that is clear from the record: labor conflicts, in the young industries and on the large farms; problems of a baronial land system still unsettled; the velvet of sentimentalism to cover the hard facts of an almost feudal way of life; some corruption in the governments of the state's two largest cities; the lies and vulgarity of many of those who speculated in luring and looting newcomers.

All this makes a sad enough total; it does not sound like a description of Paradise. Yet the deficits in some areas were more than counterbalanced by the good or fortunate things that happened to California during the same period. The state was making experiments in direct self-government—these were not all successful, but they did represent an attempt to get back to democracy; state agencies were either reformed, if they already existed, or invented if they did not already exist, to guarantee some basic economic rights; Los Angeles took a flyer in public power, San Francisco in public ownership of streetcar lines; some attention was given to the migrant, the tenant farmer, the sick, the elderly; in short, California was beginning to understand that its admirable but exceedingly varied climate, some satisfactory mountain ranges, some beautiful stretches of seashore, orange groves and orchards, fog, redwood trees, opportunities to motor around on hard-surfaced roads, to play golf, or to ski were not a one hundred per cent guarantee of an absolutely perfect life.

California was growing up and wondering about things. There they were, the devoted Californians, the new gold seekers, in what seemed to some to be Heaven with harp music—and all this, though pleasant to think about, was at times dull. The struggle to put a meaning into living—or just to endure it—went on in California as it did in less fortunate localities and islands less blessed. Mild winters did not of themselves cure humanity's age-old aches and frustrations, or right its injustices and curb its more overweening ambitions.

What gives an observer of today a little shiver of apprehension, however, is the statistical fact that the population of the entire state of California at the end of the 1910–20 decade was about half of what the population of Los Angeles County is today. (Or was when these words were written.) When we talk of California, as we have been doing in all the earlier pages of this book, we are referring to a population that was minute in Spanish-Mexican times, small in American times down to the end of the nineteenth century, and inconsiderable in the same terms until the past twenty years. What is the early history of California today? It is place names, some of them very lovely. It is fiestas, mournful and gay, recalling a manner of life that was never what it seemed and that has as much to do with life in California today as have the relics of the stone age.

For it was only yesterday that California exploded. The abundant years of 1910–20 were only a beginning—a movement of pioneers. Today we are looking at a new, sometimes brilliant, sometimes depressing, always fascinating phenomenon. The framework remains, but it frames an altered and enlarged picture.

The year 1920 was a dividing line between generations, if there ever was such a thing. The change after that time was almost as complete as when the gold seekers and merchant adventurers from the other side of the Missouri River took over. It was almost as abrupt. And at that, as we shall be seeing, it was only a curtain raiser.

13

The Big Boom

A brief and now almost forgotten recession followed the First World War. After that, the big boom exploded, and California gained nearly 66 per cent in population while the United States as a whole was gaining a little over 16 per cent. In 1929, in the first year of the great depression, the state had 5,677,000 people inside its frontiers. The second Gold Rush was under way, even when there was little or no gold to be had. It turned out that this was just a beginning—the first lappings of a Bay-of-Fundy tide. But for people who had real estate to sell it was already quite a party.

Quantitative records begin to tell the story, though they can never tell all of it. Petroleum production soared between 1920 and 1930. The state exported less than a million barrels in 1920, more than 44 million barrels in 1929. California's industries turned to oil where they could; manufactured goods reached nearly three billion dollars in 1929; oil and natural gas began to supplement the large output of hydroelectric power. Steel production, in the absence of Mr. Kaiser and some others, remained low, with San Francisco still ahead of Los Angeles. But the state was flexing its industrial muscles.

Automobiles continued to be made mostly in Detroit, but Californians during this decade were already devoted and even fanatical users of them. As many of them as could get cars went as far as they could, on whatever roads they could, as fast as they could. Where Father Serra had patiently covered fifteen or twenty miles in a day the newer Californians began to feel they were standing still if they could not do as much in twenty minutes. Immigrants who used to arrive on trains, sometimes even on freight trains, now came more and more in automobiles, no longer a rich man's toy.

The automobile opened up easy access to acres which previously had been out in the hay belt. This made it practicable for the real estate salesmen to increase their stock in trade and multiply many times over the prices demanded for it. This was peculiarly observable around Los Angeles; the same thing was happening around San Francisco, but this was, by comparison, retail business. Roads and curbs lined with red geraniums began to appear where the contemplative cow had grazed not many years earlier; these were at times a pathetic or comic sight, but after a while the land was sold and built upon. And during the 1930s a house could be built or bought, north or south, for about a sixth of what it would later cost.

These were not always good houses. A man who left Los Angeles for New York about the year 1920 told me he didn't mind when the realtors put up houses that were tacked or glued together, but he had stopped paying installments on his own Dream Home when he found it was stuck together with spit. I did not believe this, for he had a habit of overstatement, but I do think much of the Southern California building in that period was of a flimsy character.

Yet in the end the joke was on the realtor, because no matter how much he overcharged and misrepresented, he sold his goods for less than they finally came to be worth. The market, over the years, boomed and collapsed several times, but real estate bought in the metropolitan areas of California during the 1920s is now worth more than even the most credulous purchaser paid for it.

2

The farm system was technologically but not humanly improved during the 1920s and would grow worse before it grew better. But the crops were rich and varied and added to the general sense of well-being—except, at times, among the unfortunates who had to harvest them. California's great interior valleys during the 1920s would have impressed a casual traveler as being the very symbol of plenty.

It was, and is, a majestically beautiful state. Even the deserts have their magic and wonderment. And an observer at times may ask if there is some law of balance and compensation in nature, so that people who live in pleasant places, in gentle climates, are often abused and mistreated, while in rougher environments they may, like the Eskimos (and perhaps the penguins), maintain a plainer and more equitable society.

But California was booming. One of the last of our westward-facing frontiers (we have to bear in mind, also, Oregon, Washington State, Alaska, and Hawaii), it attracted the descendants of those who had fought locusts, Indians, and foul weather in the Middle West, who had kept slavery out of Kansas and abolished it by force of arms in the old South, and who had undergone dangers and torments in crossing the Plains, trailing up the Chagres River toward Panama, or rolling around the Horn. The westward tradition went straight back to Plymouth Rock, though at this point the spiritual link between the country's first immigrants and those now entering California ended.

The State was a problem and a puzzle to many of these newcomers. But they kept on coming, all sorts and conditions. This was the greatest migration in all American history.

The pity of it is, there was in it so much frustration. For the California of this century was never a pioneer community of plain and simple living, of neighborliness, and of a perfected democracy. Many gospels were heard, both secular and otherwise, but the gospel of the main chance and every man for himself was the one quite often followed. But almost to the end of the 1920s the state was booming.

New varieties of fruits, nuts, and other small crops were being cultivated. They were being cultivated scientifically, even though the migratory labor system, as followed during those years, belonged to the Middle Ages and was not efficient, even from a coldly materialistic point of view. "Cheap" labor, as many California farmers later found out, is not cheap. But an avocado or a grape vine got the kindly attention that a human migrant did not; and the results were profitable.

The increasing population made a larger and handier market, even when it pushed the farmers off the land and replaced them with commuters. For instance, the northern Santa Clara Valley used to be a dream of loveliness in spring, when the prunes, apricots, and almonds blossomed. It is nowhere near so lovely now. Yet the new "ranch houses" (where the ranches used to be and are no longer) are convenient for men who work in San Francisco or San Jose. The new suburban developments are not always ugly. One can be comfortable, in attractive style, even within the city limits of Los Angeles. But these developments obviously do cut down the open spaces and the farming lands. Or they push them farther from the cities, for the cash value of California crops went on increasing during and after the 1920s. The inflated dollar diluted the figures considerably, but there had been a great growth in bulk—and this couldn't be diluted by currency changes.

Mining went on during the 1920s, even though gold was hardly a paying venture. Other metals were useful in industry, though in some cases their very names were only recently familiar. During the 1920s it began to seem that one could find almost anything in the California earth, except an abundant and accessible supply of coal. There was even some iron.

And everybody knew, in California as elsewhere, that there were never to be any more depressions and hard times; they knew this until October, 1929, when the New York Stock Exchange and other stock markets went into hysterics, prosperity went around the corner and for some years stayed there, and the Great Depression ravaged the land.

But it took more than a depression to stop California growing.

It grew during some of the following years in pain, travail, fear, disillusionment, and injustice, but it grew. Many people decided that if they had to ride out a depression California was a good spot to choose; in some ways it was and in other ways it wasn't. But it wasn't bitterly cold there, once you got over the mountains.

3

Hollywood remained this adolescent nation's concept of heaven, even when, about the middle of the 1920s, actors and actresses who hadn't previously talked for the public ear had to learn elocution. Everybody was always happy in Hollywood, so the legend was, even though practically all the married stars were so discontented with their partners that they were continually getting married and then married all over to somebody else.

The transition to sound was painful indeed for those who did not have good or properly trained voices. One lovely lady boomed like a fog horn in her first sound movie, but later they got her down to a most fetching husky whisper, and she made several excellent audible films before she counted up her cash and decided to call it a day. I was glad they fixed her voice up, for we had grown up together—she on the once silent screen, I a rapt spectator who had often paid seventy-five or even eighty cents to get in. But the studios went on making money until nearly the end of the 1920s, not knowing what was ahead of them in real life.

When the studios began to make noises, most of the organists, pianists, and other musicians who had helped give silent films their "mood" in countless theaters passed on to other jobs, as did also many of the stars of the silent screen. But sound was probably healthful for the movie industry; it took more brains, more depth of personality, better direction, and better acting to make a talking picture than it did to make a silent one. Hollywood was never again quite as fatuous, I believe, as it had been before the sound machines were brought in.

This cinematic revolution was happening in and around Los Angeles in the final years of the Big Boom. Playwrights and writers of books went out to Los Angeles, grumbling at their hard lot, to make more in a month or two than Shakespeare did in his entire professional lifetime. They took the money to pay the grocery and other bills and some of them revenged themselves for this humiliation by writing uncomplimentary things about Hollywood, once they were safely over the mountains, going East.

Those who didn't get invited to Hollywood also grumbled. No American institution was more wittily damned during the second half of the 1920s than Hollywood and its principal industry. But for quite a while the money kept rolling in, and Hollywood nearly always had bank credit in New York to pay for films some people thought might just as well not have been made.

In 1922 Will H. Hays, Postmaster General under President Harding and Republican National Chairman, took the job of riding herd on the output of the motion picture studios. His salary was $100,000 a year—not as much as the highest-ranking stars could earn but good enough to make people in the trade look up to him. Mr. Hays was not only an honest man but looked like one; to the end of his life, sophisticated though he was, he resembled the small-town Indiana boy he had once been. The result was that the motion picture industry became audible and respectable almost at the same time.

Sound on the screen was preceded—and stimulated—in the 1920s by the development of radio. Radio was, of course, a sort of competitor of the motion picture, as television was later to become.

The motion picture in the 1920s did not generate a large fraction of the national income. Nor does it today. It was and is, perhaps, a psychic income—that is, it yields satisfactions over and above anything that can be cashed at the bank. In Los Angeles there was one good illustration of that kind of income: the Hollywood areas where the movie studios had flourished grew so swiftly in land valuations that the studios could no longer afford to stay there: this is one reason why Hollywood doesn't live in Hollywood any more.

It is probably true also (as I have said previously) that the movies gave the Los Angeles neighborhood a sort of fascination it wouldn't have had if its most glittering industry had been the manufacture of automobiles or even of men's clothing. And I think there was more of this allure during the 1920s than there was afterwards.

But the state of mind called Hollywood gave the Los Angeles area a kind of aristocratic distinction. Motion picture stars received fabulous wages, but it wasn't wholly because they were rich that they were treated like oriental potentates—it was because they had a style, an atmosphere, a come-hither, a royal way about them. This continues even as I am writing. A romance in Hollywood or its international suburbs attracts almost as much attention as a love match in Europe's dwindling monarchistic circles. But during the 1920s it was considered subversive in and around Los Angeles to poke fun at a motion picture celebrity— and if the reality was never quite as good as the pretence it didn't really matter—you could photograph the pretence and make it look fine.

4

The motion picture's beautiful but profitable unreality affected other things besides the actors and actresses. It somehow made it possible for a weirdly assorted set of people with various religious, economic, and social creeds to flourish and multiply. One was not so much aware of these phenomena in Northern California, though like tarweed and marijuana they cropped up occasionally in people's backyards. On the whole, I believe they trailed the movies, and found rich soil where the movie-makers had done their cultivating. This element of unreality keeps creeping into California life, especially in the South.

I do not mean to enlarge upon these curious cults: the subject has indeed been well taken care of by numerous authorities. Moreover, the wave of fantasy has somewhat subsided. And perhaps nothing could be more fantastic than the belief of millions of people during the 1920s, and not only in California, that stocks would continue to go up or stay up—forever.

More important things were happening in California, North and South. Like other states, this one was never chemically pure in its politics, but it had improved. The social legislation passed under the Johnson regime was expanded during the 1920s. Labor in factories and on farms was getting more protection. Prosperity made California feel rich and secure enough to be humanitarian.

The progress of San Francisco cannot easily be compared with that of Los Angeles: you cannot very well compare a city of 45 square miles with one of 455 square miles. The decade of the 1920s (again, down to 1929) was a good one for the cities of the San Francisco Bay area. For practical if not for political purposes the communities of Alameda, Oakland, Piedmont, Berkeley, Richmond, and so on were all part of the Port of San Francisco. So were Daly City and South San Francisco and the other towns down to rapidly growing San Jose, as well as the growing urban areas north of the Golden Gate Bridge in Marin County.

North and South, during this period, the state was breeding not so much a new species of American but a new kind of living for those fortunate enough to reach the Promised Land—and able to find the dollars to realize the promises.

The motorcar, and the roads it ran on, were peculiarly important in California. There were more cars per capita, for one thing, than there were in other parts of the nation. Moreover, the remarkable topography of the state opened up unusual possibilities to those who had time and money—as more and more did for recreation.

California "climate" used to mean chiefly one thing—warmth and comfort, a dry season, and a rainy season, but not a cold or snowy season. (At least, it meant this to those who had not studied the subject or had not read the fine print.) It suggested lying in the sun on a beach, or playing tennis, golf, or some other game under a clear sky. Soon, even before the motorcar conquered this new territory, California also meant Lake Tahoe and the Sierras. But going into the mountains in the early days of the automobile meant taking a long train ride, later a long bus ride, and then going in and up from some jumping-off place. The mountains were not for the lazy, the elderly or the feeble—not even Yosemite.

To take an illustration, my wife and I, living in Palo Alto, thirty miles southeast of San Francisco, about the year 1918, could reach Fallen Leaf Lake, above Tahoe, in the better part of a day. I was impressed, a few years later, to find that it had become quite an ordinary matter for Palo Altans to go up to Yosemite, or Squaw Valley, or somewhere else in the Sierras, for a weekend of skiing. *The California Information Almanac* mentions "more than fifty winter sports areas in the national forests in California." There is also a substantial state park system.

The great hills are open, even in winter, to the adventurous. A winter blizzard can close the high Sierra roads (see George Stewart's book *Storm*) but when it does so the fact is news.

Not all this was apparent during the booming 1920s, but it was beginning. It affected the whole state, North and South. A San Franciscan could not always bask in the sun (neither could an Angeleno, but that was later, when the smog began), but each could get into basking territory without annoying delay.

More than half a century ago I spent a part of a summer vacation working as a cook in a road-making camp in the San Jacinto Range. The nearest railway station to this camp was Banning. Beyond Banning, to the east, was Palm Springs. "You wouldn't like it there," a wise resident of Banning told me. "The wind blows the sand so hard that all the windows, including those in the railway station, are so cut up you can't see through them."

Some years later Palm Springs became a symbol for luxurious winter vacations, in one of the most flourishing oases in the world. Death Valley, where some forty-niners died and others suffered torments from thirst trying to reach the golden sand beyond the mountains, is also a winter resort. Eel River and the coast redwoods above San Francisco, once difficult or tedious to reach even by rail, are popular weekend resorts. On an August Saturday and Sunday the whole population of California, or so it seems, is in motion: the blistered denizens of the Central Valley come to the coast, the coastal dwellers take refuge in the Sierras.

This is the way things were going during the 1920s. With allowance for more people, more and better roads, and more automobiles, it is the way they are going today. The difference is the vastly greater magnitude. But as far back as the 1920s it was accurate to say that there never could have been in this world, except possibly some South Sea island in the pre-atomic-bomb era, a territory whose population was so largely devoted to having fun. And it was probably more fun during the 1920s than it was afterwards, or ever can be again; if the roads were not so good as they later became, they were not so crowded, there were camping grounds not yet littered with beer tins, and some parts of the floor of the Yosemite Valley, even at the height of the season, had space for a few more cars and a few more sleeping bags.

Californians also played games—as they still do. Tennis enthusiasts could bat a ball around most days in the year, especially in the South. Golf flourished, and for the same reason; if one stayed below the snow line he wouldn't miss his chance to practice; golf therefore acquired in California great dignity and solemnity; it became almost an industry. Naturally, it had to find room and occasionally it displaced some things that some persons might have wished to spare. There was once a Chinese fishing village on the Monterey Peninsula, near Carmel; as a college youth I saw it and smelled it. Now this site, or approximately the same, is occupied by a famous and stylish hotel, adjacent to an equally famous and stylish golf course. It smells better now, but some enchantment has been lost. There are so many "buts" in this business of watching California grow.

At all events, play, amateur and professional, was getting to be a large part of life in California during the 1920s—for those who could afford it and many who couldn't afford it. There was a large middle class that certainly could afford it, not to mention the motion picture stars, directors, and producers who could afford anything or had to pretend they could. It was almost a matter of State patriotism to play long, hard, and in all seasons, for this demonstrated the wonders of the climate; it showed, in the words of the old Italian song, that California was made for fun and frolic.

5

The 1920s—or approximately nine-tenths of them—were, in brief, a good decade in California—as decades go. Los Angeles passed San Francisco in the total tonnage that went in and out of her port, but this did not leave San Francisco desolate. Los Angeles grew faster than San Francisco, but there was traffic enough in San Francisco's streets to make people step lively. Southern California had the most oil, but oil shipments went out through both ports. The oil business could be corrupt—witness the conviction of former Interior-Secretary Fall for taking a bribe from an old friend, Edward L. Doheny. But Doheny was acquitted on the charge of giving the bribe, and the oil from the Doheny and other wells brought large quantities of capital into the state. Automobiles were assembled as well as driven in the Californians' frantic urge toward mobility and speed.

The whole country was in the grip of the same urge, but California felt it most, and with the most reason. Florida, it must be admitted, also drew the weary, credulous, and hopeful. But California had, and has, a variety Florida lacks; it had, and has, more natural resources; it offered more opportunities for those who don't merely wish to relax. The California of the 1920s did not much resemble the California of the 1820s, when the mountain men were drifting across the deserts and through the passes, but it had openings for the energetic at the later date as well as the earlier.

The pattern was being fixed, the future (as hindsight tells us) was evident. And in the 1920s there was still plenty of room in which the modern prototypes of the old trappers could roam, enjoy life, and pick up a living.

It was never to be that easy again.

☼ *14* ☼ ☼ ☼

The Big Bust

The great spaces were there, the seemingly infinite room to grow; the richness of the land was there; the blessings of a generally mild climate were there; but suddenly there was a darkness over the land. This was the vintage, this was the gathering of what John Steinbeck called "the grapes of wrath."

California, except for being a part of the United States, was not responsible for the crash and depression that began in the fall of 1929. Neither was she to blame for the disaster compounded of Nature's whims and human folly that created the Dust Bowl in the 1930s. Possibly the Californians had more reason than most Americans for being confident of the economic future, for their state would continue to increase in population at three times the national rate (from 5,677,000 in 1930 to 6,907,000 in 1940) during the nationally bad years.

The Dust Bowl was created by drought and the plowing of marginal land farther east—roughly west of the hundredth meridian and east of the Rocky Mountains. It affected the Dakotas, Western Iowa, Nebraska, Kansas, Oklahoma, Arkansas, and Texas; and it started a new westward migration of whole families, who came to be known as "Okies" and "Arkies," though many of them came from other Dust Bowl states. These people entered California in rickety automobiles instead of covered wagons, but it is not certain that they differed too much from the covered-wagon immigrants of the mid-eighteenth century. The trouble was that they came into a settled land which did not have work or use for them all. And they did not come as conquerors.

In view of this outcome it is ironic that this intrusion, as many of the Californians regarded it, was largely the result of the picture that previous booster publicity had created. The newcomers were looking for the land of promise, and the land was not able at the moment to keep any promises.

All the "Okies" and "Arkies" had, as a rule, was a ramshackle motorcar and a few personal belongings. Some had been share-croppers and didn't even own any tools. Others may have had title to a few acres of land, but the drought and dust had made the land unsaleable. Few arrived with spare cash—the typical forty-niner couldn't have been worse off in that respect.

2

The depression affected California industry as it did the industries of other states, but its impact on the farming system was far more visible and dramatic. The people who harvested the crops of the land of plenty subsisted on a poor and insufficient diet and lived in squalor.

The farmers had already tried many kinds of cheap labor; over the years Chinese, Japanese, Filipinos, a few Hindus, and many Mexicans had done harvest labor at low wages. Now, in the 1930s, came this other type of cheap labor—American-born of Nordic blood. Estimates as to how many came are varied: they run from 150,000 to 250,000 and up. Despite efforts by the I.W.W., the standard labor unions, and probably the Communists to organize them, they were a helpless mass, degraded by their manner of life and by the treatment given them.

The Great Plains dust storms unhappily coincided with some of the really bad depression years. When the "Okies" and "Arkies" pressed toward the California frontiers they were the less welcome because they were not needed—there was no longer any

Captain Sutter to lend them supplies or give them jobs when they came out of the big hills.

The Associated Farmers, who at that time spoke for the land-owners who needed temporary labor at harvest seasons, were themselves hard pressed. Demands for their goods had dropped and prices had fallen. They were frightened men, and like other frightened men they were driven to be cruel. They believed they could not raise wages or provide decent shelters and decent living conditions and still survive. They feared "agitators." In the end they came to regard the "Arkies" and "Okies" as an enemy in their midst and the continuous movement into the state as that of an invading army. And they were partly right. The immigrants wished no harm to anybody, but they did come in, like some of the wild tribes who pulled the Roman Empire down fifteen hundred years ago, in search of greener pastures, or pushed by forces they themselves could not resist—in their case, as perhaps in the ancient ones, a prolonged spell of dry weather.

Their arrival was not an unmitigated misfortune for the ranchers, for it produced a surplus of labor, to be bought at a bargain. By today's standards the bargain was shocking. Annual earnings, for families including children who worked in the fields, ran as high as $400, as low as $150. Thirty years earlier an unskilled worker in California (I was one during my college days) could earn twenty-five cents an hour, or two dollars for an eight-hour day. In the 1930s a migratory farm laborer was glad (if that is the right word) to get a dollar or even seventy-five cents a day.

In the very depths of the depressions something happened that must have made the pale wraith of Frank Wiggins shiver with horror. Mr. Wiggins had done his best to lure people to California. California had cured him of what ailed him, and he wanted others to have the same good fortune. He assumed, of course, that they would bring a little money with them, but in his day that was hardly a problem: except for a few hardy souls who "rode the rods" or traveled free in an empty boxcar, few came west without some money to spend.

Now the whole picture was changed. Southern California, not to mention the Central Valley, was no longer smiling and hospitable; Southern California, and especially its mother city, Los Angeles, showed the face of a snarling watchdog guarding a private preserve.

And a huge preserve it was, for Los Angeles, occupying 455 square miles in a state containing 156,000 square miles, took it upon herself to guard the entire state against invasion from the north or east. Los Angeles police, sometimes deputized as sheriffs but otherwise without legal justification, took control of all the main inward-leading passes. It seemed, and still seems, incredible, and it was, but it happened. The operation had a name: it was called "the bum blockade." It was an old-fashioned vigilance committee with brass buttons and badges. But Los Angeles, as the saying goes, got away with it.

John Steinbeck treated of these matters in *The Grapes of Wrath.* In a pamphlet written for the Simon J. Lubin Society of California, he asked bitterly: "Is it possible that this state is so stupid, so vicious and so greedy that it cannot feed and clothe the men and women who help to make it the richest area in the world?" His novel and his pamphlet, together with publications by other authors, answered his question. California did and does have a conscience. But some of the things that happened in the 1930s remain a blot on the page. They spoil the rhythm of the poem; they give a sad twist to later eulogies; they sour the wine; they rot the golden apples of the Hesperides.

But Greek history had its wretched incidents, too, and those who ponder the course of events in modern California may find some comfort in that thought.

3

During the depression California formed the habit of voting Democratic in Presidential years. It voted all four times for Mr. Roosevelt, even in 1940, when the amiable Wendell Willkie was running, and the two-term tradition was being (temporarily) squashed. However, it was already apparent to even the most casual observers that Los Angeles and its tributary communities tended to go Republican, and that San Francisco was instinctively Democratic. This was easier for the Republicans to bear, because there are more people and more voters in the Southern counties than in the Northern.

On the other hand, the Southern counties remained the home of original and often startling political doctrines as well as of a variety of curious religious doctrines, concerning which a lay man is possibly not qualified to write.

California during the 1930s had a Criminal Syndicalism Act, passed in 1919, which was supposed to discourage violent attempts to overthrow the Government but was sometimes actually used to prevent strikes. Almost any minority belief was made dangerous by this law; under it that gentlest of Utopians, Upton Sinclair, was arrested for reading the United States Constitution audibly in public. Mr. Sinclair did not have to go to prison for this offence (for the Constitution is an inflammatory document, if one takes it seriously), but the incident did help turn him into a politician. In 1934 he offered himself as Democratic candidate for Governor on a ticket called EPIC—which stood for the slogan, "End Poverty in California." One of his demands was for a pension of fifty dollars a month for those who needed it. Another was for the issuance of scrip, which had to be spent within a certain time.

Mr. Sinclair did not win. Perhaps in no other state, however, could he have come so close to winning, so close it apparently scared him, for he did not really want to be Governor. He received 879,597 votes, as against 1,138,620 for his conventionally reliable antagonist, Frank F. Merriam. If Mr. Sinclair had been a little less extreme, a little better organized, if he had more closely followed President Roosevelt's Democratic platform, he might have become Governor. But his relatively heavy minority did give the professionals a jolt, showed that many thousands of Californians, even in the conservative South, were uneasy and resentful, and possibly prepared the ground for later Roosevelt successes in the state.

The Townsend Plan, fathered by a retired Long Beach physician, Dr. Francis E. Townsend, had ultimately a nationwide appeal and considerably less chance of success than Mr. Sinclair's modest proposals. Dr. Townsend's program demanded a pension of $200 a month for all persons over sixty, on condition that this sum be spent within three months of issuance. Practically, it would have compelled the young and middle-aged to support the elderly. It would also have been inflationary and in the long run might not have amounted to much in actual value. The "Ham-and-Eggs" project, which called for thirty dollars a week for all unemployed persons over fifty, came a little later and never really got off the ground. Social security, current pension plans, plus the decline in the value of the dollar have made the financial figures of the Townsend and "Ham-and-Eggs" proposals seem less absurd today than they did then.

Though not accurately recognized at the time, there was also beginning in the less than golden thirties an influx of young people who were not especially tired, and eventually, as the depression let go a little, there was an increase in the number of jobs available. These jobs first began to show up when the Roosevelt Administration began to spend money on public works as well as on some forms of relief that were tied in with actual work. These were often described in unflattering terms—does anybody remember "boondoggling"?—by Mr. Roosevelt's political enemies, but they did give people, in California and elsewhere, something to do.

And some work of substantial and lasting value did give employment in California and other states during those dark years.

4

During the depression years the spotlight rested on San Francisco for a crisis or two and several magnificent achievements. The crisis, in the spring of 1934, began with a longshoremen's walkout, in which the unions were master-minded by Harry Bridges. In this strike San Francisco was a focal point. As the strike went on, other workers left their jobs in sympathy, the police swung into action to (as they said) repress or prevent violence, and, in doing so, not for the first time in police history, they were themselves unjustifiably violent. Not since the days of the Gold Rush had San Francisco Bay been so full of idle ships. Rarely before had there been such bitter feeling in a labor dispute—although in that city it had never been common for either side in such a quarrel to use ladylike language.

On the day after Independence Day, 1934, the police killed two pickets and wounded many others while attempting to break the union lines and get nonunion men on the docks. Nine days later practically the whole organized working force of the city— estimated at 150,000—walked off their jobs.

Thus this became a general strike, which, as a management spokesman later explained to me, is revolution. Governor Merriam sent in militia, ostensibly to protect state property, actually to keep order. This was a force no labor union could oppose, and after three days the general strike began to break down. It had to break, if the city were to be fed and enabled to go about its daily business. The maritime unions stayed out, however, for some months; they felt they had real grievances, as in fact they did. In the end some of these grievances were corrected.

On the whole, the right of employees to "bargain collectively through representatives of their own choosing" was due to be recognized at this time; and it was so recognized, all over the country. Except in the harvest fields, California was growing more democratic. Employers in the Bay areas came to respect Harry Bridges, if only because he could control his unions. I might anticipate the story a little by stating that toward the end of the Second World War, I spoke with a Chamber of Commerce official in San Francisco who had a kindly word for Mr. Bridges and praised the manner in which he was cooperating with the war effort.

Like every prominent and successful labor leader in California, Mr. Bridges was accused of being a Communist; but this neither the Dies Committee on Un-American Activities nor any other suspicious person or agency was ever able to prove. There the matter has to rest.

Meanwhile, the depression and the accompanying labor-management collywobbles did not prevent San Francisco from changing her own physical character considerably and altering her relations with neighboring cities, by bridging both the Bay and the Golden Gate.

She did this on borrowed money but not on a Federal dole, for it proved possible to operate both bridges at a profit. Mrs. Fremont Older, in her book, *San Francisco: Magic City*, reminds us that that picturesque character, "Emperor" Norton, once wrote out a check for $3.5 million and commanded the contemporary Mayor to "bridge the Bay." The Bay Bridge, begun in 1932, completed in 1936, cost a little more than the Emperor had calculated, for there had been some inflation; it was considered cheap enough at $77.2 million.

So far as is recorded the Emperor did not order any bridge across the Golden Gate—it may have looked too difficult, even to his not altogether realistic eye. This is significant, for San Francisco did quite a few of the things that were commanded by its pet eccentric during his flourishing years, 1859 to 1865.

However, the Golden Gate did get bridged, with construction starting in January, 1933, and finished in June, 1937. Thus, within the space of five years, the water barriers that had frustrated Portola and other explorers as well as modern travelers disappeared. One could drive or ride a bus, at a fairly fast clip, from San Francisco to Marin County on the north or to Contra Costa County on the east. Before this there were no land routes into the city from north or east. San Francisco had been a peninsula, almost an island. Now it was a crossroads corner on an increasingly busy tangle of roads.

The effect of the bridges was twofold (as everything is in San Francisco): sentimental and economic. San Franciscans had loved the ferry boats almost as much as they loved the cable cars; but ferry boats could not be, and were not, practicable on a purely sentimental basis. One or two lingered for a while to make transcontinental train connections, but soon these too disappeared.

An older generation will recall these craft and miss them as long as its members survive; they were elegant boats; they carried lunch counters where one could breakfast luxuriously on coffee and those sweet buns called snails, or on eggs, or bacon if one were rich enough; the gulls followed them, and there were always four gulls aboard, one on each of the flagpoles fore and aft; in the morning fogs there was always the chance of a transbay voyage ending in a collision with an incoming steamer from the Orient; on the long Sausalito run one saw Alcatraz, where a Federal prison then was, and sometimes one had a clear westward view to the Pacific. But even San Franciscans had to admit that romance was extravagant when you could wangle yourself two bridges and tangle up traffic in the city without any direct cost to the taxpayer.

The bridges made San Francisco and Los Angeles more alike (one hates to admit this, for in California contrasts are part of the joy of life) in that they were a product of the age of speed and mechanism. They linked the city, a gray-white miracle as one came into it from the north, with its tributary cities and valleys; and to some extent they took away part of its isolation and a bit of its charm; the modern steelclad knight jogging down into many-towered Camelot had to look to his road and not to the towers; in plain words the bridges made it possible for the traveler to scoot the whole length of the state, from Oregon to Mexico, without catching more than a glimpse of anything but other motorists.

The bridges were, and are, wonderful; they are poems in steel; and they came, with a gesture the forty-niners would have loved, out of the depths of that dry gulley, full of fool's gold, known as the Great Depression. They expressed a feeling about roads (for a bridge is merely part of a road) more intense than men had experienced since the fall of the old Roman Empire. The automobile made the roads necessary, the roads made more and more automobiles not only necessary but practicable, and the frenzy of travel seized almost everybody, like the tarantella dance that we are told swept Naples three centuries ago.

San Francisco celebrated the ending of one dream, the old easygoing dream of romance, and the beginning of a newer dream, half ecstasy, half nightmare, by holding another World's Fair, opened on filled-in shoals adjoining Yerba Buena (or Goat) Island, in February, 1939. The actual site was called Treasure Island. Perhaps there was less to rejoice over than the San Franciscans of 1939 believed, for if the depression was losing its grip the Second World War, in February, 1939, was not far off.

Just as San Francisco would never be the same again, once it had made itself a passageway rather than a destination, so the earth could never be the same again after Mr. Hitler's bloody buffoonery and Japan's fantastic cooperation in it. Treasure Island itself was to be put to warlike uses within the next two and a half years.

But people had fun at Treasure Island, on the eve of the Second World War, just as they had had fun along what is now called the Marina, in the first year of the First World War. California, in the Central Valley, in the Salinas lettuce fields, and in the broiling Imperial Valley, did not seem a totally happy commonwealth, nor a totally civilized one, but at Treasure Island it was, at least locally and briefly an earthly paradise. That was the sort of dream that wouldn't die in California, soon or later; Queen Calafia should have had a special evening at Treasure Island.

However, things were being planned in Tokyo, in Berlin, in Rome, and in Moscow that would bring California to and over the Big Divide. Treasure Island celebrated an achievement, to wit, the building of two bridges, but it also commemorated much that was to disappear—much that was bad and some that was good—all along the length and breadth of California.

☼ *15* ☼   ☼   ☼

The Great Divide

The Second World War removed the last traces of California's isolation; it increased her manufacturing output, measured in dollars, more than three times over; it established her as the center of American aviation, military and civilian; and, because a Japanese submarine popped out of the ocean one day and took a random shot at a pier near Santa Barbara it made her the only State in the Union to lose even a few slivers of wood by enemy action.

Since the Second World War was a two-coast affair California's part in it was direct and visible, and since the Japanese surrendered some months later than the Germans California had a longer war, more glory (whatever that is), and more worry than did the states in the Middle West and along the Eastern Seaboard. And California gained a vast flood of immigration out of the conflict: in 1940 she had a little under seven million people; in 1950 a little more than ten and a half million.

Such changes, I should like to repeat, are not merely quantitative inflations. As the California population grew larger, it grew more vigorous and ambitious. Southern California especially needed energy and ambition, and it got them. The average age decreased. The hold of venerable traditions loosened. Even in San Francisco people didn't look back to the Gold Rush or to the "Earthquake and Fire" as earnestly as they used to; they looked forward; after all, they did have those bridges. In Los Angeles the annual Iowa picnic would never again be the event of the year.

However, all this did not happen overnight. Or smoothly.

2

After the Dominguez Field meet in 1910, near Los Angeles, every one knew that Southern California was a favorable area for aviation. If you kept away from the mountains there was no snow; for a large part of the year there was no rain; the winds were commonly not too bad, and since the early flying machines were delicate affairs, not very stable and subject to the mechanical equivalent of influenza and indigestion, these points were important. Also, if an aviator were bold enough and had a machine good enough to trifle with the mountains he could find lower passes in the south than in the north.

As the airplanes grew more robust and acquired a longer range California still afforded advantages in manufacturing and testing. Lindbergh's "Spirit of St. Louis" was built in San Diego. By the opening of the Second World War Douglas and Lockheed were in full stride, and even before we went into the war the huge Federal program for defense had made California a manufacturing center for airplanes.

With this development California's historic isolation ceased forever. She was no longer, and never would be again, an island. The size and speed of planes were startlingly increased, until in a few incredible years no place on earth was far from any other place, measured in travel time. Aviation was no longer a thrill, it was an industry and a weapon, and California, now nearer New York than Detroit used to be, was getting the contracts, profits, and employment to pan out the possibilities. It was Sutter's Mill all over again, and surer.

Immigrants from outside the state, however penniless, were now as welcome as the kindly fruits of the earth; if they could not be used in the fields they could be employed in the factories, and even at relatively high wages they were profitable to hire. Government orders flowed in and California manufacturers welcomed them. The manufacturers earned good returns on their investments, labor's pay kept rising, and the Government got the needed aircraft, ships, military hardware, and other goods it needed to fight a war. Ships were built from Richmond and Marin County to Los Angeles and San Diego.

A shipyard in Marin County, which I saw toward the end of the war, was turning out merchant vessels like motor cars on an assembly line; the superstructures were being built separately and hoisted aboard in one piece. It was ships such as these that carried the immense burden of supplies needed in the Pacific part of the war.

In camps both north and south soldiers were being processed for the desperate fighting believed to lie ahead of them. One such camp, near San Francisco, was known as "The Slaughterhouse." Young soldiers sailed out of San Francisco and Los Angeles harbors with no farewells and no parades. The transports lay at the piers behind guarded barricades, and ships and men went out to their uncertain fate whenever a convoy could be assembled.

All this was a fine, patriotic effort. With it went an act of stupid injustice. Even at such a time the dual character of California, half generous and noble, half childish and brutal, showed itself.

3

I am referring, of course, to the round up, concentration, and exile of citizens of Japanese ancestry. It is common practice in time of war to put enemy aliens under control, and in California this was accordingly done. But the action against the Japanese race in California went further. Many members of this group had been born in the United States. Most of them felt just as loyal—or at least acted just as loyally—as citizens of German or Italian descent, who were not identifiable by skin or eyes. Under the law, all had the same rights as though their ancestors had come over in the Mayflower.

There was no basis in law, nor as it now seems in necessity, for interfering with these people. In Hawaii, where there were thousands of residents of Japanese derivation, the Federal Government was able to pick up a few spies and dissenters but the vast majority went free and cooperated fully with the "war effort." A battalion of Japanese ancestry went to Italy, where its members felt they had to do something special for their adopted country—and did.

The action against American citizens of Japanese descent was taken, to be sure, by military order—and we all know what a fearful and wonderful thing the military mind can be when it is staked out to graze on a long tether. The order to "relocate" the Japanese (for this was the beautiful word applied to a high-handed outrage) came from the boss general of the Western Defense Command. However, there was strong support for "relocation" among various assorted lots of self-appointed patriots, including labor unions. Thus American citizens accused of no crime or misdemeanor were hustled out of their homes, even in San Francisco and Los Angeles, and shipped to remote areas in Wyoming and Utah.

Once in concentration camps, they were not harshly treated. So far as I have heard, nobody proposed to gas them. They had enough to eat, provided they raised some of it themselves on the arid soil around them. But they had been dislodged from their businesses and occupations and deprived of their homes, and though they were citizens they were treated as second-class or third-class citizens. In another category were about one-third as many who were not citizens; a few of these, but certainly not all of them, were hostile to the United States Government. However, the Government was within its rights when it rounded up these technical aliens.

One argument given in support of the relocation policy was that it was a humane measure to save people who looked like enemies, whether they were so or not, from hostile public reaction. Another argument wasn't given, except in whispers: if a Japanese had to leave his property and go inland, some white American whose foreign ancestry was not so visible was likely to profit by the transaction—as many outwardly white Americans did.

Prof. Andrew F. Rolle (in his *California: A History*) says that "the Japanese-Americans suffered a property loss of $365,000,-000." I have talked with persons who did not pretend to know the total but who did know, whether in Auburn or in Los Angeles, many Japanese-Americans who had lost practically everything they owned. In later years one could hear a Californian (not himself a beneficiary of this transaction) express regret at what had been done to innocent fellow-citizens. But no redress was made. Thousands of exiles never came back. Most were released when the first hysteria was past, but they went East, not West. They had had enough of what must have seemed to them the land of broken promises.

In California, as usual, the economic factor was at work. Those who had wanted the Japanese-American property got it—at a good price, as their predecessors long ago had gotten the old Spanish-American land grants. Japanese labor was not needed, for a sufficient deluge of white labor was pouring in from the East. A little injustice would soon be forgotten (it was) and, as in the old days when the miners drove the Mexicans, Chileans, and Chinese out of the gold camps, the white man would profit by it.

This is human nature, not California nature. I believe, however, that there was a frankness about the procedure that expressed the pioneer spirit, just as did some other and more admirable episodes of the World War. It was old-fashioned claim-jumping, which was all right if men with enough artillery did it.

4

War of the sort carried on between 1941 and 1945 is largely an industrial enterprise. The heroic and sacrificial qualities shown on the front line have to be sustained by an abundance of hardware, explosives, and other supplies and an effective system of transportation and communication. California supplied these materials of war in increasing abundance. At the beginning of the Second World War (to cite again the *California Information Almanac*) the state stood seventh in the Union in value of manufactured products, but it came third in the value of war contracts between 1939 and the end of 1944.

One reason for this swift growth was of course that California's products could be fed directly into the hungry maw of the Pacific campaigns, with no dangerous voyage down the Atlantic side and through the Panama Canal and without further clogging of the overloaded transcontinental railways. Another reason was the old lure—the climate. Except for the absence of usable coal and the relative scarcity of iron, California was admirably suited to modern manufacturing. She had plenty of petroleum; there was still much good but unused land; and the roads were excellent. For passengers of sufficient importance California was within a few hours' flying time of the East Coast.

With an astuteness that Frank Wiggins would surely have admired, and with a patriotic fervor that might also have moistened his eyes, the ruling generation of California businessmen went into action. They more than tripled the dollar output of manufactures between 1939 and 1944. They gave the state an economic place in the Union that it has never since lost.

Typical of what happened in California during this period was Henry Kaiser's steel plant, which replaced a vineyard at Fontana, in San Bernardino County. The workers in this plant and in others up and down the state (though there was, of course, only one Henry Kaiser) had to be housed, and this required the expansion of old towns and the building of new cities. In the swift rush of population and in the money that flowed in, these towns and cities resembled the mining towns of the old Mother Lode. In another sense they were different; the people had come to stay; the gold they brought in could not be exhausted by even the most intensive mining; it came out of taxes, not out of the beds of ancient rivers.

Nobody labeled this a new Gold Rush. Nobody so far as I have noticed thought of it in that way. Yet that was what it was. It brought new population in, by motorcar, by train, by airplane, and this time the new arrivals were welcome. It altered the face of the land, just as much as the old Gold Rush had done—only in different places. That quaint and jovial organization, the Native

Sons of the Golden West, dwindled by comparison into a puzzled and overlooked minority. New California was being born. Without any preambles and whereases, and almost without notice, a new State was coming into the Union.

The old traditions still remain, and on such occasions as Admission Day (a legal holiday in California) they would be romantically remembered. But the old days and the old gods, the Spanish cavaliers, the pre-movie movie actor Frémont, the red-shirted miners, the old happy-go-lucky times, the tumult and the shouting of the state's adolescence, these were retreating into the mist.

California was a big state now, in population and in ambition. The last of the old-fashioned kind of wars had given California its opportunity to flex its muscles. If it had stopped being a Paradise it had become an astounding workshop; Pan didn't live there any more, but Vulcan did.

5

And it was a workshop in which, for the time being, everybody labored together in peace—an almost unbelievable phenomenon in California. Some animosity had been expended on the exiled native Japanese, with resulting new opportunities for the white-skinned home folks; if there remained any lust for strife it could be diverted against the fighting forces of the Japanese Empire— which in early 1945 were nearer surrender than even the wisest generals suspected.

The only time during the Second World War when part of the labor movement in California dragged its feet was between September, 1939, when Britain and France were in it, and June, 1941, when Hitler attacked Russia. During this interval American Communists seemed to regard Hitler as an ally of Russia, and so far as they could influence the labor unions they discouraged the prewar preparedness drive. I don't mean to say that all American labor unions, or all labor unions with members in California, or most of them, were controlled by Communists. Some of them, however, were influenced, I am sure, by undercover Communist sympathizers, and in some instances these sympathizers succeeded in wagging the union labor dog: that is, they touched off strikes in the preparedness industries. There were strong indications that this happened in the aviation factories in Southern California. But when Herr Hitler was foolish enough to march on Russia he became an enemy of the Communists as well as of the rest of humanity. Our domestic left-wingers then went all out for "defense," then for war.

The men who have to face the enemy and the enemy's weapons have no reason to like war, and I don't believe many of them do or did. The civilian taxpayer and consumer suffers, too, though in a less primitive way. But if war were ever good to a community it was good to California. That is, it was good to those who owned California land, those with money invested in California industries or farms, and also those who worked there at war wages. Fifteen cents an hour would not buy much in the form of field work after Pearl Harbor.

Curiously enough, many of the soldiers, sailors, and marines who trained in the state did well, too, for many of them arrived too late to get into the hard fighting. Many, it was said, announced that if they survived they would never go back home to stay—they would return to settle in California. Frank Wiggins could not have devised a more effective scheme to bring in not the aged, doddering, and modestly well off, but strong young men with a capital investment of energy and health. In this way the armed services and the war industries operated together to augment the population.

For some months after the German surrender it was necessary, of course, to keep building up California's industrial and military strength for what was expected to be the final desperate thrust into the main islands of Japan. It was almost as though this were a sectional war—California against Japan.

6

Our troops did not have to fight their way into the main island of Japan, but the memory and foreshadowing of the enormous atomic tragedy must long remain in men's minds. As a journalistic visitor to California in 1945 I saw some of the preliminary stir, heard more than could be seen, learned slightly more than could be written, and felt much that could not easily be put into words.

The elevators that gave access to the roof of the Mark Hopkins Hotel, on Nob Hill in San Francisco, the "Top o' the Mark," as it was and still is called, were sealed in by long waiting lines in the early part of 1945, and in these lines there were more privates and non-commissioned men of all services than there were with bars, stars, or chickens on their shoulders.

These men were not saving their money, for they were not sure they would ever need much more money; they were not embarrassed in those luxurious surroundings by their own comparatively modest rank; they merely wanted, as they said, to give their girls a good time—a last good time, maybe. "They think they are going to die," a San Francisco newspaperman said to me. They did not die, not in that war; it ended before the grand assault that was scheduled to cost two million casualties. But that was California in 1945, too, the doomed young men, the enchanted glitter of lights all around the Bay, the dark hulks of transports lying at their barred docks; laughter and danger, love and youthful bravado; and I don't believe the forty-niners, most of whom bought their women as they went along (or went without), ever had San Francisco evenings as innocent and poignant as these.

It was the same in Los Angeles, too, and in San Diego and any port from which the transports sailed. It was a part of the history of California. It was outsiders looking in—and under the circumstances seeing peace and plenty in this Paradise from which they were invisibly barred.

I was not in California when the first units went out, and I know that many thousands of the first waves were killed or wounded in the horrible fighting through the islands to the Philippines. But the later ones, though they did not face this fate, thought they did and must have gone in the same mood and with the same cheerless expectations. I suppose that is why so many of them remembered California as an almost lost Heaven and came back to it when peace gave them the chance.

The state to which they returned after the war was not Heaven —it merely resembled it in some superficial and meaningless ways. It had its aches, worries, and apprehensions, sweat and early rising; it had its disillusionments and disappointments, the same as Arkansas and North Dakota. But it held most of its new settlers. They did not hanker to go back East.

So the war came to its end, with the mass slaughter at Hiroshima and Nagasaki to punctuate it all.

7

The conference that produced the United Nations Charter met in San Francisco on April 25, 1945, thirteen days after the death of its chief architect, President Roosevelt, three days before the death of Mussolini, four days before Hitler's suicide. Most of its major meetings were held in the Opera House, although it did assemble in the vast convention hall known as the Cow Palace just over the San Mateo County line.

Los Angeles would have been just as good a half-way point between the two mutually suspicious halves of the world as San Francisco was; but Los Angeles did not have the facilities, the background or—let us face it—the significance of San Francisco. History rolled in with the fog in San Francisco: here the Russians had at least dreamt of an extended empire in the old groping days; here the British had felt their rather gentlemanly ambitions, never pushed to the point of rudeness; here the Spanish had belatedly explored, here they had established their church and fort when the going was tough. This was a natural meeting place of nations.

Moreover, San Francisco, perched visibly above the deep-rolling Pacific, was in itself a mystery that suggested a solution (even though perhaps there was and could never be a solution)— certainly not always and everywhere beautiful, comfortable, or even respectable, but always spectacular.

So the diplomats and their staffs came, the journalists descended from half the world, a subsequently familiar hodgepodge of United Nations observers, and so began the struggle to make an international organization more sensible and more durable than the lamented League of Nations had ever been. This time the work began before the World War was over and the defeated were not present in chains, even figuratively, nor were territorial bargains openly discussed, as they had been at Versailles in 1919.

One's mind might have gone back to Colton Hall, Monterey, in 1849, where the first California Constitution was drawn up. This was a fairly rational interval in an irrational generation. Ten years later I heard Dag Hammarskjold, then Secretary General of the United Nations, speak of "the spirit of 1945." I think there was such a spirit, in spite of all the arguments and intrigues, and notwithstanding the fact that the Russians did not seem as keenly bent on world-wide peace as some had hoped.

But the Russians had been horribly punished during the war, and if they did not long for democracy or any new Bill of Rights they did at the moment long for security. A hard-boiled newspaperman of my acquaintance (I use the adjective as a compliment) told me when I paid a visit to the press side of the 1945 conference: "I think the Russians are not quite so ornery about all this as they seem. My theory is that they understand English or French all right, but they understand Russian better. They don't get all that is said, even when their own people put it back into Russian. They're not exactly cooperative, but they're not quite as mean and grasping as they seem."

This man was leaning over backward to be fair. The Russians were really tough, at San Francisco and afterwards, at least until Stalin died. Any Russian, or anybody else who had read the history and myths of California might have remembered at this point that visit of Nicolai Rezanov to the old Spanish Presidio in 1806 and his supposed romance with Concepcion Arguello, daughter of the Spanish Commandant. The lady was no doubt beautiful and Rezanov may have been attracted by her, but this did not take his mind off his work; he dutifully counted the guns the Spaniards had at the mouth of the Bay.

In short, this was not Russia's first official visit to San Francisco, and on this later visit they were no more humble or pliable than they had been in the old imperial days. But they did sign the Charter of the United Nations, though they may have been, even then, planning to pick up real estate in Asia or Central Europe, by means not strictly in accord with the Charter's provisions. There was a kind of faith about the ceremonies, in some men's minds, a hope that this time a way might be found to settle differences of opinion without butchery.

One day I heard a youthful brass band playing near the Opera House, where the flags of fifty nations were flying in a fine salt breeze. The musicians were drably dressed in khaki, as though about to march off to war, but I could not make out whether they were high-school boys, or just old enough to enlist in the army that was, as we thought, about to conquer Japan. I think they were too young for that—though not too young to get into the sad, far-off, dreary, and sacrificial warfare that was to break out in Korea five years later. But that war wasn't expected or threatened in the spring of 1945. The bands in front of the Opera House in San Francisco played, in so far as they were able, the music of all member nations.

But California looked somewhat dourly westward: there lay the East; there lay the road to India (or Japan); there was old Senator Benton's shattered dream; there still roared the flames of war.

8

The day the Germans surrendered, May 7, 1945, I was in the Yosemite Valley, on a legitimate journalistic errand. We drove all day, in a Government car, down the San Joaquin Valley and then up the Sacramento Valley to the City of Sacramento.

The other news we had that day was that the United States sea and land forces were still entangled in the death grapple of Okinawa, in which they were to lose more than twelve thousand men, dead and missing, 36 ships, and 763 airplanes. This slaughter had another six weeks or more to run, and those most familiar with what was going on projected the casualties into the far more massive attacks beng planned for Japan's main islands. Not all the facts, naturally, were available to the civilian public, or to the men who were to do the fighting and dying, but in California, to which this war came close, there was dread in people's hearts, even on V-E Day.

All day long we rode northward, through lands that were fabulously productive when they were given enough water. Our guide, a veteran newspaperman in the service of the Department of the Interior, told us of the Central Valley Project, by which surplus water would be taken out of the Sacramento River, carried across the delta and the mouths of two rivers, and delivered into the dry areas of the San Joaquin. This was part of the future of California: the more water the more people, the more well-being, perhaps even the more justice and enlightenment. To these majestic proportions had evolved the old dry-country practice of damming up the arroyo in order to save a trickle of the spring's overflow.

It was a warm day, but not too hot for comfort. The news from Germany had made us all cheerful.

But never once, all the way from Yosemite to Sacramento, did we see or hear any sign of celebration in that quiet countryside. It was not until we were lodged in our Sacramento hotel, long after dark, that we heard some shouting in the streets.

There wasn't too much to shout about. California's war had not yet been won.

16

Ring Out, Wild Bells

And now California entered the most startling period of her history. What had happened prior to the summer of 1945 was hardly more than a prelude and invocation. It was a curtain raiser. Now the hurrying years overran the land. Cabrillo, Drake, Portola, the saintly Padres, Frémont, the forty-niners, the Big Four had been strolling characters in a leisurely pageant compared with what was now to come to pass.

This was not foreseen, of course. People talked of the Pacific War and of what everybody hoped would turn out to be a pacific conference.

The war went on, for a while. Meanwhile, the United Nations Conference, after making some very fine speeches and drawing up a charter that would end war if every government lived up to its principles, adjourned on June 26.

The young men whom I had seen on the Top o' the Mark, saying good bye to their girls, did not have to die in battle. On the other hand, many California war contracts were terminated, many thousands of jobs in California faded away, and not everybody thought this was a good thing.

On the basis of experience, the end of the Second World War

should have been followed by a terrific slump all over the country, and an especially terrific one in California, which had absorbed more than her per capita share of war business. But there was no general economic collapse in the country, and in California there was a continued increase in population, a shift in employment but not a catastrophic decline.

It was as though California had devoured what H. G. Wells, in one of his earlier scientific romances, described as "The Food of the Gods." The only danger, as in his story, was that this swift growth would produce a monstrosity. And indeed, that is still the danger.

But the psychology behind this growth was anything but obscure. People who had had war jobs in California—and the total dollar value of industrial goods had increased nearly four times over during the war years—might foresee unemployment when the fighting stopped; but this was felt to be the case everywhere. If one had to be unemployed why not in a comfortable environment, with accessible beaches and dramatic mountains in the background? Men honorably discharged from the armed battalions when no more dying was required of them may have felt the same way. We are a foot-loose people, and the tumbleweed is our national plant. The next big migration may be to the outer islands of Hawaii. Who knows? As long as there can still be migrations, who cares?

At any rate, great numbers of the war migrants did not go home. They seemed to be inquiring, in the current vernacular, how long has this been going on? They had the wide-eyed aspect of the old Mountain Men of a century earlier who gazed at the Sacramento Valley in delight and infinitely preferred to spend a winter there than holed up in the Rockies or the Sierras. In effect, though not consciously, the later generation of migrants, the twentieth century trappers and diggers displaced the existing inhabitants, or made them move over, and took over the land. They have been taking it over ever since.

The Native Sons of the Golden West began to seem a little out of date, though they did manage to hold on to some choice acres and some profitable positions. One might say that what was happening was the natural sequel to the landing of the Pilgrims at Plymouth in 1620. The westward tide had traveled far and taken on majestic proportions. California was a bright new star among the states—new after more than a century of formal existence as such. She was hardly a state any more: she was becoming what destiny long ago seemed to have marked her for, a nation.

2

California was in fact getting to the classical point where the inhabitants could live by taking in one another's washing. It was a rich producing area for civilian needs. It was also a consumers' market of majestic dimensions. Its progress might have been less hectic if the Korean War had not broken out five years after the end of the struggle with Japan, but nothing, not even profound peace, could have held California back very long.

Two things did happen that shaped the future. First, California became a staging area for the Korean War—a smaller war than the preceding one but serious in its cost in life, in goods, and in its implications for the future. Second, the Korean episode led to a new "defense" drive which resulted in new and rewarding contracts for the state's industries. And the manufacture of military equipment, however essential, however patriotic in its intentions, gives new jobs and often yields substantial profits; but this is not the best basis for any community's economy. In this instance it was the final wind of destiny that turned California away from any possibly recapturable pastoral or idyllic culture and swept it into a sternly materialistic bleakness. The old dreams died, the new arose.

If we look at the years between 1945 and 1950 we shall find them drifting toward this decisive moment. The keynote of the new era which the Korean trouble precipitated was industrialization—and this phase was just as dramatically apparent on the farms and ranches as it was anywhere else. The old problem of getting men to work in the harvest, at wages too low for decency and under inhuman conditions, continued; it would be dealt with for a while by importing Mexican labor, and many jobs once performed by men would be taken over by machines. And the trend of real wages, in the fields as in industry, would be upward.

In industry California had had some exceedingly shrewd operators. Steel production was going up, though California's share was not (and is not) a large fraction of the national output. Wise manufacturers, however, using what was handy, switched from war goods to the smaller household articles that were becoming "necessities"; these included various kinds of refrigerators, kitchenware, plumbing, and radios and (as time went on) television equipment. Automobile parts were assembled in vast quantities in California; it might also be said that they were disassembled there also, so enormous was the increase in the number of cars wildly driven and in the highway mileage available. Per mile driven, however, the state remained as safe as most of the rest of the Union. The catch was that there were more and more people, more and more of them drove motor cars of various vintages, and speeds were high.

The State went into what seems to be the modern paradox— one might almost say neuroticism—of producing too many cars for the road space, and then making it possible to bring still more cars into operation by adding to the amount of road space. This also happened on the Eastern Seaboard, but California did it more exuberantly and perhaps with less thinking. Nobody anywhere, except a few recluses who didn't like anything modern, objected.

During the early postwar years this process set the pattern for long years to come, including years that have not even yet arrived: virtually the entire population was to be unstable, footloose, continually in motion, seeking employment in one direction, recreation in another.

A new breed of Californians was coming into being: a typically modern breed, with little disposition toward fixed habits, or fixed abodes, urban rather than rural in inclination and occupation, using the vast background of ocean, valley, and mountains for play, fiercely ambitious and correspondingly energetic, with incomes above the national average, with climate as a fringe benefit —but having available enough varieties of climate to fit out and furnish a half-dozen hells as well as the same number of heavens.

The climate had been there all along, of course, but these modern *vaqueros* were putting it to full use: enjoying the desert, if they could afford it, at Palm Springs or even Death Valley, skiing in the big hills, lolling on the beaches.

Population in California could not immediately reach the density that prevails in lower New York State, New Jersey, or lower New England. It will take a long time to clutter up the landscape to that extent. There are about one hundred million acres of land available, and even today this means more than five acres to a person. Nevertheless, the population of the state, per acre, multiplied nearly five times between 1920 and 1960. This would worry Dan'l Boone, who felt cramped when he could smell a neighbor's fireplace smoke.

In 1920 it might have been reasonable to imagine a representative Californian sitting under an orange tree, a prune tree, or an apricot tree (and a sun-ripened apricot, just off the branch, is not too bad) and taking his leisure moments in an Edenlike atmosphere. Automation was in the air, even then, though not called by that name.

It is true that the whole United States had been turning from the land to the cities, with fewer farmers needed to raise and harvest the crops. California was merely following this path with a sweep that was accelerated after the end of the Second World War. The mass of people who went there to inhabit were clearly not looking for a bucolic life; they swarmed into and expanded great metropolitan blobs. They didn't hunt quiet and didn't find it. Quiet didn't lie at either end of the nerve-racking freeways that were being bulldozed and power-rollered out of the landscape: factories are usually noisy places in which to work; and really modern homes, in crowded sections, with radio and television going full blast, are not quiet places in which to live. Of course, there are even now quiet places, such as Alpine County, with 776 square miles and (in 1960) 397 inhabitants. Too quiet, possibly—men leave such areas in order to find jobs and opportunities in the big towns. Modern man, with nearly two square miles at his individual disposal, may be scared and lonesome. He may actually *want* noise. He may long to have somebody step on

his toes or scrape his fenders on a blind curve. Walden Pond isn't
what it used to be.

3

Attempts to analyze such an episode as California's melodra-
matic increase in population are bound to end in confusion. Like
the rest of the world, the state had a high birth rate and a declining death rate. Likewise, it was affected, like the rest of the
world, including the Communist countries, by the tendency of
persons living in rural areas to migrate to urban areas.

Persons who want jobs go where they think the jobs are, and
even if an industry is established in what has been a rural district,
such as Henry Kaiser's Fontana steel plant, that very fact pro-
duces urban conditions.

At the same time, there was in California as in other regions
not only movements of people from rural into urban areas but
also from urban areas into suburban areas. San Francisco, for
example, lost a few bedtime inhabitants in this way when the
bridges were opened and peripheral industries were established
around the Bay—as well as peripheral beds. This was something
like New York City's Borough of Manhattan ceasing to grow in
nighttime population, or even losing a little, to the bedtime communities across the East River, or up the Hudson, or in the states
of Connecticut and New Jersey.

Thus more and more the city became a place to work, the
country an arena for recreation. (It is true that the so-called
"shopping centers" sprang up in what had been rural territory,
but such neighborhoods did not long remain rural.) Today few
persons actively earning a living in California are likely to live
more than a relatively short drive, measured in time, over good
roads, from something that can be truthfully called a city.

The roads, of course, are all-important—as every good Californian, and I suppose every loyal American, knows. And the roads
of California have been going forward at a great pace—as are the
cars using them—since the end of the Second World War. The
roads and cars together have changed things in the United States
more than any other factor, and they have changed them more in

California than in any other state: of this I am convinced, though I hope no reader will ask me for the supporting statistics and diagrams. California, with its great distances and the restless nature of its population, seems to have been created for the motorcar —and vice versa.

Some might argue that the radio and televison have altered daily life more than the automobile. Or that the airplane, abolishing distance, has done so. But hearing far-distant sounds or seeing far-distant images, carried inaudibly and invisibly through the air, is merely another form of reading. And air travel is for those who are able to pay for it; it does not move multitudes. So I put my money, for good or ill, on roads and motor cars.

The roads began early to be good (that is, to permit rapid and dangerous travel) but the real change gathered its strength after 1945. It is difficult for those who have seen both worlds—the preautomobile world and the postautomobile world—to believe in their own memories. Mine, for instance, include walking an old coast trail between the Big Sur country, just south of Monterey, to San Simeon, the site of Mr. Hearst's famous palace—now turned into a museum. The trail has been replaced by a scenic highway, and the old poetic lonesomeness is, of course, gone, too. But what rural Californians desired, like rural people all over the United States, was not an old poetic lonesomeness but a chance to get somewhere else in a hurry.

4

California did not invent roads, but the climate, or the landscape, or something else of a more subtle nature (if anything in today's California can be called subtle) has given its people something of the urge from which the old Romans suffered. And in which they gloried. The Romans built roads mainly (or so it is said) for the purpose of moving the legions along the Italian peninsula and into subject lands beyond. They also built them in order to enable Roman patricians and their friends to get out of Rome in the hot months without too much discomfort.

The two countries (as I shall call them, meaning Italy and California) are not too far apart in area: California has 158,693 square miles, Italy, 116,372. If California were as fully inhabited as Italy it would have a population of more than seventy million people. Let us bear this figure in mind; it is something to think about, and worry about, at four o'clock in the morning. Of course such a population would require more roads, in order to get away from itself—but would not succeed in doing so.

California's freeway system, to get back into the stream of history for a moment, came into full flood after the end of the Second World War. It was not seriously interfered with by the Korean War. It was stimulated by the defense orders which a benignant Federal Government poured into the state after the Korean fighting.

Felix Riesenberg, Jr., writing in *The Golden Road*, was of the opinion that the freeway was invented in Los Angeles. If any city on earth needed this device Los Angeles did. The concept of heavy duty roads running straight through the middle of towns and cities, bringing trade to the stores which fronted on the highway, was out of date; the days of by-passing centers of population, of restricting access, and of turning through-routes into something resembling railroads, though without rails and certainly less efficient than railroads, were arriving; all this was bound to come out of the motorcar itself, which was less and less limited in speed and whose drivers had learned to accept the risks of the traffic battle with a soldierly fatalism.

The historic fact is that freeways were invented and developed; whatever may be said against them they were and are an improvement over the old type of winding, narrow road; freeways were good for the automotive and cement industries; the ordinary citizen sometimes complained because they spoiled the beauty of the land, but he would miss them now if they disappeared. He would miss them because the dear old winding roads would be solidly jammed with vehicles and nobody would get home until after midnight—if ever.

The beginning was comparatively modest, like the spread of the boll weevil. The program adopted in 1945, after a long legislative wrangle, called for spending what would now be considered the modest sum of $2.4 billion. Sam Taylor, as quoted by

Mr. Riesenberg, argued that "the freeways carry three times the traffic of a similar surface street, twice as fast and fives times as safely." He added: "The initial cost, while high, is the last cost; freeways are a permanent investment." This is an optimistic view, for any road, even a freeway, has to be kept in repair. But in a land where no frost pushes stones up through the ground, freeway surfaces are durable. Too durable, some critics complain.

The freeway, wherever it is carved out and plastered down, changes the landscape. Its honeymoon in California was while it was relatively uncrowded, and everybody was delighted, except those who were dispossessed to make room for it, or those who were shut in by holiday traffic so that they could not get out of their own front yards, or those who loved trees and quietness.

It may be said that if you loved peace and quiet, if you wished to do a bit of meditating, you could get to the right spot sooner on a freeway than on one of the older types of curly roads, where the trees arched over and shadows lay morning and afternoon. But so also could thousands of other people. Then it wasn't quiet any more.

For a while the freeways were fun. They were free in the sense that you didn't pay tolls, except at bridges. They were also free because they let down the bars of earthly and linear space. You could, maybe, escape. But what happened was that there was no more privacy in California, except for the athletic.

5

The freeways and express highways were soon to make it possible for multitudes of Californians to visit places they wished to visit. They have made it possible to bring some order, at least for a while, into the cosmic sprawl of Los Angeles. And though they sometimes interfered with an existing city park, or seemed to require cutting down a few ancient redwoods, they did make the surviving state and national parks more accessible.

Such parks are an increasingly important part of the play facilities of California. The state is by no means all working space or likely to become so. Thirty million of its hundred million acres, or roughly about the equivalent of the area of New York State, are for the grown-up boys and girls to play in; this is a consoling thought as one watches the holiday traffic on Junipero Serra's old trail.

John Muir loved and glorified Yosemite Valley. He wanted other people to see and enjoy it likewise. Now they do: in 1963 more than one and a half million persons visited it; more than 778,000 others went to the national park in King's Canyon; 631,000 to Sequoia, 369,000 to Lassen. During 1963 four million persons who wanted to visit California's parks, state and national, were turned away—there was at the moment they arrived no camping room for them.

Thus, though the automobile can be and has been improved, and though highways get better and more and more numerous and direct, the total recreational area of California, vast though it is, grows smaller and smaller when it is measured per capita.

I do not mean to belittle the Californians' love of nature. This is a heritage which was already strongly cherished nearly sixty years ago when I first set eyes on California and its inhabitants—such as they were at that time. The impulse to go and look at strange, beautiful, and unspoiled scenery is an honorable one, as is the desire to cook, eat, and sleep in the open, and to invent hardships and look around for danger.

In the end, I fear, these tendencies will be self-defeating, because such great throngs will be succumbing to them. The lovely wild places of California will be like the precious but tame attractions of Central Park, Golden Gate Park, or Boston Common. Perhaps the perfection of a safe, cheap, and easily operated helicopter will be the final touch, in which case reservations will have to be made far ahead for spots on top of Mount Whitney or down in the rugged King's River gorges.

At any rate, the outdoor tendency and the inclination to get places fast are prevalent in California today, and the new development is not the desire but the improved means by which more and more people seek to gratify the desire. And these new means —the roads and vehicles—have done more to and for California than any other influence in its history—and have done it largely since the end of the Second World War. As those who have made repeated visits to the area have found, California is almost a new country every two years or so.

The framework of mountains, deserts, fertile plains, rivers, and seashore remains—almost all else in California is transient. Even the historic relics—the Missions, for example, cannot really remain unaltered. How can a Mission with a parking problem retain the spirit of its old lonesomeness, its lost tranquillity? How can we fit poor, limping, heroic Father Serra into the age of crowded movement and congested roads? Remember, the twenty-one Missions were about a day's journey apart. Now, by hustling, an experienced and fearless motorist could pass by them all in perhaps two days.

6

If the Californian or the visitor is young enough and vigorous he can walk the Pacific Coast Trail, a true wilderness promenade, the California portion of which extends from the Mexican boundary to the state line of Oregon. During the summer season he will seldom be rained on, and will be that much better off than if he were following the magnificent Appalachian Trail on the other side of the continent. I read that nearly one and a half million fishermen catch an average of about a dozen trout each year in California; and that nearly a million hunters take out licenses, and one out of eight shoots a deer. These are just samplings. Californians also play tennis, golf, and baseball rather more enthusiastically than Easterners seem to do; they swim in the chilly salt water of their native (or acquired) shores; they ski in the right places and season. They have a wider choice than anybody else, so favorable is their climate and terrain.

They do not live in the Garden of Eden, but they act as though they did. Sometimes, indeed, the observer may conclude that today's Californian, if employed at a comfortable wage, is the real playboy of the Western World.

7

Play is a form of pretending that what isn't so is so. Therefore it shades over into drama. In this way we arrive at the motion picture (and in recent years the television) world. The climate in

Southern California suited these forms of the drama; and in turn the celluloid and airborne theater was influenced by its surroundings. Queen Calafia, though not often seen, sat on her golden throne, with peacock feathers in her hair, and ruled the roost.

The entertainment industry is complicated, and the relationships between the motion picture and television have made it almost incomprehensible. It was found, of course, that many persons would rather sit at home and watch television than go out in the rain or the darkness of night to see an equally bad movie at a theater. It was also found that for quite a number of reasons motion pictures made abroad had advantages, both atmospheric and economic, over those made at home. This did not end the making of pictures in California—it merely presented new problems for the picture manufacturers. Finally, the motion picture industrialists seem to have reached the conclusion that the more it cost to produce a film, the better the film would be and the more impressed the public would be.

All we have to worry about here, fortunately, is what effect new conditions in the picture factories had on California. The effect was not primarily economic. Even in the most lavish form of the motion picture, with the wealth of the Indies poured out to make details right when the total effect was misleading and vulgar, even the most sumptuous gold-spattered creation hardly represented real money when compared with an electronic factory. But the motion picture industry, symbolized by the word Hollywood, was not doomed to be killed by television, nor by gigantic expenditures of film money abroad, nor by the glamour of electronics.

The movie, in short, found its place, or kept it, in California, in the postwar, television, electronic world. It achieved a marriage of convenience with the television system. It scooped up a great deal of the gravy, without itself dying of indigestion. Hollywood found it possible to sell old motion picture films to the TV industry. Los Angeles retained some cultural prestige because so many entertainers and performers found it convenient to live in that vicinity.

When in the mid-fifties it became possible to put on nation-wide television in Southern California, using available actors, studios, and weather, the output of TV on the Coast began to build up. Television operatives may or may not be as alluring (apart from a handful of celebrities) as movie actors, but they are likely to earn enough to pay for the groceries. And I believe they add tone to the communities associated with them. Make-believe, we must not forget, is just as much an asset as real estate.

8

In 1955 my wife and I returned to California after a ten-year absence. I had the pleasant task of helping to cover the tenth anniversary meeting of the United Nations. Mr. Hammarskjold was there, hopeful and diplomatic as he always was, and full of an almost mystic zeal; President Eisenhower and former President Truman made speeches; and the city seemed its old, buoyant self, without that tremendous boost in population that Los Angeles was showing. The ferries were gone, but the cable cars, backed by a wave of true San Francisco sentimentality, were still there on two of the old routes.

I made a mental note that this was an abiding city, not easily spoiled even by its two bridges or by the swaggering elevated structures that fed in and out of them. San Francisco had not lost its personality. Los Angeles, on the other hand, had exchanged an old, relatively easy-going atmosphere for one more combative, almost ferocious. This is Detroit in a semitropical setting, somebody remarked. Or maybe Chicago.

The two cities, North and South, San Francisco and Los Angeles, seemed doomed to one common fate, to love romance and to have less of it. Of the two, San Francisco, held within limits by its political boundaries, kept more of its old character—as when it rose almost in a cultural revolution, to retain its obsolescent cable cars and to raise millions to prevent the Palace of Fine Arts, relic of the 1915 Exposition, from being destroyed. Meanwhile, Los Angeles threw away the old red Pacific Electric cars, with all their utility and charm—perhaps they were *too* red for the color-sensitive eyes of the Angelenos.

At all events, Los Angeles was not doing much in 1955 to remind itself of the glorious or glamorous past. In fact, it had no glorious or glamorous past. If it had been destroyed by an earthquake and fire no journalistic genius such as Will Irwin would have been able to write about it so fond and moving a piece as "The City That Was." In that sense it wasn't and had never been; it was just there. On the other hand, it wouldn't have been there if a multitude of people hadn't wanted it to be: you cannot indict a city as large as Los Angeles.

As one out of a myriad visitors I had seen it in 1910, in 1912, in 1916, and fairly often during succeeding years; it was at each recurring visit a little bigger, a little more difficult to move around in, a little less coherent, a little sillier in some of its political and theological ideas, a little more appealing, like a gigantic child playing with blocks—its freeways and highways, the Hollywood Bowl, some high-class as well as low-class motion pictures, some good community theaters, some reputable music, some outstanding research institutions, colleges and universities, and quite a lot of water, hauled over incredible distances by some of the world's most ingenious engineers.

By 1955 you could not always see Mount Wilson from the downtown district of Los Angeles: the smog obscured it. The smog had not been there before the vast modern increase in factories and motorcars. It had not been there when the first motion picture producers arrived breathless on the then enchanted scene. But now there were spring and summer days when the sky was slaty, not robin's-egg blue; there were days when one's eyes smarted; there were days when one coughed. There is a price for being industrial, making a lot of money, and attracting vast new populations; and this price Los Angeles was paying.

San Francisco had a touch of smog, also, but not so much. It is not of course the fault of the people of Los Angeles County that some millions of them live in a fairly deep bowl with a closed ring of mountains about it, and that when the air temperatures are just right (or just wrong, one might say) the polluted air in this basin cannot get out.

San Francisco, on the other hand, has always had fog. Fog kept its great harbor from being discovered during a period of two centuries or so, for a sailing ship would stand far out when passing a shrouded coast. To this day a mariner living in retirement in the Santa Clara Valley, thirty miles or so southeast of the Golden Gate, will tell you by the look of the mists along the crests of the Santa Cruz Range to the West that it is thick going outside the Heads. The San Francisco fog is produced, as everybody knows, by the heated air of the Central Valley luring in and condensing the cold air of the sea. But there is circulation here: in and out of the Golden Gate, up and down the rivers, in and out of the mountain passes; the fog cannot linger.

Even in this case no partisan can boast that the air of San Francisco is wholly free from humanity's contamination. There is no magic except self-restraint that will keep a city's air, a valley's air, in an industrial area completely pure. There is a smog index, sometimes published in the San Francisco newspapers, that shows when it is time for the Argonauts' successors to cough and weep.

The hand of man is at work on the land, north as well as south, changing the results of the historic labors performed by the hand of God. The California earth, wherever it is smooth, fertile, and convenient, is becoming one large city or series of cities. The atmosphere is being perceptibly adulterated by various intense activities. Population presses upon the arable soil, not in the old-fashioned oriental way, in which each spadeful of earth is closely stirred and cherished, but in the large, mechanical fashion of the late twentieth century; California may already lead the world in mechanized agriculture; if she does not yet do so, she soon can.

A new kind of human living is coming into existence in this once dreamy island of Queen Calafia. One wonders whether there has ever been anything in the world like this since the Romans conquered Italy and made the Etruscans give up their old, jolly, shiftless ways and compelled them, in what was then considered a modern, efficient manner, to get down to work.

This is what has been going on in California since the end of the Second World War. I would like to take another look at the how and the why; although anybody who tried to answer these questions in full would need ten years and a five-foot shelf.

First, let us take up the How of the great change in California. Then we may feel vigorous enough to tackle the Why—if there is any.

17

The How of It

We are now talking of California between the year 1945 and the year 1965—and of necessity projecting our thoughts forward somewhat. The Second World War, the Korean War, and the resulting national defense policies (and contracts) did not determine the line of development California has taken, but they did accelerate that development.

No matter what the news displayed on the front pages of the newspapers, it was inevitable that this warm western slope, with no real winter below the snow line of the high mountains, should see a new birth of the modern industrial system. The first industrial revolution occurred in a very bad climate, indeed, that of Britain. It flourished in bad weather—and some of its furious energy may have been owing to the fact that people compelled to live in shabby, picturesque, rheumatism-breeding huts in the English Midlands were almost happy to have their minds taken off their other discomforts by working in wretched, dangerous, dismal, ill-ventilated factories.

The modern factory worker enjoys almost luxurious ease and comfort compared with his (or her) predecessors. Much drudgery has been eliminated by what is often abusively called automation; the hours are shorter; the wages buy more; and more provision is made to ease the risks and burdens of accident, illness, and old age. Karl Marx's sinister predictions simply did not come true.

But the California worker, whose employers are no rougher, no milder, and no more grasping than those of other parts of the United States, is provided, without extra charge, with more comfortable working and living conditions than most other workers in this country. There are ugly slums in San Francisco, in Los Angeles, and in other California cities. There are rural slums. But the average state of well-being is higher. Frank Wiggins was not telling a complete lie when he said settlers would do well to come out to the Coast; the "Okies" and "Arkies" of a generation ago had a torturing time of it, but the instinct that took them West was sound; and the industries that today try to attract competent craftsmen to California do not have to shanghai them.

California would have grown in wealth and population, even though barbed-wire fences had been erected by the Federal Government (or by the Los Angeles police) along its borders. It did grow faster because the Government had defense work for the State to do.

Senator and Mrs. Leland Stanford, donors of the University named after their son, would hardly know what to say about the two-mile linear accelerator which Stanford has constructed for the United States Atomic Energy Commission, at a cost of many millions of dollars, on 480 acres of the Stanford Campus. I mention this enterprise, not because it accounts directly for much employment but because it shows a direction in which the minds of highly gifted men are turning in California. The atomic and electronic industries are not merely experimental—they change the landscape; they alter our lives; they foreshadow the future. And California is ideally suited for that sort of thing. Its future is far more important than its past.

2

This doesn't mean that Californians are much different from the rest of us. In fact, they are the rest of us, a sort of porridge or stew made up of all the ingredients the country has or has had on hand. California's situation and the environment, the climate and the spaces, have attracted scientists and technicians, together with the industries that spring from their work, thus furnishing employment for the new kind of factory hand. Out of science and technology, out of an almost feudal hierarchy of skill, comes increased employment for masses of men and women—and a new population.

The state, and especially the South, where the weight of population is, has more splinter religions and curious philosophies, I imagine, than the rest of the country put together. Its people are not dumbly ignorant, but they do go aggressively askew on the basis of what they know. (I don't intend to say they are mistaken because I or anybody else, or millions of others, don't agree with them; their peculiarity, as shown in polls, elections, and organizations of various forms, is in arriving at conclusions that have no relationship with the given premises.) They are a complicated and unprecedented cultural mixture, ranging from the depths of vulgarity, architectural and otherwise, to some extremely high levels of achievement.

It is the technology that has replaced much that was, or seemed, romantic and dashing. The Californian of legend shows us a cavalier, jingling and gaudy, riding the vast ranges. The significant Californian today (though he is naturally not numerous) is a man in a laboratory. Outside his laboratory he often lives in an atmosphere of the most extravagant foolishness—lives in it and possibly ignores it.

And the population streams in, almost without plan or foresight. Cities are planned in California; roads are planned; and industrial developments are planned. Despite this, the whole campaign of California's future is not planned. The significance of modern technology is often obscured by the technologist's extreme interest in one small corner of experiment and exploration. This key figure, this modern Calvinist, austere and concentrated, has made possible a society which is exciting, sometimes hilarious, usually constructive but sometimes mean and depressing. That is California. The population is made up of the usual assortment of weak, fallible, foolish, wise, heroic, and nonsensical human beings, but the society, the species of community, is, I believe, something new in the world.

It has grown with unbelievable speed. Statistics are inescapable, dodge them though we may. Every figure in the total sum, every rise or dip in the curve, is made up of human lives. These are *persons,* each one unto himself the center of a universe, whirling into a new adventure—at the rate of about eighty arrivals every hour, day and night. The great clock ticks loudly and its hands cannot ever be turned backward.

3

When the population of California rose from more than ten and a half million in 1950 to more than 15.7 million in 1960, the rate of increase was nearly three times that of the United States as a whole. Of this increase about sixty per cent was by immigration. The rate of growth was—and is—spotty: in the San Francisco metropolitan area a little over 24 per cent; in the San Jose area about 121 per cent; in the Sacramento area 81.4 per cent; in and around San Diego, 85.5 per cent. These percentages may be deceptive. If, for example, 1,000 persons were to move into Alpine County, counting population on the basis of 1964, the increase would be about two hundred per cent, but it would not distort the population curves of California to any marked degree. Los Angeles County gained only a little over 45.5 per cent during the same period, but the individuals expressed by that figure came to nearly two million.

The trend lines bulge here and there (sometimes because government contracts are given, withdrawn, or withheld), but the drift and concentration is southward. In the middle of 1964 four Southern counties—Los Angeles, San Diego, Orange, and San Bernardino—accounted for more than half the state's population. And in spite of gains in the North this disparity has been increasing.

Politically, this means that the South governs the state. Socially, culturally, and economically, it means that the South, despite its vast expanses of mountain and natural desert, has been the first to develop the symptoms of over-crowding, including the crowd neuroses. If crowding is to be humanity's future, the Southern Californians will be among the early victims, in the Western World.

Industrial development in this section has much to do with climate, of course, but it has much more to do with ease of access. As railways spread within and into the state during the last quarter of the nineteenth century, it was easier to reach Los Angeles with heavy freight than it was to get into San Francisco. San Pedro Harbor, when the engineers put it together early in the present century, opened up the Pacific, north, south, and west, and enabled Los Angeles and its neighboring communities to profit by the Panama Canal. Though coal was lacking and iron limited, the discovery of oil was a dividend for industry. San Diego had most advantages together with a natural port, more modest in size than San Pedro but provided by Nature rather than by Federal funds. In our own day, freeways and express highways supplemented, and in some cases supplanted, the railroad. Today the interstate trucks carry about half the normal freight load.

There was plenty of room for people and factories throughout the southeastern portion of the state. Kaiser, building his steel mill at Fontana in San Bernardino County, could haul his ore from Eagle Mountain in Riverside County and his coke from Utah. The operation was smooth and ingenious. Naturally it required workers, who had to be housed and fed; and who were more inclined to play golf in their leisure time than to throw horseshoes in a dusty park.

Much could be said of the growth of industry and population around San Fancisco, in the San Joaquin and Sacramento Valleys and along the coast northward and southward from San Francisco. This has not been and is not a stagnant area. Its percentage growth may even exceed that of some of the congested southern counties. The difference is that it has a smaller population base than Southern California, and the actual number of persons added is not so impressive.

The boom growth of the South may not have been wisely and

solidly planned. There may have been more concentration on the quick dollar than on human satisfactions. There is no mellowness in the results.

It is the rapidity of the change that startles even a casual observer. What is the use of romanticizing about California, especially about Southern California, when a new and basically unromantic society has developed? What possible relationship is there between a man in what passes for an old Spanish costume, riding a silver-mounted saddle on an obsolete horse during a so-called fiesta in Santa Barbara—what connection is there between this motion picture actor, this fugitive from television in all his trappings, and the modern Californian who roars along the speedways at three times the greatest speed ever attained, even briefly, by a galloping horse?

4

While Southern California was outnumbering the rest of the state, the northern counties, as I have tried to indicate, were developing in a reasonably normal way. In spite of local booms (such as that around San Jose) the growth in the North has not been an explosion. In so far as it concentrated upon a city, the city was of course San Francisco. She is a mother city, as the Greek and Italian city states were, not a conglomeration. This is a factual and descriptive judgment, not a moral comment. San Francisco may be an obsolete urban type. It may be an accidental and sentimental survival. But for good or ill it is a complete city, that can hardly take in much mor population. (It gained a trifle between the middle of 1963 and the middle of 1964, rising by 5,800 to a total of 755,700. Tall apartment buildings may put more people into sleeping quarters on the golden acres, but not many more.) The city's function today is to serve the cultural, economic, and financial needs of a great outlying area. The bank clearings are high, out of all proportion to the city's population— in 1962, for example, the ratio of bank clearings in San Francisco to those in Los Angeles was, to put it simply, a little more than two to three. On a strict county population basis it should have been nearer one to eight and a half. There are satisfactory explanations for this, but that is what the figures say.

San Francisco and its neighboring communities are obviously not just sitting there and taking life easily. The northern complex of cities is bound to grow, and it does. It cannot help growing, for the land and the resources are there. It was opened up to swift and easy communications and access, just as the South was, by the new state-wide road system. The tireless highway engineers, seeming to hold almost dictatorial power over the state's destinies, slice through ancient redwood groves in order to reach the Oregon frontier in a hurry and no nonsense, blandly propose to mutilate San Francisco's Golden Gate Park, unroll their cement on the western shore of Tahoe, invade seashore beaches above and below San Francisco that used to be the wildest and loveliest in the country. Some persons in Central and Northern California like this sort of thing, just as most persons in Southern California appear to do.

The Central Valley of California is not the most beautiful area in the world, unless you look down on it from the foothills or the mountain tops of the Sierras. It is flat, or rolling, or interrupted by irregular ridges, and in summer it is hot as the hinges of hell. But it is lavishly productive and getting more so as the years slide by. In these later days it is being engineered in a massive fashion, with water taken from the Sacramento's abundance to fill out the San Joaquin's deficit. As the water is brought in more people can live on the land. Ocean-going ships can reach the Port of Stockton —my wife and I have voyaged to New York on one that did. Sacramento is likewise linked with the Pacific by a deepwater channel. Most of California's rice goes through this port, just as petroleum issues in great quantity from the Port of Los Angeles.

As one looks at the map it becomes clear that the North has advantages in water routes from the interior, and that the South has easier connections with the East by railroads and truck highways. The artificial harbor of Los Angeles is magnificent, but nobody will ever sail up and down the Los Angeles River, except in time of flood.

The North goes by what Nature gave it. Yet Humboldt County's population grew by nearly 50 per cent between 1950 and 1960; Mendocino by more than 40 per cent; Monterey County by 52 per cent; Marin County by 71.5 per cent (credit mainly the Golden Gate Bridge); Sonoma by 42.5 per cent; Sacramento by 81.4; Tehama, up the Sacramento river, by 31.3; San Joaquin by 24.5.

All these rates might be considered normal for California's growing population. Except possibly in the Santa Clara Valley, whose climate is something to exclaim over and whose industrialists did latch on to some extensive Federal defense contracts, they were not extraordinary. It seemed, somehow, as though those newcomers who could live and find jobs in the South did so. This is a puzzle. It is as though the populations of the New England, Atlantic, and Central states chose to move in enormous numbers, not merely into Florida, where it is warm and the swimming is good, but into Virginia, Alabama, South Carolina, Arkansas and—yes—Mississippi.

One should not be captious about the habits and preferences of eight, nine, or ten million people. What happens happens. Human beings, like fruit flies and rabbits, tend to increase and multiply; unlike fruit flies and rabbits, they make what they regard as individual choices. The sum of these choices in California tilts the weight of population southward.

5

Despite the wide difference between the two sections, at whatever point one may choose to divide them, they have remained similar in a few respects. The freeway system has tied them together, not only literally but figuratively.

Another respect in which the two sections resemble one another is that they like to amuse themselves—or rather, to be amused. Hence music, the drama, and all kinds of sports, including riding to hounds, flourish within the state.

They also worship education with almost a Scottish tenacity and devotion. The development of higher education in California has been astounding. David Starr Jordan, first president of Stanford University, related in his memoirs that when this institution opened its doors in 1891 a New York newspaper said that there was "as much need of a new university in California as for an asylum for decayed sea captains in Switzerland." Others accused Senator Stanford of using the new institution as cover for "a real estate speculation." The University of California in that year had only 400 students—enough higher education, possibly, for a population of about a million and a quarter according to the standards of the day.

Fortunately Senator and Mrs. Stanford went ahead with their plans; and today four out of every five students who apply for admission to Stanford University are rejected—there is no room for them, and the school can afford to pick and choose. The state has had a remarkable flowering of institutions of the higher learning in recent years, and the demand is still running ahead of the supply. Today's California has 182 or more institutions above the high-school level. It has 66 four-year colleges, public and private, and this number is increasing. It has more secondary-school students than the state of New York.

Thus if Californians, especially in the South, do sometimes wander into strange, devious, and eccentric ways of thinking, this is not because they have not been exposed to education. A part of California sometimes acts like a part of the state of Mississippi, which just hasn't the money it needs to create a modern type of school or college, but the reason is different—the reason is not pure ignorance of American history and of the facts of life. In terms of the numbers attending colleges and universities, the Californians of this generation ought to be in step with today's civilization and today's Western World culture. One example: in the fall of 1964 the University of California was asking a budget of over $200 million to meet the needs of more than 76,000 students whom it expected to enroll on its nine campuses. Stanford took up some slack with about 10,000 registrants. More than 269,-000 full-time students, however, were in the tax-supported colleges and universities—and this figure, it is stated, represented an increase of 100,000 in five years.

Education and culture are not the same thing. People who can't read can have culture, if the word is widely defined. And there has been a great deal of culture in California for more than a hundred years. San Francisco, when it was the state's leading city, was admirably hospitable to traveling singers, instrumentalists, actors, and artists. Always sentimental, the city made a heroine of Lola Montez, the Irish dancer with the Spanish name and a background half scandalous and half romantic; Lola came to California soon after the Gold Rush. Almost any real San Franciscan will grow moist-eyed even today over Lotta's Fountain, given to the city by Lotta Crabtree, who sang, danced, and acted more than a century ago.

Los Angeles hasn't as long and poignant a tradition as has San Francisco; but when that city heard about culture it set out with considerable money, many good intentions, and some good taste to buy it. San Francisco has long had a symphony orchestra, and a good one. So has Los Angeles. Both orchestras go on extended tours. You can hear good music and see dramatic productions in both cities. Music and drama are emphasized at the colleges and universities. There are little theaters of various sorts and conditions all over the thickly settled areas. There is opera in San Francisco; its musicians often threaten to strike, just as they do in New York, but they play well, and they get to do quite a lot of traveling. Nobody in the urban portions of California needs to go without entertainment comparable with what he might find around New York, Chicago, or Boston—provided he has a car or can thumb a ride. Easterners need not feel snobbishly superior when they visit the Coast; they will find some funny people around, just as they do at home, but they will also find many quite as sophisticated as themselves.

California culture may be big, brassy, and fast moving, but it is there. It is not precisely a native culture, such as might have been developed if the settlement, growth, and communications system of the region had proceeded at a slower pace and not at jackrabbit speed; it is largely imported, but the very best is imported along with the remainder.

Pan will not play his pipes in those woods; no Thoreau, in homelier style, will look for a Walden conveniently close to the village store and the Emerson residence; quietness is dying, just as it is all over the world. But nobody can honestly simplify Cali-

fornia by calling it a cultural jungle. It isn't. Not even Los Angeles. Not even Orange County.

Looking back over what I have written, I can see that I have
scarcely described how California became what it is. Except for
politics, which tend to divide the South from the North, the recent history of the state is every day a little more of the same—
every day a new wagon train, rolling into the Promised Land—
and rendering it a little less promising; every day a new factory;
every day money added to or subtracted from a Federal contract;
every day a few more miles of hard, wide road.

One decisive factor, as I might reiterate, has been the drive in
Southern California to bring in enough water for current needs;
as this has been done the population has rushed in to use and
overuse this water; then it has seemed necessary to bring in still
other supplies of water; the population has arrived to use these
new supplies and buy the land they irrigate: there is seemingly
no end to it all.

The Owens River, the Colorado River, the Feather River, possibly some of the Sacramento, which has already been partly diverted into the San Joaquin; very soon water diverted from the
western slopes of the Trinity Range to flow eastward through
tunnels into the Central Valley, power if not water from the
Columbia River: the list and litany is a long one. And the more
people Southern California has, the louder the voice she can raise
when she wants anything or objects to anything. Desalinization of
sea water may be the final answer; at the moment the cost per
gallon is too high, but when the Pacific Ocean is finally tapped it
will last a long time.

San Francisco and the other Bay cities and their suburbs have
also taken whatever water they needed and could lay hands on;
naturally, they have not been as hard pressed for water as has the
Southland, for they get more rain. The real estate operators were
active around the Bay, too, buying and selling at a profit when
new supplies of water sent the prices of land up.

Water, roads, people, industries, modern inventions, the inflated importance of cities—these factors created the modern
State of California, and they are still working it over. What began

at Plymouth Rock nearly three and a half centuries ago culmi-
nated at San Francisco's Seal Rocks and the San Pedro Break-
water; it took a long time, and often it traveled slowly, but it got
there. One wonders what Elder Bradford would think of it all.

6

There is about as much resemblance between the California of
today and that of the late Mexican and early Gold Rush period as
there is between the Massachusetts of today and that of William
Bradford as seen from Plymouth. Nevertheless, today's Californians cling with pathetic nostalgia to what they imagine is the
state's past. They do not find the Mexican *bracero* romantic,
though they do find his field labor for a few weeks of harvest very
useful. As this is written they have been worrying as to what they
will do if the Federal Government refuses to let this humble Mexican citizen come in when needed, returning to his home country
when not needed. They do not find romance in those parts of Los
Angeles solidly inhabited by Mexican-Americans nor in the remarkable fact that the present Mexican-American population of
the state (about one and one half million, as measured by the
Spanish names they carry) is about equal to the total population
of California in 1900. The Mexicans they find romantic are either
rich or dead.

But they do adore the days and ways that are no more, even
though, as sensible people, they would make any sacrifice within
reason to prevent those days from returning.

Many years ago, I saw a historical pageant in Monterey in
which, in re-enactment of an episode in the Mexican War of 1846,
a detachment of sailors and marines landed on the beach and
seized the Custom House. This pageant was good practice for the
men from the ships, and it was good to see the flag go up again
where it had already flown for more than sixty years. This small
historic drama was also, no doubt, good business for the worthy
merchants of Monterey, whose problem at the time was not to
regulate traffic but to bring traffic into their stores.

The Californians—at least the vocal ones—love this sort of
thing, for picturesqueness is just as much a crop as oranges,

prunes, cotton, rice, lettuce, or a plump defense contract; it brings in cash, just as does the manufacture of electronic equipment, missiles and the assemblage of motor cars.

A San Francisco firm was starting, early in 1964, to develop three hundred homes on the outskirts of the city. One selling argument was that this site (prices for modern houses ranging from $24,950 to $29,950) was probably that from which Sergeant José Ortega, coming north with Portola's expedition, in 1769, discovered the Bay of San Francisco. This discovery was a setback for Ortega, since he had hoped to reach Point Reyes, and the water gap frustrated him. But the people in the new houses can now cheerfully discover San Francisco every morning for themselves—weather permitting—and will enjoy doing so; they can also reach Point Reyes by way of the Golden Gate Bridge with no trouble at all.

I have ventured to suggest that the less one looks at the Bear Flag episode the more heroic it seems. However, the fun-loving Californians celebrate it still, especially at Sonoma, where William B. Ide's play actors raised their banner on June 14, 1846.

Some less foolish and debatable incidents are also celebrated. Early in 1964 a group of mule riders, many of them women, were retracing the old trail down Baja California to La Paz on the Gulf of California. They were doing, on an average, 18 miles a day— about the pace of any mule expedition in any dry country; seven hundred miles of this promised to take up a lot of time. Snakes, rabid animals, and a scarcity of water made this adventure almost like the good old times; and I was moved to take off my hat to the ladies and their patient steeds.

A less precarious excursion into the poetic past was a reproduction of the freight haul from Virginia City, Nevada, home of the fabulous Comstock silver lode, to Placerville (alias Hangtown), California. This was a hundred-mile, seven-day trip, along what was described a century ago as a highway solidly jammed with wagons carrying silver ore out and bringing in explosives, provisions, and (I believe) liquor. Mark Twain said of this road, which then as now continued into Sacramento, that "its long route was traceable across the deserts . . . by the writhing serpent of dust it lifted up." Nevertheless, it flowed on and finally helped build the great gaudy mansions that decorated Nob Hill in San Francisco.

The Hangtown Grade was a jolly way to travel, if you didn't mind dust, but life for travelers and freight haulers became easier when the railway—then a new and revolutionary device—was put through from the Missouri River to Sacramento. Today railroads are beginning to be regarded, by some misguided souls, as quaint. Californians celebrate the driving of the Golden Spike at Promontory Point, Utah, now approaching its hundredth anniversary; then they get into their automobiles and drive back to San Francisco; the railroad companies get up arguments that may persuade the regulatory agencies to let them abandon a few more branch lines; and the air companies increase the speed of their jets to a point where San Francisco and Los Angeles, about an hour apart by air, are also commuting towns on the fringes of New York.

Every Californian's eyes moisten a little when one mentions the Golden Spike. They do not wish to go to Virginia City by a four-horse stage, in a cloud of dust, along the Placerville Road, although they may drive the route in a high-powered car. They often avoid the railroad because there is so little time, though the Union Pacific has done quite a number of things to make rail travel fast and pleasant. But all true Californians turn toward the past, provided they do not have to live in it any more.

California has had real historic characters, even in recent times. In April, 1964, an eighty-five-year-old lady was buried in the Mt. Olivet Cemetery at San Rafael. One mourner attended the funeral, for as far as was known she had had no surviving relatives; and her last days had been spent living very simply in a hotel room in Los Angeles.

She had, however, a great significance for California. Readers of *Two Years before the Mast* may remember that when young Richard Henry Dana came into San Francisco Bay in the year 1836 in the brig *Alert* he noticed, on the peninsula side of the bay, a single structure between the Mission and the Presidio—"a shanty of rough boards put up by a man named William A. Richardson, an Englishman who was doing a little trading between the vessels and the Indians." This shanty (Richardson built an adobe in the following year) is now thought to have been the first private house in San Francisco.

Richardson had arrived as mate of a whaler and had stayed behind when his ship departed. Later he became a Mexican citizen, was baptized into the Catholic faith, and married a girl of Spanish ancestry. He did well enough in his business, not having any competition, and seems to have drawn up the first town plan for Yerba Buena—the hamlet that grew into the city of San Francisco.

There were no stately ceremonies when the old lady named Josephine Richardson was buried at San Rafael. There were no cavaliers, no parade, no speeches. But Josephine Richardson—so short is California's history—was the granddaughter of William A. Richardson, San Francisco's first white, civilian settler, after whom Richardson's Bay was named.

Nobody had remembered to write a part for her in the pageant.

18

The Domestic Manners
of the Californians

For this chapter I have borrowed with a modification, the title Mrs. Trollope gave to her book about the United States, published in 1832. I do not think she will mind. Moreover, Mrs. Trollope irritated our predecessors of more than a century ago by the acidity of her comments; she had failed in a sort of "notions store" she had tried to run in Cincinnati, and this made her querulous. Finally, she was, and remained, a trueborn Englishwoman; whereas this reporter has been a Californian at several periods of his life and is one now. But even though I am a tiny part of the thing I now contemplate, even though my wife and I were portions of the population bulge that has turned the state into a nation; even so, we Californians are not (thank God) all alike, and we ought to be able to look at our state and its inhabitants with some detachment.

The first point I wish to make is one that has been in my thoughts for some time: this is that California is not really the Far West. (Let us ignore the map for a moment.) It has some western traits, as has, indeed, the state of Maine, but if you really yearn for westernness it is better to get off the train or plane somewhere in Texas, Arizona, Nevada, Utah, Idaho, or Wyoming.

Western Kansas and Western Nebraska are fairly western, too, as is Colorado. But California isn't. It has real cowboys, but if it weren't for Hollywood and television, they would starve.

The part of California we hear most about, which is the coastal stretch from San Francisco down, with its coastal valleys (as distinct from the great Central Valley), resembles parts of New York, Pennsylvania, and the lower peninsula of Michigan, transplanted to a better climate. They are close-knit, thoroughly organized communities. Their inhabitants ride horses sometimes, but they do not place a canter after the cattle among life's supreme joys. They wear suspenders and on occasion put on cowboy hats, but this is not because they are western—it is because they think it is cute. In some cases, female ones, it really is cute. They also go into the Sierras, in winter as well as in summer; the Sierras are about the best mountains in the world, but they differ in quantity and altitude rather than in charm from the Adirondacks, the Green Mountains, and the White Mountains.

I have seen cattle being raised in California, in a careful, far-seeing, highly scientific manner. But those who follow the cattle for a livelihood do not worry about being buried on the lone prairie. They use comptometers and rarely write poetry.

2

The automobile rather than the horse is naturally the Californian's way of getting about. People in a hurry take the supersonic jets, as they do in other parts of the world. For short runs—a few hundred miles or so—a semisupersonic drive on the freeway suits a Californian quite well.

The superways remain, in a sometimes grisly sort of way, fascinating. In 1959 California adopted a twenty-year freeway and express highway plan. A prodigious network of fast communications is to permeate the entire state—and nobody will have to stay where he is for any length of time—assuming he has an engine, chassis and wheels, and money for the gasoline.

In fairness to the California driver and to the engineers who designed the freeways and other modern roads he uses, it should be said that motor vehicle deaths in the state per 100 million vehicle miles are below those of Alabama, Arizona, Georgia, Idaho, South Carolina, South Dakota, and some other states— and less than half the rate for Puerto Rico. On the other hand, the Californians drive more miles per capita per annum; thus they rolled up a total of 4,121 dead in 1962, as contrasted with New York State's 2,362. The California total is nearly twice that of the Union soldiers killed in action at Antietam in what Bruce Catton thought was "the worst single day" of the Civil War.

On the other hand, pains are taken to protect the pedestrian, who is much safer in most urban streets in the state than he is on a Manhattan one-way avenue. Perhaps this is ordained on the theory that if he is kept alive, he may buy an automobile. Even those midget cars that sound like a battery of field artillery will not deliberately run him down—the state law says they ought not to do so.

Meanwhile, the freeways and other heavy-duty roads follow their preordained courses. If they threaten to vulgarize Lake Tahoe, mutilate Golden Gate Park, spoil a section of the San Francisco waterfront, destroy the quietness of Mission San Luis Batista, turn Los Angeles into an immense traffic jam, if they do things like these it is just too bad. The age of winding roads is mostly past.

One effect of all this road building, in California as in other areas, is to destroy or cripple the railroads. California has gone further than New York or New England, but in the same direction. Enter a new section of freeway, exit an old branch line— such is the formula.

In the summer of 1964 the U.S. Bureau of Public Roads reported that California had nine million licensed drivers, the largest number of any state in the Union. New York State came second, with only 7.7 million. This means, I think, that if every California car were fully mature and not of the puppy or compact variety, then the entire population of the state, with a little squeezing and some use of buses and trucks for the more corpulent, could be on the road at once.

At any rate, distance means little to a Californian. He is the end product of the historic Westward Movement. After about three and a half centuries he has arrived. There is no further westward road, except by air or water, but he cannot settle down. He loves his home; but he loves his car and his carport more. (His carport, which is a kind of covered car stable, open at both ends and looking somewhat like what the farmers on the Cumberland Plateau in Tennessee—and probably elsewhere in the Southeast—call a "dog trot," is a status symbol.) On the spur of the moment he will dash to the Sierras or cover the shore route between Los Angeles and Crescent City, by way of San Francisco.

He lives, one may say, in Nomad's Land.

3

He loves Nature, but the characteristic expression of this fondness is not quite what it used to be. The Sierra Club, a rugged institution, some of whose members can climb the side of a skyscraper, still exists; but the typical out-of-door enthusiast in California is a man who takes a trailer along and is annoyed if there is any desirable objective he cannot reach with it. About 25,000 campsites minister to this impulse, each site a little community with many comforts. On shores, in valleys and mountains, among the great trees are some thirty million acres of land, two-thirds of it Federal, set aside for recreation. In the height of the season this does not permit a solitary communion with Nature, for millions will be on the road. Nature has almost too many friends.

Nature is, however, preserved, even though her virginity is threatened. She is respected and courted, except when ancient redwoods bite the dust in order to widen or straighten a highway to enable more motorists to roar through the forests. Some fast-moving drivers will stop at a park among the redwoods to listen to wild-life lecturers who will explain Nature to them—often eloquently, always informedly. But the redwoods keep going down, in spite of all that the Save the Redwoods League and other devoted groups can do.

However, Californians really do love the out-of-doors, except in cases where loving it too much would cut profits and put men out of work; this is the argument put up by the lumber industry. It takes money as well as diplomacy to save the trees.

But outdoor life in California will be popular, I believe, until and unless, in some final madness, all the trees have been butchered and all the flat places paved with concrete. The urge to have a picnic is aided by the climate. In most parts of California it simply cannot rain, except during the official rainy season—though there may be some pretty wet fog along the northern coast. The camper need rarely take a rubber poncho. He can make some progress every day toward that great objective which binds the nation together, uniting East and West, North and South, Republicans and Democrats—the effort to become properly sunburned. The athletic, woodsy type is popular in California: male or female, it expresses youth and—shall we say?—hale middle-age also.

Attire, even in city streets, restaurants, hotels, and places of entertainment, is informal. This informality is, to be sure, modern and national, but California—perhaps with a little help from Florida—invented it and gives it the widest scope.

California is not a huge retirement home, although there are plenty of retired persons there. As Dr. Clark Kerr, President of the University of California, has said: "The state has a smaller proportion of the very young and the very old, and a higher proportion in the productive ages twenty to sixty-five than the country at large." California's population, in short, is growing younger. Neil Morgan, in his *Westward Tilt*, cites the state's purchases of outdoor sporting goods at half a billion dollars annually, which works out at about $28 a head. People are young enough to need exercise.

They are also able to pay for the apparatus that stylish modern exercise demands. It seems to be true that personal incomes are higher than the national averages: weekly factory pay, for example, was reckoned in 1964 at an average of $112 as against a national average of $97, and all personal income at an average of $2,871 annually against a national average of $2,357 annually. It is risky, of course, to put out such figures: if an Easterner or a Middle Westerner can have not only the climate and scenery of California but also more pay, why should he stay Eastern or Middle

Western?

A true Californian will not be able to understand why some persons might actually prefer to live in some other state; this way of thinking, or nonthinking, is a California folkway. So also, as has been pointed out, is the Californian's habit of assuming, in all modesty, that he helped God invent the climate and the scenery.

Dana wrote of things and people he saw when he came back to California in 1859, twenty-odd years after his first adventures there; one of the old friends he met was a man whom he had known as "a strict and formal deacon" of a New England church; this man was still a deacon, but "gone were the downcast eye, the watchful gait, stepping as though he felt responsible for the moral universe . . . [now] he walked with a stride, an uplifted open countenance . . . his voice strong and natural—and in a short time he had put off the New England deacon and become a human being."

Something of the same sort happens even today to some persons who come to California from more rigid and frigid environments. There is a tendency to relax. There is also a tendency, in certain religious and political fields, to get up and howl. The classic motto, Nothing in Excess, is not the admonition that California instinctively follows—especially in the South.

4

Yet the sharp differences between the sections may be tending to blur, perhaps because people move around so often and so far. It may also be that the physical framework of California—that is, the part of it which is not obscured by highways, houses, business structures, factories, and laboratories—can imprint itself on the inhabitants and is actually doing so.

But this theory overlooks the fact that California is a region, not a place, and certainly not a unified commonwealth. It could be split into two states as easily as were the Carolinas and the Dakotas. The Central Valley would actually belong with neither slice of pie—and that Valley is divided between the Sacramento, which is relatively well watered, and the San Joaquin, which is dry. The great Sierra Range is a kind of Switzerland or Tyrol; the

Coastal Valleys are wetter than the inland ones, and smaller; the actual seacoast grows damper and wilder as one goes north. In short, this is a diversified land, a little Europe.

And of course there is no special reason why all Californians should be alike, even now. It would be as reasonable to expect citizens of Mississippi, of both colors, to resemble those of Vermont. Californians, though they have some things in common (including being a long way from either Mississippi or Vermont) are not like peas in a pod—they just talk that way sometimes.

The geographical peculiarities of the state compel a wide variety of land uses, bring about a vast difference in land values from one area to another, and produce differences in folkways. A steel worker does not think or act in quite the same way as an oil operative, much less an orange grower or picker; and none of these much resemble the old-style individual who has gone to California to settle down and do nothing on a small income.

But the whole of California has one thing in common: it is a land of great magnitudes. Its principal valleys are continentally vast. Some of its mountains reach heights not equaled in the United States outside of Alaska. Its main river system, the Sacramento-San Joaquin, is no Mississippi drainage basin, but it is majestic. Hidden valleys and quiet nooks exist, but they are not characteristic. As at sea, the eye rests itself upon distances. The tongue of the true California booster wags with boasts of bigness —most of them true: the biggest and oldest trees, the biggest natural harbor, the biggest artificial harbor, the tallest hills, the longest sea coast, the longest growing season.

The Californian can be a cautious, unimaginative man, but Nature encourages him not to be. North or South, he has a bear by the tail and loves every minute of it. His most vulgar representative is the realtor who rejoices when he sells so much of the earth that a community is too crowded for civilized living. His poet is John Muir, who loved the mountains and the valleys passionately and who described solitude in such glowing terms that now there is no solitude; John Muir has been dead more than half a century, but his soul goes tramping and climbing on.

John Muir also dealt in real estate, though not in the Yosemite

Valley. But a great deal of the land he had to traverse on foot can now be followed at high speed by the motorcar. And he helped, as Frank Wiggins did, to create a certain type of Californian—the man who feels equally at home in the middle of Los Angeles and on the now sometimes equally overcrowded floor of Yosemite.

What this all adds up to, perhaps, is that there is no immediately recognizable Californian (Texans are easier to detect, as are Kansans and New Yorkers and a few Bostonians) but that almost all Californians like distances, heights, extremes, and contrasts. They can be picked out, just as an Italian can be, though nobody looking and listening carefully would confuse a Lombard with a Sicilian. So, at a distance, a San Franciscan and an Angeleno may blend, though nearby an experienced observer can readily tell which is which.

5

Californians also resemble the Italians in their sectional rivalries. If the region had been let alone long enough (this is one of my favorite and most futile thoughts) city-states would undoubtedly have developed, with Los Angeles and San Francisco playing the roles of Rome and Florence; and Santa Barbara, San Diego, Stockton, Bakersfield, and Sacramento enacting lesser but robust roles; and stern, visaged, fog-dripping seafarers sometimes coming down from Eureka and Crescent City to plunder the softer and richer communities; possibly there would have been sturdy tribesmen in the lower Sierras, descending to raid the lowland cattle herds, and a sort of Arcadia, seldom visited but full of magic, on a roadless coast below Point Sur.

One can let one's fancy play, but such things did not happen. There is not much mystery any more, and the rivalries take a gentler form. As I write this I read a rather wistful story in a San Francisco newspaper, to the effect that members of a visiting Russian track team who had inspected both cities expressed a preference for San Francisco over Los Angeles. One of them said —and it sounds familiar—that in San Francisco "he loved the white houses and the view of the bridges and the hills"; but that Los Angeles "isn't really a city, it's just a spread-out village." He also said there was "too much smog down there"—although San Franciscans are a bit cautious in talking on this subject, now that they themselves have a little "too much smog."

For many persons there is little hesitation in choosing between the two major cities as places in which to live. But beauty and charm are not the whole story or, in California, even a major part of it. San Francisco, for example, is in certain lights, gray and dismal. Sometimes, in the fog (not the smog) that Nature herself sends in, she is not even visible. She has too many high-rise buildings and is acquiring more. What counts on the California frontier is not the view from San Francisco's Telegraph Hill or the wilderness of freeways and unimaginative dwellings in and around Los Angeles; what counts is power, which can be translated into terms of jobs, and profits, power that is economic, financial, finally governmental. Perugia cannot really challenge Florence; Florence cannot throw down the glove to Rome; when it comes to a test of brute strength Los Angeles and the sunny Southland will always, as far as can be seen, win out.

This is the law of survival; you leave Chester and Plymouth to go "up" to London; you leave Bordeaux and Marseille to go to Paris; you leave Seville, which is lovely and historic, or Barcelona, which is full of fire and pride, to go to Madrid—if you want something, London or Paris or Madrid is likely to have it. So with Los Angeles; not so much so nowadays with San Francisco.

The California Southland is well fitted for electronic and other high jinxes that the necessities of defense—and maybe also the advances of peaceful civilization—have forced upon us. It will therefore get the bulk of profitable Government contracts in those fields in the state, though the Santa Clara Valley has had quite a boom out of them. As time passes Southern California will have a proportionately heavier representation in Congress and more influence there; it will be able to outbid the North as New York can outbid Connecticut. In that part of life which can be measured, weighed, paid out in profits and wages, the South will outbid the rest of the state.

But, as we know, it is not always the great power centers or the great masses of population that count most in human culture.

There is a sense in which Scotland, Ireland, Switzerland have left and are still delineating an extraordinary mark on history. In cultural values the North in California is still dominant, even though the South is definitely not the barren cultural desert it is often assumed to be. Indeed, Los Angeles has, or soon will have, as much culture as money can buy. Poets may not be born there, but they will go there—poets in words, in sounds, in shapes, in colors, in scientific ideas that will move and shake the world.

The Southerners have a hankering for what they do not natively possess. On long holidays they are likely to drive North, where the great natural glory is. Heavy casualties during the July 4 weekend of 1964 occurred on the northern highways of California, and police attributed the sudden rise to "the great influx of Southern Californians" who drove North for the holiday.

Despite these losses, Los Angeles keeps right on growing, at the reported rate of a thousand persons a week. It is said to be the airplane manufacturing capital of the nation. It is dotted with electronic plants. It is astride the ridge of Time and looking onward and upward. There is no indication that it knows where it is going, but it is surely going somewhere. All the resources of science, renewed each morning, are being used to keep Southern California, and especially Los Angeles, well supplied and vigorous.

The city of Los Angeles is not a conspiracy, a half-witted political party, or a well-thought-out plan—though at times it shows the symptoms of all these entities. It is a natural force. It is a sort of mass hypnotism. Time flows by it like a river, and all its people, yesterday's, today's, and tomorrow's, are caught in the swift current. Father Serra, when he established the Mission San Gabriel, did not contemplate any such horrific miracle as this, nor did Frank Wiggins, when he tried hard to get people to come to Southern California and get rested and feel better.

This is not a city with a past. It is a city with a future, at which we will have to take another look before we close our lesson books and go home. And I don't mean a "future" in the conventional sense of a glittering success. This future for Los Angeles may or may not make people happy. What I am sure of is that it will not much resemble anything that has happened on earth before.

6

The fallacy in comparing Los Angeles with San Francisco is that it is an attempt to compare a metropolitan area—and a new kind of metropolitan area, at that—with a city and, perhaps, an obsolescent kind of city. One could come nearer by including the whole tributary region of San Francisco, including the Bay cities, the Peninsula as far down as San Jose, and Marin County at least as far up as San Rafael. What can truthfully be said is that somewhat less than 800,000 San Franciscans are a recognized community with traditions and a rough and unforgettable poetry of its own. Let me try to illustrate what I mean.

It is not necessary to go back to the days of Lotta Crabtree, Lola Montez, or the Emperor Norton to find the evidence of honest sentiment—or, if one prefers, sentimentality—in San Francisco. Two modern instances will do. One is the cable car. This was in its day a great invention, for it predated the electric trolley and the motorcar. It was also a humane device, for it removed the brutal necessity of making horses haul vehicles up and down such cruelly precipitous streets as California and Mason. It was never a really comfortable form of transportation, except for the young and rugged. At the rush hour a cable car looked like a swarm of human bees; it always seemed remarkable that so few people fell off. At times, in the somewhat artificial prolongation of their working life, the cable cars are still crowded in this fashion. As I write, there have been a few accidents and near accidents caused by the grip slipping on the cable, but these, though they call for a shutdown for repairs, would not lead a true San Franciscan to propose that they be abandoned. Indeed, with a gesture of defiance of fate, they were declared a National Monument late in 1964.

San Franciscans love them, mainly because they are a sort of trade-mark of the old city. A bus, with good brakes and plenty of gears, will climb any hill in San Francisco where a road runs. But when it was proposed to do the sensible, cold-blooded thing and let the cable cars disappear the city rose in an almost revolutionary fervor to save them. Devoted San Franciscans sat down, read Gelett Burgess's "Ballad of the Hyde Street Grip" (or listened to it on a playing record), wept a little into their beers or martinis, and rose more or less as one man to swear that the cable car should be exterminated only over their dead bodies. The cars still run on two lines (except when being repaired); and not only do the tourists love them but many staid citizens ride them habitually to and from their jobs and cheerfully chip in an extra tax penny or two to help meet the deficits. The city gains by the tourists, of course, and loses on the residents. On the whole, sentiment, not profit, keeps the cables running and the cars, sometimes by jerks, moving.

Another example of San Francisco's devotion to the beautiful or traditional was the long and finally successful campaign to save (by duplication) one of the loveliest relics of the Panama Pacific Exposition of 1915. This was Bernard M. Maybeck's Palace of Fine Arts, built, like other Exposition structures, of impermanent materials.

Fortunately or otherwise Mr. Maybeck made this edifice so admirable, so appealing to the eye, so full of dreams, that nobody could bear to tear it down when the rest of the Exposition site was cleared for housing—and a wonderful housing site it is, with a wide view of the Golden Gate, Tamalpais, and the Marin hills.

After a generation and more the beauty still lingered, though the stucco began to fall on the heads of people who went too close to the enchanted gardens. At about this time a man rose to remark that he had fallen "in love with this building forty years ago. . . . It is a building with a soul. . . . It refused to die." This man's name was Walter S. John; he did not merely express an opinion and heave a sigh but offered a check for two million dollars toward a restoration.

For a time the outcome was uncertain, for two million dollars was not enough to do what had to be done. Other private citizens, encouraged by a generous example, came forward with lesser but numerous donations. Finally the city gave way to popular pressure and provided what was still needed. The lovely old edifice has been torn down, indeed, but the drawings and measurements have been carefully saved, and it will live again in a more nearly permanent material.

I do not suppose that Mr. Maybeck's Palace of Fine Arts will ever be judged as beautiful as the Parthenon, but as long as it stands it may symbolize the fact that San Francisco is a city and not a haphazard encounter of purely utilitarian glass, cement, and steel.

It is not, of course, a modern building. Neither will today's modern buildings be such after another generation. It may not be needed—San Francisco has other museums. But it is a gesture, a banner in the wind. It is San Francisco.

19

Trail's End

If you come into California by land, from the East, you may find yourself curving down out of the Sierras and catching your breath at the first sight of the vast Sacramento Valley—possibly with the Marysville Buttes in the hazy distance. In late spring, summer, and early fall the prevailing color will be brown, with a little red in it, shading off into ashy white. After the rainy season—lowland California's "winter"—has started to do its magic there will be an ecstatic green: this, you may tell yourself, is an enchanted land.

By the southern approaches you will have many miles of sand and sand-colored rock, beautiful and terrible, the sort of deserts that cost Anza so much toil, then the artificial green of modern cultivation, as one may call it, the dreary shores of the Salton Sea; you will come at last to a species of Paradise, half agricultural, half industrial; this may not seem enchanted, except at the rising and going down of the sun, but its riches burst swiftly upon you.

When you begin rolling into Los Angeles you will find little magic for the eye to gloat and wonder over, but you will see that this is a plump and well-tended land. If you continue you will find a noble array of beaches, many of them accessible to the wandering public; though few of them have been protected from the blare and glare of the modernized, vulgarized, intensively developed California world. You may experience more of the ancient enchantment if you go out to the Seal Rocks, on the far frontier of San Francisco. There may be fog—the same fog that for so many generations protected the Bay of San Francisco from being discovered. If you are looking for the cheap and gaudy you can find them, but the rocks are real and the entrance to the port, the Golden Gate, was cut through, ages ago, by the hand of the Creator.

At San Pedro or at the Seal Rocks, it used to be accurate to say, here ends the United States. One does not say this any more, out of deference to one's Hawaiian friends. But these shores are really the end of the trail. The "cut-offs", the by-passes, the grim passages across the deserts and through the mountains, the sins and glories of the railway builders, the realized dream fantasies of the highway engineers, the swish of the great winged vehicles that go luxuriously in minutes where men endured a long damnation in the deceptively romantic days of old—these now terminate. Here is California. Here America, cocky, proud, and scared, turns and looks back at itself. There is a rock somewhere, with the fog horns blowing in the white obscurity of the future, there is a rock that is twin to the one at Plymouth.

We are at the end of our journey, on this coast. Here we dig in and plan to hold the line. Here, indeed, as old Benton said, here lies the road to India; but India is no mystery any more, no treasure house; India is a problem.

And here we continue hopefully to arrive. Such is one California point of view. Another state of mind, not so often shouted in the streets, is one of bewilderment: what are all these people doing here? What will they all do when government defense contracts (as they may) begin to peter out? Consider Santa Clara County, south of San Francisco, where in 1963 23,400 persons were engaged in electrical manufacturing and 26,200 in producing military hardware. The Santa Clara Valley used to be renowned chiefly for its prunes and apricots.

The same problem on a larger scale can be found in Southern California. No doubt jobs can be found for skilled workers who will be displaced when military orders fall off—assuming they do. And perhaps an economy depending largely on armament production is invariably somewhat unhealthy. But what is California going to do with all its people? What are they going to do with California?

2

California can, of course, provide for the elementary needs of many more people than live there now. If Italy, with about 116,-000 square miles of territory, can maintain about fifty million people, California, with about 158,000 square miles, might support even more. This would not be a picnic by today's American standards—it might be very rough, indeed—but one might still find a place to lie down if one went far enough from the freeways. (I note with a shudder, however, as I write this, that there is talk of legalizing the practice of motorcyclists in riding their vehicles along some of the trails in the National Forests.)

The state is in serious danger of overpopulation, with a consequent deterioration of all the qualities (except some phases of climate) that make it attractive. If the Census Bureau is accurate in its predictions, more than nineteen million people will be in California when these words are in print, nearly twenty-five million in 1970.

The figures are not merely impressive—they are appalling. But it is misleading to treat statistics of populations merely as statistics. Statistics are people and tangible things.

The increase of population in California is, for example, a man and his wife, who many years ago bought a home on the shores of San Francisco Bay, near Palo Alto. They were quiet there; they planted a garden, as it were, westward in Eden. Now the road in front of their house is becoming a main thoroughfare, approaching the freeway to San Francisco or south to San Jose; a high-rise apartment is being built next door, and taxes are going up to a point where they will soon have to sell and hunt for quietness somewhere else. They do not know where they will find this quietness; or how long, if they do find it, it will remain uninvaded.

The population increase, plus the highway intensification, has done other things in this area. When my wife and I lived in Palo Alto many years ago we used to walk to and from the campus of Stanford University along an almost unused road called the Embarcadero—which means, in Spanish, a route leading to a pier or place of embarcation. The Embarcadero is now a roaring link with a much-traveled freeway and is therefore itself much traveled. One walks there, after dark or in daytime, in deadly peril.

There used to be a foot-and-horse trail along the coast below Monterey; following this, one could reach San Luis Obispo, although the final stretch, passing Mr. Hearst's fabulous castle at San Simeon, was by road, as were also the first few miles. But it was wild country—and peaceful country too. A high-speed road has now superseded the old trail, and the borders of the route are being settled—as they doubtless should be, but there is no wildness any more.

The old Camino Real—Spain's "Royal Road" or "King's Highway"—running from mission to mission in the picturesque days we like to remember, with no fear they will come back, is almost solidly lined for mile upon mile south of San Francisco with a roadside architecture invented by some maniac in order to make America hideous. The nearby freeway is a little better protected, but there is clutter and overcrowding beyond the fence.

Up and down the valleys, orchards have been cut down to make room for houses; these are lavish and comfortable if the buyer has enough money; but slums are being built also. These houses used to be stuck together without any heating equipment except fireplaces. Now they are likely to have central heating, for it can be cool in California at night and in winter, even down at sea level, even in Orange County and areas like that. But the expensive houses will not be—and need not be—as solid as an equivalent dwelling in New England or the Texas Panhandle; and you can stick a pin through the cheap ones.

These houses, up and down California, and especially between San Francisco and San Diego (a long stretch, but it leaves out a lot of the north coast) multiply like rabbits. They breed and flourish and the green or brown earth is obscured with them. For people do have to live somewhere, and it is hard to make orchards pay enough to resist the prices offered for residential acreage.

Of course there remains much rural land in California. There has to be some (if you call a milk factory, a lettuce factory, or a fruit factory rural), for the total cash income from California farms has been running about three and a half billion dollars annually, and the total farm acreage is roughly about one third of the state's area. But farming in California will of necessity become less and less "rural" in the ancient meaning. The state tends to become what might be called a mechanized China: every arable acre cultivated, though, wherever possible, with machines instead of coolies. This is practicable and sensible. It is not romantic. Nor was the plight of the "Arkies" and "Okies" during the 1930s romantic.

As California becomes more crowded, more prosperous and perhaps duller it naturally becomes less enchanting. The farm labor problem remains, but in a different form. In late 1964 the problem was how to continue with the bracero system—the authorized temporary importation of Mexican laborers after the relevant Federal law ran out. The braceros were a luckier lot than their predecessors: they generally were adult men, so that child labor in the fields was not involved; they did not get as much pay as American workers but they got enough to send back to their families in Mexico—about $35 million annually, perhaps a little under $200 apiece. This meant much more in Mexico than in the United States.

The bracero system also had an advantage for the farmer: under the law and agreement the Mexican laborer could throw up his job at any time, but if he did, he had to go back to Mexico. American citizens, even if they could be persuaded to do "stoop labor," were not handicapped in the same way: they could quit at any moment and work at something else. Thus some of the farmers and all of the braceros regarded the importation system as a gift from the gods.

Increasing mechanization will take care of part of this problem. One enlightened rancher told a group of visitors that an improved tomato-picking machine might replace some labor; the trouble was that existing models would pick only about twenty per cent of the crop. This rancher, who used machinery wherever he could, including milking his cows, had friendly letters from braceros who came year after year to work a few weeks for him. But there was real worry at that time about harvest labor. Six per cent of all California workers—about 650,000—were then unemployed, but they could not easily be induced to work in the harvest; most harvesting by hand makes a person's back ache; I have tried this and I know—and I find it hard to blame others for preferring some other kind of exercise.

If the population increases enough, of course, and if land and jobs do not keep up with the increase, the native son or adopted stepchild may be persuaded to lower his pride and weary his spinal column by picking melons, celery, or strawberries. But I suspect the solution will be mechanical. Mr. McWilliams' "Factories in the Field" may echo to the clackety-click of an overworked but uncomplaining apparatus, for which no protective labor laws are needed and no sympathy required. Farm labor may then be skilled operatives, with nothing to do but push buttons and pull levers, which is fun if you like it.

On the whole the state's problem is more likely to be to find jobs for its burgeoning population than to get the needed work done. Barring catastrophe, this is the modern dilemma, and California is bound to be afflicted with it in an aggravated form. The Californians of today are no Donner Party, stranded in the pitiless wilderness. They are not driven, except possibly in a political or economic way, to eat each other. One of their dangers may be that they will fall into the plight of the traditional South Sea Islanders, who did not have to work at all, because Nature furnished them all that they found necessary. This would be a calamity, of course.

3

Water supply will not set a limit to population growth or even to potential well-being. The Northern coast will never lack for it. The Sacramento Valley will be able to get all it needs, provided the thirsty South, with its excess of votes, does not grab it. In the summer of 1964 it was estimated that between the Russian River and the Oregon boundary ten million acre-feet of water were annually poured into the sea. An acre-foot of water will cover one flat acre one foot deep; this amount of water would be more than enough to put that amount on every foot of ground now devoted to the state's principal crops.

Much of this water could be profitably used in the upper—or Southern—San Joaquin—and will be; all that is required is a little tunneling and new or heavier caliber feed lines across the delta and estuary between the Sacramento and the San Joaquin. The rest could be shipped—can anybody guess where?—by means of a state-owned nuclear pumping system carrying it over the Tehachapi Ridge, at an estimated cost of thirty per cent less than present pumping systems. So the experts say.

The project is no daydream. Governor Edmund H. ("Pat") Brown stated in 1964 that on the basis of a current study "a nuclear plant would mean savings of more than $2.50 an acre-foot of water at the farthermost reaches of the California Aqueduct" —meaning, of course, that more industries could be served in Southern California, more acres irrigated, more industries operated, more population supported than is possible today. One atomic pumping plan, it was thought, might be ready in 1972, another by 1973.

These measures, in using water to create more opportunities for profit and employment, will naturally create an increasing demand for water; this, vicious or beneficent, is the circle that events must follow. When Northern California has been drained so dry that not even Southern California dare ask it for more, resort will be had to the limitless supply available in the Pacific Ocean.

In 1964 the Metropolitan Water District of Southern California approved a twelve-month study for a huge desalting plant. The Department of the Interior and the Atomic Energy Commission were expected to share the initial cost of $5,000,000—not much, to be sure, compared with the expenses of a Mars or moon shot. This plant would serve a population of 750,000 at a rate of 150 million gallons a day. If it could be made to work well enough and cheaply enough it could be duplicated as often as necessary. There is no question about man's ability to turn salt water into fresh water: it is being done; the question is how much it will cost. This, or some subsequent, experiment will succeed: Southern California will not die or dwindle from thirst.

Nor will Southern California, or any part of California, suffer from lack of mechanical power. What coal could not do in this almost coalless region, what petroleum, however abundant, did not do, atomic power can and will do.

This is what it says in the papers and in the scientific reports. The two necessities of water and power will be provided. So will food, for many more millions of people than will exist, even with a continued population explosion, during our time. But the riches of the earth, even in California, are not limitless.

What has to be considered, for the immediate future, is not so much a quantitative element as a qualitative one. How good a life, what kind of culture—actually how much fulfillment, how much fun?—can this stupendous experiment, this crossroads in history, this deliberate planlessness provide? Is the State of California a normal part of the Western World, or is it something different, something ahead of the general line of march, perhaps a sort of wrong turning—a modern Hastings' cutoff, with only desert, and snow, and death at the end of it? Is this the future we all, in all states, will have to face, we and our children forever?

4

Before trying to answer such questions we ought to look at the assets today's California has to offer besides food, water, shelter, roads, and playgrounds. Education is one of them. If California takes the wrong road she will not do so ignorantly. I don't suppose there has ever been so large a population so exposed to learning at all its levels—particularly with learning that has to do with man's use of natural forces. I don't see much poetry lying around in today's California, but it is impossible to miss the evidence of a high, lucid, and inquiring scholarship in all the technical fields.

Dan Kimball and Harry Ashmore, speaking in the fall of 1964, pointed out that California "has had to build colleges faster than ivy can grow"—hence, few academic traditions. The result is, they added, "the largest coordinated system of tax-supported education in the world." Five out of six Californians who go to college at all go to tax-supported institutions; there were more than a quarter of a million such students in 1964—a rise of 100,000 in five years. State and local expenditures, plus private gifts, plus Federal aid, bring California's expenditures for higher education to half a billion dollars a year; this almost equals what the State spends on roads. Good roads, of course, make it easier for the students to get to college.

In principle, at least, California has come close to fulfilling Thomas Jefferson's proposal that every individual, regardless of income or rank, be entitled to as much education as he (I don't recall that Mr. Jefferson put a feminine pronoun in) can profitably use. There is a Master Plan for Education, just as there is one for water and one for roads. The State will have to run hard to keep up with the inflowing and native waves of population, but it is trying to do this.

In other ways a careful observer can detect a continuing cultural advance. To measure education, or any other aspect of culture statistically is of course dangerous; to measure such things qualitatively is difficult. All that can be truthfully said, perhaps, is that a large number of young Californians, numerically and in percentages, are exposed to the main flow of thought, information, and techniques available in today's America. This ought to reduce some of the foolishness, occasionally noted in California, that arises from pure ignorance.

A layman may look with awe at some of the industries of the electronic age. He may, for example, learn that the Stanford Research Institute, in Menlo Park, near Stanford University, is spending $40 million a year, employs 2,400 persons, and is planning to expand. Pasadena used to be known for its venerable elderly inhabitants and its roses and other posies; now its California Institute of Technology has a jet propulsion laboratory. Dr. Melvin Calvin of the University of California, a Nobel Prize winner, is bold enough to speak of "the research industry" as "California's greatest resource." We can understand why, for though it may involve only thousands of workers it can add to the productivity of millions.

From the modestly paid worker in the fields to the skilled laboratory technician is a long jump, but both are parts of today's California. It is not easy to grasp: this stir of mental and muscular energy; it does not explain why California votes as it does, or follows after curious economic doctrines or strange gods; it may, indeed, suggest a future wildly different from the present. California is in the rush of a dramatic transition. Tap a strange passer-by on a street in San Jose or San Bernardino; he may be fairly young; he may hold a degree from the Massachusetts Institute of Technology; he may know nothing about Iowa, except that you may pass across it or over it on your way to California; in fact, he may not in any degree resemble the Californian of fun or fiction—or of the year 1930.

This man, and his lady love, and notably the children who will be born to them in California, will justify watching. He is the successor to the Spanish don who rode the range in sombrero and leather pants; he is the modern equivalent of the forty-niner who came roaring down to Market Street in his red shirt and boots with mud up to his knees.

This man is taking bits of the universe apart and putting them together again in what he or his employers believe will be a more useful form. He is not romantic. Not in the old, restful way.

5

But romance, or something so labeled, continues. Indeed, as California comes nearer and nearer to some strange future, some electronic heaven or hell, more and more of her people cling to memories of the days of old. Some will go up to the Mother Lode country and pan a few flecks of gold, just to say they have done so. Many years ago, I saw a store in Oroville, Butte County, on the Feather River, that had scales on the counter for those who wanted to buy groceries with their gold dust.

There are those who love the old ways and days, or pretend in a playful sort of way, to do so. Nobody wants to have the old-fashioned California flea back in circulation, but this, and possi-

bly the old-fashioned dust from unpaved highways, are almost
the only features of California life a half century or so ago that
somebody has not attempted to dramatize or revive.

San Francisco's devotion to its Palace of Fine Arts (1915), to
its cable cars (1873), and to the Ferry Building (of purely sec-
ondary importance since the completion of the two bridges in
1936 and 1937) is genuine and touching. So is its preservation of
Fisherman's Wharf, though here there may be as much fishing for
tourists as for fish. So is the ferocity with which many San Franciscans protested against the proposal of the State Highway
Commission to (as the critics said) mutilate Golden Gate Park in
order to hurry freeway traffic through the city.

San Francisco is indeed full of memories and loyalties that may
interest visitors but do not really bring in much money. The poets
of the city are not all or nearly all Beatniks; they are often ordinary citizens with jobs and without whiskers, who wash regularly;
they have homes and they worry about things; but they do get an
extra dividend out of believing they belong to no ordinary
Metropolis—which is true. The electronic age will change these
people, but a little at a time and never completely. Some of them
may move to the suburbs, for San Francisco is developing
blighted areas—but they will be San Franciscans still. You can't
cure or abolish a San Franciscan, except by force.

Sentiment—sometimes sentimentality—runs as far South as
Santa Barbara, which after the big earthquake of 1925 ordained
that buildings restored or constructed on its main streets conform
to what is thought to be the true Spanish-Mexican-Californian
style of architecture. The effect is pleasing.

Near Oroville a tree said to be the oldest living orange tree in
California had been growing at Bidwell's Bar for more than a
hundred years; $15,000 was spent to get it out of the way of the
rising waters behind the Oroville Dam on the Feather River. It is
odd that the tree was not only way up north but that it stood near
the fantastically rich gold riffles that John Bidwell and two others
found on July 4, 1848; there will be no more mining on that spot,
but the impounded water, drained off to the southward, will be
worth infinitely more than all the gold.

The visiting fireman or out-of-town buyer may tour California, or at least the northern three-quarters of it, without paying too much attention to such prosaic matters as industry and business. He can see—or think he sees—"Old Spanish Days" at Santa Barbara; he may in season go to Squaw Valley and wallow in the snow; he may witness a Pioneer Day parade in Chico; he may, if he wishes, attend festivities in honor of Kit Carson at Jackson, up in Amador County in the Mother Lode neighborhood; he may witness the Jumping Frog contest at Angels Camp, and perhaps suspect the ghost of young Mark Twain wandering around and enjoying itself; he may like to take a look at the Monterey Peninsula, if anybody will let him move slowly enough; there he may do a bit of daydreaming about what went on there in the old days—or even in the less elderly days when John Steinbeck's fascinating bums inhabited Tortilla Flat. He doesn't have to watch a golf tournament at Pebble Beach or buy abalone shells and contorted pieces of driftwood at Carmel if he doesn't want to. He had better visit Carmel Mission, whatever his religion, for brave and sacrificial men labored heroically there to do what in the end couldn't be done—and left a restorable beauty behind them.

But these glimpses into the past, except by accident, are not today's California. They are no more a part of today than the Colosseum is a functioning part of today's Italian Republic. Today's California has little to do with yesterday's, except in fond make-believe.

20

And There,
on a Golden Throne—

As I was saying a while back, California may easily have been named after a character in a romance published before Cortez landed in Mexico. This yarn was called "The Exploits of Esplandián," and in it there was a queen called Calafia, who lived and ruled on an island called California. In this kingdom or queendom: "The weapons were all of gold, and, the island abounded with gold and precious stones, and upon it no other metal was found."

As any metallurgist knows this situation would have created difficulties. You can't dig gold without iron—every forty-niner found that out. But I think the symbol of the island and the gold means something for us today. For many centuries California was harder to get to than any island; she did produce quantities of gold a hundred years and more ago, and gold—in the sense of easy money as well as of a single metal—has been one of the guiding incentives, though not the only one, in her history: easy money, easy living, an easy climate in the right times and places, these are the facts and myths by which California has thrived and drawn population down to this present year.

The isolation is all gone, but the peculiarities that made Cali-

fornia California and not Florida, Pennsylvania, or Michigan remain. What we are witnessing in our time is a demonstration that
a highly modernized—indeed, modernistic—superindustrial, materialistic, pleasure-seeking culture can be imposed on what was
once a land of dreams and vagaries. The realm of Queen Calafia
is something the world has never seen before; it is an electronic
Greece, a sunny Manchester, a sort of Heaven, and a sort of
boobyland, according to the elements you choose to emphasize.
It is noisy, hurrying, harrying, exciting—and at times dull. Many
of its details are planned; but the whole, the total impact, could
not be foreseen and was not premeditated.

Modern California is a kind of accident, a product of blind
forces and a confusion of individual impulses. It is precariously
balanced on a number of fortuitous elements, chief among them
the astounding improvements in devices for communication and
transportation, the rise of critical situations in the Pacific, the national defense emergency, and a sudden and not generally foreseen increase in the whole country's population. This is the end of
the continental Westward Movement. Henceforth it can only turn
back upon itself. Here, like a migration of lemmings, we stand
upon the salty beaches, and listen to the ominous thunder of the
surf.

And the water, as the cautious bather soon finds out, is somewhat chilly.

2

When a big businessman says, as one distinguished Californian
did in some promotion material I have been reading, that "Californians have a distinctive philosophy of life: they do not live to
work, they work to live," he had come a long, long way from New
England, Samuel Smiles, the Alger boys, and the nineteenth century. The sentiment might express the feelings of an unskilled and
underpaid worker (I know, because I was one once), but I do
not believe an eager salesman, a dedicated technologist, let alone
a worker in an experimental laboratory, tiptoeing each day on the
verges of infinity, would put it that way. I am convinced that
most men really like to work, if they can find work they care for.

But there is no question that what is called "play" is a large and profitable industry in California.

The world may be approaching a stage in which relatively little routine and unavoidable labor will be required; it may be on the frontiers of a Tennysonlike lotus land in which the day will always seem afternoon; California may be nearer this destination than most other communities. An old and pleasant theory is that in such a case this leisure will be used creatively. Another theory is that it is not being so used and will not be.

This is not to say that creative individuals may not flourish in California. Local situations may attract and encourage such individuals. Hollywood, for all its sins and foolishness, has given some of them a chance to flourish. Science and technology may not have produced them but have attracted them and given them opportunities. What I am thinking about is the general tone of the California culture, which is often highly appreciative of the very best in the arts that money can buy but does not seem to stimulate a native and spontaneous cultural expression. California is more a cultural market place than a cultural workshop. As I write this I have just been reading about the new music center and art museum in Los Angeles County; and every now and then somebody predicts that Los Angeles will soon have as good an opera company as San Francisco has—and perhaps better. These reports raise my opinion of Los Angeles but do not suggest that that city or county is about to turn into a new Athens.

A Californian or a visitor to California can do the following things: he can ski or watch skiing in Squaw Valley; he can visit the redwood groves; he can speed along the western shore of Lake Tahoe; he can admire the lake's somewhat polluted waters, which have lost a little of the "marvellous transparency" Mark Twain saw in them a century ago; he can buy a cottage and a lot in a development on the lake shore if he desires; he can camp in Yosemite if the valley is not full when he gets there; he can attend symphony and other concerts in San Francisco, Los Angeles, and other cities; he can visit art museums, historical museums, and scientific museums in almost any sizable community; he can see and hear well-produced and well-acted plays not only in the cities but on college and university campuses; if he keeps going there need never be a dull moment for him.

Thus it is plain that Californians with a dollar or two in their jeans do not have to be content with the more prosaic aspects of the modern world. They can escape, and they do. Queen Calafia does not have them in thrall; they do not palely loiter.

The question is, what are they so busy escaping from? Is their constant activity a flight? Are they creating a culture or avoiding one? One might think of culture as one of two things: first, as a warmth, an enthusiasm, pervading a whole society, which was the way Henry Adams thought of it when he wrote *Mont Saint Michel and Chartres;* second, as a way of getting out of a real world into a less real but more satisfactory one. I suspect culture in California at the moment belongs in the second variety. This is not wrong or even illegal; it is just another bit of evidence that even in California there are tedious facts that have to be faced. (This may be true of Heaven, too, if it is anything like what the reverend fathers of various faiths have said it was.)

3

Many persons must have wondered what would have happened to California if its development had been at a more leisurely pace, less spectacular, not so devastating. Actually the commonwealth was not even lightly populated by Europeans until close to the end of the eighteenth century; it changed little and was little known to North Americans until close to the middle of the nineteenth century; and then, with the Mexican War and the Gold Rush, emerged with dramatic suddenness as an American State. Literally, it went from rags to riches overnight. All this happened after generations of neglect by Spain and decades of lackadaisical Mexican government; California had been an island too difficult to reach and was all at once drawn into the main tide of continental events.

Let us suppose, for a few moments, that she had had an extra generation or two to grow up before the forty-niners, and their sons and sons' sons, descended upon her. She might have mellowed into a distinctive culture of her own, more allied with Madrid and Rome than with Boston, New York, and London; more

Mediterranean, less aggressive, perhaps lazier, more like what one sees today in outlying parts of Mexico, such as Oaxaca and Yucatan. But because California, Queen Calafia's island, was so hard to reach, and because without the Gold Rush there would have been no hurry to reach her, California might have kept a special quality of her own. The United States in 1849 didn't need more pastoral or agricultural land, though its statesmen believed the nation did need sovereignty all the way to the Pacific. A real settlement and exploitation of the area would have come in time, but more slowly and later. The population of the entire United States in 1850 was not much over twenty-three million: there was room enough.

On an agricultural basis California could have done fairly well, without much contact with the outside world. Much of the land was naturally rich; little of its valley land was forested or rocky; much of it could have easily been irrigated when necessary, and the melting snow from the Sierras took the place of rain during the dry months. The state as a whole was admirably adapted for a population of about two million people—a level it did reach during the first decade of the present century.

The conquest was an incident—almost an accident. Sooner or later the land was sure to fall under the control of the United States, not by right, but because the Westward Movement demanded it. There is no profit, therefore, in musing as to what might have become of it if Mexico had continued to claim title to it; or if it had become independent of Mexico (as, in fact, it almost was in 1846) without being annexed to the United States. It might have become another Greece, another Italy, another Never-Never Land of some sort. Growing in dreamy languor it might have made a new, slightly different contribution to world culture. But dreamy languor is the last expression one may truthfully apply to California. For all its make-believe, California is today —and has been since the Americans moved in—a tough, realistic, hurrying community.

It still might have been less such, even after the railways began to haul human freight into her territory at fairly low fares and no risk. Settlement had to jump the intermountain arid lands before it could congest California; the true frontier of the Far West, after the Indians had been pacified and somewhat reconciled to their hard lot, was the land of short grass and little rain. Dan'l Boone had less trouble getting over the Alleghenies into the dark and bloody ground of Kentucky than the wagon trains had in crossing the Salt Lake Valley and going over the Placerville grade into California; and the railroads of the late nineteenth century, though certainly convenient, did not produce a really massive transcontinental migration.

But the motorcar and the hard-surfaced road intervened. These are the devices, with some help from the Panama Canal and the increased attention the United States was paying to the Pacific Ocean, that caused the population of California to flood the fallow acres of the state. The airplane helped, not at first massively, but selectively. The Second World War, the Korean War, and preparations against a third war increased almost to a frenzy a population movement which in numbers can be compared with the greatest in the world's history. These were the hordes of Asia, these the new tribes wandering into what would never again be a wilderness, these were the new crusades—pick your own figure of speech, but there they were.

We cannot have too firmly in mind the fact that California's modern growth—indeed, its growth since the end of the Second World War—has not been normal, has not been altogether wholesome, and cannot be continued, at its present rate, without catastrophe.

The quality of life in the state has not yet been grievously impoverished, except for those who like peace and quietness and now find them hard to achieve. Wages, salaries, and incomes in general have been augmented. The artificial and man-made amenities have been enriched. One can amuse oneself. One can live a good life—an almost tediously good life.

But—.

4

The danger is not that California, like the rest of the habitable world, will soon acquire more people than it can adequately support. That can come later. This is still the land of plenty—for a while and up to a certain point. It is the land of open space and far horizons, again up to a certain point. It can support, in a decreasingly comfortable fashion, millions more people. But there could be an end to all this, an end to comfort, an end to true civilized living.

There is no formula precisely adapted to keeping California anything like a paradise. If we are in for a period of overcrowding, many will prefer to be overcrowded in California rather than in Connecticut. One need not yet be physically overcrowded in the intermountain states—for instance, in Utah, Nevada, Idaho, New Mexico, or Arizona—but since a human being cannot subsist on sand, or without water, the oases in those states may come to have, so to speak, standing room only. On the other hand the oases area of California is vast, indeed.

The population surge might be somewhat checked by a guard along the border—though this device did not prevent the fall of the Roman Empire. And not even the Los Angeles police, however deputized, are likely to take on the task of reducing births inside the state, when caused by the acts of solvent and legitimately resident parents.

The old-fashioned real estate man still continues to have his influence (sometimes, as in the 1964 election, in influencing people to vote for a segregation amendment to the State Constitution); he does not wish to drown his community in a flood of new immigrants, but he does like to keep prices up and sell land and houses at a profit; this is why he is in business, of course.

Industries, likewise, will look on this area as a happy hunting ground, not because raw materials are always cheaply available but because people like to work and play in an agreeable environment.

Thus all the obvious influences make for more population, and there is no visible or logical effort to prevent overpopulation. The learned, the wise, and the compassionate who have written upon this subject, the lovers of beauty, the poets, the social scientists, the legislators, the engineers do not any of them seem able to tell the rest of us what needs to be done and how to do it. All that is certain, if disaster is to be avoided, is that sooner or later some master plan must be established. Can any such plan preserve the basic freedoms? Is it possible to be entirely free within the framework of an increasing world population, and particularly within the frame and under the urgency of what is happening in California?

We have to believe that this is possible, or else we have to stop believing that mankind can peaceably and righteously control the essentials of its own future.

There may be some brief easement of the growth problem. If the Federal Government relaxes its moon-shot or Mars-shot program, or is able safely to get along with fewer missiles and fewer fighting planes, California's development, after a painful slump, might resume a more normal pace. An acceptable means of reducing the birth rate might also help, though this would do nothing to prevent persons who have already been born and who do not like cold winters from migrating westward across the Sierras.

The fact is that remedies for overexpansion are not welcomed in California or in any other American community; they run counter to some of our most cherished traditions. From San Francisco to San Diego any proposal to cut Federal expenditures for defense is received with cries of indignation and alarm. Overpopulation may be regarded as an evil, but in California what the word means is too many people for too few jobs; it is only the idealists who grieve because an orchard of prunes, apricots, cherries, almonds, oranges, limes, or lemons is cut down for a factory or for homes for the men and women who will be dependent on another factory. But if enough millions of people have homes or work in factories on land that used to produce edible crops, what then?

5

Two conclusions seem evident to me: (1) that what has happened to California since the end of the Second World War—that is, the extraordinary increase in population—is more important than all that happened in that area prior to that date; (2) that this development, so far, may be a gain or a loss, according to one's tastes in such matters, but that it cannot indefinitely continue without unhappy results.

Those of us who knew the state when it had about ten per cent the population it has today are likely to lament many phases of the vanished past. This is human nature: we were younger then. I have argued this point elsewhere and shall not debate it again now. All of us accept the modern conveniences, such as getting from the coast to Yosemite or Tahoe in a day's easy drive; or flying almost anywhere, east or west, in a few cheery hours (with motion pictures in flight to take our minds off the scenery); and no doubt we should accept the inconveniences, such as too many cars on the road and a full house when we arrive at our destination in what used to be wilderness.

But Queen Calafia would not know her island any more. Existence in California has ceased to resemble what it was in her golden days. The idyll is finished. The wild woodland poetry is heard no more; the tiny pipes do not sound; the mountains and forests are no longer haunted.

Something better may be taking the place of the old lazy dispensation. A humane twentieth (and twenty-first) century may wipe out the inequities and iniquities, the follies and sins of the generations we have known. The older California was no Arcadia —though it might have been.

The majestic framework of one of the world's loveliest— perhaps the very loveliest—lands endures. The mountains cannot be torn down, not even by the most fearful of our tools and weapons. The snows, the rivers, the majestic hills, the wonderful plunging shorelines, the welcoming sands, the procession of colors in the natural grasses, the fog and wind, the upland lakes, the vast and luminous distances—these will remain for what mankind calls forever. This is a land to love, in spite of all that has been done to spoil and vulgarize it.

And in California, where so many varieties of religion claim to be the best, men's thoughts may go to the last verse of the eighth chapter of Genesis: "While the earth remaineth, seedtime and harvest, and cold and heat, and summer and winter, and day and night shall not cease."

The Almighty has done His part. Only the long procession of

the years can tell whether or not, taking rude possession of this Garden of Eden, man will have the patience and fore-sight to do *his.*

. . . Meanwhile Queen Calafia, who never existed and is therefore the more real and the more secure, sits brooding on her golden throne. She is a dark queen, so the story has it, but this would cause her no embarrassment if today she walked abroad; she was a broadminded queen and would not have thought the white invaders an inferior race.

But she would ask, What are you doing to this island—and why? Are you still, as Montalvo said more than four centuries ago, "very near the Terrestrial Paradise"?

I wouldn't like to have to answer these questions.

T H E   E N D

Bibliographical Note

I shall mention only a few books, all of which I found useful. Some of this material, though not much of it, overlaps a field I ventured into more than a generation ago (*The Santa Fe Trail*, 1930). My list may be conspicuous because it overlooks the massive products of Hubert H. Bancroft's so-called "history factory." I looked into Bancroft when I was a graduate student at Stanford (M.A., 1911), but I did this because the professor suggested I do so and was never tempted to go back.

The days of Spanish exploration and colonization have produced a Mother Lode of books. Of these I have relied mainly on Professor Herbert E. Bolton, who was for a time, during my undergraduate years, a teacher and researcher at Stanford University; and on Zoeth S. Eldredge. Bolton was a lifelong scholar in the Southwestern field. Eldredge, a retired banker, wrote *The Beginnings of San Francisco*. I had the good fortune to know both men—as a young and extremely modest inquirer into their fields. Bolton's *Outpost of Empire*, with its account of Anza's land journeys from Mexico to California, was especially useful and most interesting.

The best picture I know of life in California in the middle

1830s is contained in a book I first read more than half a century ago and have been rereading at intervals ever since—Dana's *Two Years before the Mast.* The literature of the so-called Bear Flag Revolt of 1846 and of the Gold Rush is astoundingly rich. Two trail books, indicating what the overland immigrants had to face, have been published by the Princeton University Press; I mention them because they especially appealed to me. They are: *Route across the Rocky Mountains* by Overton Johnson and Wm. H. Winter, from the edition of 1846; and *The Emigrants' Guide to Oregon and California* by Lansford W. Hastings, reproduced in facsimile "from the original edition of 1845." My authority for some statements about John C. Frémont is in an appendix to Eldredge's book. Many years ago I had researched a bit for an *American Mercury* article on Frémont, but frankly I do not believe he is worth fussing about—except as an interestingly neurotic character.

I will mention two useful books on the Gold Rush period itself: *The 49ers* by Evelyn Wells and Harry C. Peterson, and *Anybody's Gold* by the late Joseph Henry Jackson. Mr. Jackson, incidentally, also edited *The Western Gate: A San Francisco Reader,* in which he carried the story of his favorite city from its founding to the Golden Gate Bridge, with wise and informed comments of his own. Parkman's *Oregon Trail* was not inspired by the Gold Rush, but it gives a glimpse of conditions on the Great Plains at the beginning of the Mexican War. It is interesting to compare it with Mark Twain's *Roughing It,* which is based on conditions during the 1860s on the transcontinental stages, in Virginia City during the Comstock silver excitement, and in San Francisco and the old California gold fields. The dazzling episode of the pony express is dealt with in a brief but interesting volume by Howard A. Driggs, *The Pony Express Goes Through;* Mr. Driggs was diligent and energetic enough to pick up some quoted narratives of former express riders.

An excellent picture of California during the Civil War period can be found in the journal of William H. Brewer, who was later, for almost forty years, Professor of Agriculture in the Sheffield Scientific School at Yale: *Up and Down California in 1860–1864.*

This is a classic, though it never won the fame of Dana's book, the only one (though a dramatically different one) with which I would rank it. Josiah Royce's *California: A Study of American Character*, is also a classic in its different way, though it was written more than eighty years ago (my copy was issued in 1886) and of course came too soon to cover the most significant period of the State's growth.

A curious phenomenon is the number of really excellent books about San Francisco and the comparative rarity of the same sort of affectionate, even sentimental volumes about Los Angeles. Gertrude Atherton's *My San Francisco;* Mrs. Fremont Older's *San Francisco: Magic City;* Evelyn Wells' *Champagne Days in San Francisco;* and Oscar Lewis's *This Was San Francisco*, a collection of "first-hand accounts of America's favorite city," are all good modern examples. And seemingly no traveler, from Bayard Taylor, more than a century ago, down to yesterday's latest foreign journalist with an expense account, has been able to visit this metropolis without being moved to words, sometimes admiring, sometimes pungent, but nearly always copious in supply. I shall mention only one book about Los Angeles, though many others exist. *Los Angeles: From Mission to Modern City* by Remi Nadeau (1960) is a well-informed, unslanted account by an author whose roots are in the city. It seems as natural to be satirical about Los Angeles as it is to be sentimental about San Francisco; the result in one case is as far from stern historical fact as it is in the other.

The novels of the late Frank Norris tell a good deal about the California of the latter nineteenth century; just as John Steinbeck's *Grapes of Wrath* gives the immigration of the mid-1930s. Carey McWilliams' *Factories in the Field* is an honest, indignant, sensational, and non-fictional description of the same problem.

Among general histories of California I made special use of Robert Glass Cleland's *From Wilderness to Empire; Thirty-first Star* by James A. B. Scherer; and *California: A History* by Andrew F. Rolle—the latter published in 1963. *The Golden Road* by Felix Riesenberg, Jr., is subtitled "The Story of California's Mission Trail," is supplemented by chapter-by-chapter references to sources, and can hardly help being a history of California, not merely of California's roads. I recommend it now, as I did in a book review when it was first published, in 1962.

I should give particular acknowledgment to the *California Information Almanac*, which contains more information about California, past and present, than any other book I have run across.

Finally, I have relied on current newspapers, chief among them the *San Francisco Chronicle*, to keep me up to date.

This, let me repeat, is a selected list of sources—and a short one. Those who desire a complete bibliography of books about California will have to take a year or so off to get it and a century or so to skim through the material.

Queen Calafia's Island

Miles
0   75   150

OREGON

UTAH

NEVADA

California Trail

COASTAL

SIERRA

Feather River

Sacramento R.

L. Tahoe

Coloma
Sacramento

Stockton
Sonora
San Joaqui.
Livermore
Santa Clara

YOSEMITE
NAT'L
PARK

Mt. Tamalpais
Pt. Reyes
Drakes B.
San Francisco

PACIFIC